taste of home
TAILGATE
cookbook

taste of home

TASTE OF HOME/READER'S DIGEST BOOK

© 2012 Reiman Media Group, LLC
5400 S. 60th St., Greendale WI 53129
All rights reserved.

Taste of Home and Reader's Digest are registered trademarks
of The Reader's Digest Association, Inc.

EDITORIAL

EDITOR-IN-CHIEF: Catherine Cassidy

EXECUTIVE EDITOR, PRINT AND DIGITAL BOOKS:
Stephen C. George
CREATIVE DIRECTOR: Howard Greenberg
EDITORIAL SERVICES MANAGER: Kerri Balliet

EDITOR: Christine Rukavena
ASSOCIATE CREATIVE DIRECTOR: Edwin Robles Jr.
ART DIRECTOR: Gretchen Trautman
CONTENT PRODUCTION MANAGER: Julie Wagner
COPY CHIEF: Deb Warlaumont Mulvey
COPY EDITOR: Alysse Gear
CONTRIBUTING LAYOUT DESIGNER: Holly Patch
RECIPE CONTENT MANAGER: Colleen King
RECIPE TESTING & EDITING: Taste of Home Test Kitchen
FOOD PHOTOGRAPHY: Taste of Home Photo Studio
EXECUTIVE ASSISTANT: Marie Brannon
EDITORIAL ASSISTANT: Marilyn Iczkowski

BUSINESS

VICE PRESIDENT, PUBLISHER: Jan Studin, jan_studin@rd.com
REGIONAL ACCOUNT DIRECTOR: Donna Lindskog,
donna_lindskog@rd.com
EASTERN ACCOUNT DIRECTOR: Joanne Carrara
EASTERN ACCOUNT MANAGER: Kari Nestor
ACCOUNT MANAGER: Gina Minerbi
MIDWEST & WESTERN ACCOUNT DIRECTOR: Jackie Fallon
MIDWEST ACCOUNT MANAGER: Lorna Phillips
WESTERN ACCOUNT MANAGER: Joel Millikin
MICHIGAN SALES REPRESENTATIVE: Linda C. Donaldson

CORPORATE INTEGRATED SALES DIRECTOR: Steve Sottile
DIGITAL SALES PLANNER: Tim Baarda

GENERAL MANAGER, TASTE OF HOME COOKING SCHOOLS:
Erin Puariea

DIRECT RESPONSE: Katherine Zito, David Geller Associates

VICE PRESIDENT, CREATIVE DIRECTOR: Paul Livornese
EXECUTIVE DIRECTOR, BRAND MARKETING: Leah West
ASSOCIATE MARKETING MANAGER: Betsy Connors

VICE PRESIDENT, MAGAZINE MARKETING: Dave Fiegel

READER'S DIGEST NORTH AMERICA

PRESIDENT: Dan Lagani

VICE PRESIDENT, BUSINESS DEVELOPMENT: Jonathan Bigham
PRESIDENT, BOOKS AND HOME ENTERTAINING: Harold Clarke
CHIEF FINANCIAL OFFICER: Howard Halligan
VP, GENERAL MANAGER, READER'S DIGEST MEDIA:
Marilynn Jacobs
CHIEF MARKETING OFFICER: Renee Jordan
VICE PRESIDENT, CHIEF SALES OFFICER: Mark Josephson
VICE PRESIDENT, CHIEF STRATEGY OFFICER:
Jacqueline Majers Lachman
VICE PRESIDENT, MARKETING AND CREATIVE SERVICES:
Elizabeth Tighe
VICE PRESIDENT, CHIEF CONTENT OFFICER: Liz Vaccariello

THE READER'S DIGEST ASSOCIATION, INC.

PRESIDENT AND CHIEF EXECUTIVE OFFICER:
Robert E. Guth

"Timeless Recipes from Trusted Home Cooks" is a registered
trademark of Reiman Media Group, LLC.

"Cooking, Caring, Sharing" is a registered trademark of
Reiman Media Group, LLC.

FOR OTHER TASTE OF HOME BOOKS AND PRODUCTS, VISIT US AT
TASTEOFHOME.COM.

FOR MORE READER'S DIGEST PRODUCTS AND INFORMATION, VISIT
RD.COM (IN THE UNITED STATES) OR SEE RD.CA (IN CANADA).

INTERNATIONAL STANDARD BOOK NUMBER (10): 1-61765-126-5
INTERNATIONAL STANDARD BOOK NUMBER (13): 978-1-61765-126-7
LIBRARY OF CONGRESS CONTROL NUMBER: 2012934550

COVER PHOTOGRAPHY
PHOTOGRAPHER: Rob Hagen
FOOD STYLING MANAGER: Sarah Thompson
FOOD STYLISTS: Leah Rekau, Shannon Roum
SET STYLING MANAGER: Stephanie Marchese

PICTURED ON FRONT COVER (left to right):
Baja Chicken & Slaw Sliders (p. 25), Steak Teriyaki Quesadillas (p. 95).

PICTURED ON BACK COVER (clockwise from top left):
Tailgate Sausages (p. 119), Grilled Glazed Drummies (p. 42), Roasted
Potato Salad (p. 235), Chocolate Peanut Butter Cake (p. 296).

PICTURED ON SPINE:
Honey-Glazed Chicken Kabobs (p. 91).

PRINTED IN CHINA.
1 3 5 7 9 10 8 6 4 2

Table of Contents

CATCH THE **TAILGATING SPIRIT** WITH FUN FOOD FOR FANS!

There's nothing like packing up the cooler, heading to the stadium and tailgating before a big game. Just imagine the cheers and laughter of family and friends, the sizzling sounds of the grill, plates of great eats and coolers of refreshing drinks!

Now you can make the most of any sports event, family picnic, outdoor gathering or neighborhood party with 406 of the very best recipes from family cooks who know how to have a good time with great food.

Recipes are simple to prepare and easy to take along for tasty meals on the go. Whether you want a basic party menu or an extravagant spread, you'll find what you need right here!

Wondering where to start? Check out our tips and secrets about what to bring and how to pack and serve it. Get the inside scoop on must-know outdoor food safety. And read up on expert grilling techniques for perfect results every time.

So get ready for any sports season with **TASTE OF HOME TAILGATE COOKBOOK**. Turn to these recipes when you cheer on your favorite teams, and you'll be the champ with family and friends every time!

GET YOUR **GAME ON** WITH THE PERFECT PARTY MENU!

The easiest way to guarantee tailgating success is to start with an irresistible menu of foods. A little planning will go a long way to making certain that friends and family are well fed and energized before the big event begins.

Guests won't be expecting a fancy seven-course meal at this kind of casual get-together, so keep your tailgating menu simple. Pick three or four homemade dishes to serve, including one or two entrees plus sides, then fill in the menu with purchased items like chips, dips, cookies and beverages.

Depending on the length of your gathering, the anticipated weather conditions and the appetites of your guests, add an extra side or fill-in snack to keep hunger at bay. But don't plan too much food—a sudden shower could leave you scrambling for cover and wasting extras! (See "Estimating Food Quantities" below.)

When selecting recipes to serve, look for foods that are easy to eat while standing up or sitting in a lawn chair. Also, dishes made without perishable ingredients (such as mayonnaise) travel best. Rely on foods that can be made ahead and brought to the event or that can be cooked there on the grill.

If you're feeling ambitious, handle all the food yourself, dividing the cost among the group if you wish. Or assign a food item to each person attending. It's best to offer suggestions on what to bring so you don't end up with too many sides and not enough desserts!

Plan on eating at least 45 minutes before the game starts, so you have time to clean up and pack things away. If you like, save dessert for after the game. That way you can linger in the parking lot while others are fighting the traffic.

ESTIMATING FOOD QUANTITIES

These guidelines can help you determine about how much food you'll need per person.

APPETIZERS
- 8 to 9 pieces when served as the meal.
- 2 to 3 pieces when served before the meal.
- Cheese cubes—4 to 6 cubes.
- Vegetables—5 to 8 pieces.

MAIN COURSE
- Cheese—2 to 3 slices for sandwiches.
- Meat, fish or poultry—6 to 8 ounces.
- Hot dogs, hamburgers or sausages— 2 pieces.
- Sandwiches—1½ sandwiches.

SIDE DISHES
- Breads—1 to 2 slices of bread; 1 roll, biscuit or muffin.
- Potatoes—5 ounces.
- Baked beans—¾ cup.
- Salads—1½ cups green salad (a head of iceberg for six people); ¾ cup fruit, potato or pasta salad.

- Pasta—2 ounces.
- Vegetables—4 ounces.
- Condiments—3 to 4 pickle slices or 1 pickle spear; 3 olives; 1 ounce ketchup, mustard and pickle relish;1 teaspoon butter or margarine.
- Chips—1 ounce.

DESSERTS
- Cake or pie—1 slice.
- Cookies or brownies—1 each.

BEVERAGES
1. Calculate how many people will be drinking at the event.
2. Multiply this number by four to determine the maximum number of standard servings you need.
3. Translate this number of standard servings into cans/bottles of beer, wine and liquor.
4. For soft drinks, juices, lemonade or bottled water, plan on 24 ounces per person.

BETTER SAFE THAN SORRY WHEN IT COMES TO OUTDOOR DINING

Whenever you serve or handle food, keep in mind these rules of food safety:

 Keep everything clean, including hands, utensils, plates and work surfaces. Anything that comes in contact with raw meat juices should be thoroughly washed in hot soapy water before reuse.

If you won't have access to soap and water at your gathering, bring along antibacterial wipes, hand sanitizer and plenty of paper towels.

Keep foods separate. Don't cross-contaminate foods, which means allowing the juices of raw meats, poultry and fish to come in contact with other foods.

Keep dishes at the right temperature. Keep hot foods hot, cold foods cold and cook food to the proper temperature. Cooked foods and uncooked foods that require refrigeration should be left at room temperature for only up to 2 hours, 1 hour if it is a hot day (90°F or warmer).

To keep foods hot, use insulated containers. When you have access to electricity, use warming trays, slow cookers or chafing dishes. And if you're tailgating with your RV, you can also serve a small amount of the hot food and replenish the dish as needed, while the rest of the food stays warm in a 200° oven.

 To keep foods cold, place dips, cut-up fruits and salads in a plastic bowl and set in a larger bowl filled with ice cubes or crushed ice. Replenish the ice as it melts.

the 3 rules

1 Keep it clean.

2 Keep it separate.

3 Keep it at the right temperature.

PACK YOUR COOLER LIKE A PRO

Coolers can act as portable refrigerators for any outdoor party. These tips will help your coolers—and the items inside—stay well-chilled for the duration of your gathering.

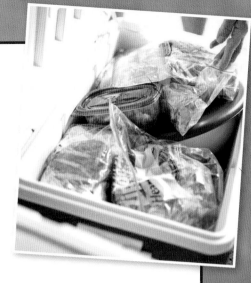

GETTING READY

Since ice blocks take longer to melt than ice cubes or crushed ice, make some a few days before the event. Use a disposable aluminum pan or pans that fit the bottom of your cooler. Place the pan on a baking sheet, then fill it about three-fourths full with water and freeze. For smaller ice packs, fill resealable freezer bags with water and remove as much air as possible before freezing. Don't forget to place gel-type ice packs in the freezer.

Foods and beverages that need to be chilled should be thoroughly chilled in the refrigerator before placing them in the cooler. Chill the coolers beforehand, too, by placing a few ice cubes inside and closing the lid about an hour before filling.

Wrap raw meat, poultry and fish separately from cooked foods. Place raw meat in airtight plastic containers or resealable plastic bags to contain meat juices. Wash fruits and vegetables just before packing them up. Place them in plastic containers with lids or resealable plastic bags.

Beverage coolers tend to be opened frequently, so use one cooler for beverages and one for the other foods.

If you made ice blocks, place in the bottom of the cooler. Add the cans and bottles to the beverage cooler, then top with ice cubes. Pack the food cooler in the opposite order of how you'll use the items. The foods you need first should be on top so they're easily accessible. A full cooler will stay colder longer. So once the food is in, fill the open spaces with the homemade ice packs, frozen gel packs, ice cubes or crushed ice.

Pack warm foods in a separate, insulated cooler lined with clean towels. Wrap warm dishes individually in clean towels or newspapers, then pack them tightly in the cooler.

Don't place coolers in the trunk. They'll stay colder in the back seat of the car. On warm days, run the air conditioning to keep it even cooler.

AT THE PARTY

If possible, keep the cooler out of direct sunlight. Keep food in a closed cooler until needed.

To avoid leftovers, grill only what you need and grill in batches so the food is always hot.

Replenish the ice in the cooler if possible. Otherwise, leave the melted ice water in the cooler; it keeps things cold almost as well as ice.

GOING HOME

When you arrive back home, promptly refrigerate all perishable items. If they are wet or not cold anymore, toss them out.

Drain the cooler and wash it in hot soapy water. If meat juices have dripped in the cooler, you can clean it with a solution of 1 teaspoon bleach to 1 quart of water. Let the solution stand in the cooler for about 10 minutes. Drain carefully to avoid splashing, and wash the cooler. Leave the cooler open until it is completely dry before storing.

LIGHT UP THE GRILL FOR
CLASSIC TAILGATE TASTES

Most folks wouldn't consider it a tailgate party without a grill. While you can enjoy plenty of foods without the flame, there's something to be said for the smell of burgers, brats and steaks sizzling on a charcoal grill. To avoid under- or over-cooked foods, turn to these handy tips and charts.

GRILLING SAFETY AND TIPS

- Place your grill in a well-ventilated area on a level, solid surface away from fences, shrubs, grass and overhangs.
- Store charcoal in a dry place.
- Do not use gasoline or kerosene to light briquettes. Once the coals are lit, do not add lighter fluid.
- To grease a hot grate, fold a paper towel into a small pad. Moisten the paper towel with cooking oil; using long-handled tongs, lightly coat the grill rack.
- Soak wooden skewers for at least 15 minutes in cold water before using to prevent them from burning. Leave a little space between pieces of food as you thread them onto the skewer to promote heat circulation and even cooking.
- Don't crowd food on the grill. Allow some space around each piece for even cooking.

- Always place cooked meat, seafood and poultry on a clean plate—never on a plate that held the uncooked food.
- When basting with marinade, reserve some for basting and add the meat to the remaining marinade. Discard the marinade from the meat. Any marinade that came in contact with uncooked meat, poultry or seafood should be discarded.
- Brush on thick or sweet sauces during the last 10-15 minutes of cooking, basting and turning every few minutes to prevent burning.
- Wear long barbecue mitts to protect your hands and arms from the heat. It's best to have two pairs of long-handled tongs—one for moving the coals and one to turn food.
- Always have a water bottle handy to spray any flare-ups.
- When you're done, cover the grill, close the vents and let stand until cold. Don't discard the ashes until they are completely cooled.

TESTING THE TEMPERATURE OF YOUR GRILL

Cautiously hold the palm of your hand 3-4 inches above the grate. Count the number of seconds you can hold your hand there before the heat forces you to pull away.

TEMPERATURE	NUMBER OF SECONDS	COLOR OF COALS
Hot (at least 450º)	2 seconds	coals glow red
Medium-hot (400º)	3 seconds	coals are gray with a red underglow
Medium (350º)	4 seconds	coals are gray with a hint of red
Medium-low (300º)	5 seconds	coals are gray with a faint red glow

GRILLING DONENESS TESTS

When grilling meats, fish or seafood at your tailgate, take along this handy chart, which indicates doneness temperatures or tests.

MEAT	DONENESS TEST
BEEF, GROUND BEEF & VEAL	
Beef Cuts	145° (medium-rare)
	160° (medium)
	170° (well-done)
Ground Beef and Veal	160°
Veal Cuts	160° (medium)
	170° (well-done)
CHICKEN	
Breasts	170°
Ground	165°
Kabobs/Strips	Juices run clear
Whole	180° (measured in thigh)
FISH & SEAFOOD	
Fillets/Steaks/Kabobs	Opaque and flakes
Scallops	Opaque
Shrimp	Turns pink
LAMB	
Chops/Steaks	145° (medium-rare)
	160° (medium)
	170° (well-done)
Ground	160°
PORK & SAUSAGES	160°
TURKEY	
Ground	165°
Kabobs/Strips	Juices run clear
Tenderloins	170°
Whole	180° (measured in thigh)
VEGETABLES & FRUITS	Until tender

SEVEN ALL-SEASON
TAILGATING TIPS

#1 To get an early start in the morning, pack the car the night before with nonperishable food, chairs and tables. Don't forget supplies like a blanket or tablecloth to spread over the tailgate, and a variety of paper products (plates, napkins, utensils, paper towels, trash bags, resealable plastic bags, etc.).

#2 True tailgaters proudly show their support of the team, so dress in team colors or jerseys!

#3 Just before heading out, pack the food and beverage coolers. Covered plastic containers work great for all kinds of food because they prevent leaks and won't break during transport.

#4 When you get to the parking lot, fly a team banner so other tailgaters in your group can find you. Or keep in contact by cellphone.

#5 Plan on eating at least 45 minutes before the game starts. This gives you time to clean up and pack things away.

#6 Before heading into the stadium, make note of your parking location so you're not lost in a sea of cars afterward.

#7 Instead of fighting traffic jams when the game is over, linger in the parking lot for an hour or so. Rehash the highlights of the game over a snack or dessert.

- ☐ Food
- ☐ Beverages
- ☐ Ice
- ☐ Coolers
- ☐ Two sets of cutting boards, grilling utensils and platters
- ☐ Meat thermometer or instant-read thermometer
- ☐ Clean foil, plastic wrap and resealable plastic bags
- ☐ Paper plates, napkins, cups and plastic utensils
- ☐ Trash bags
- ☐ Paper towels
- ☐ Hand sanitizer and moist towelettes
- ☐ Grill, charcoal, lighter fluid, matches
- ☐ Chairs and tables
- ☐ Blankets or tablecloths
- ☐ Sunblock
- ☐ Hats, jackets and other outerwear
- ☐ Insect repellent
- ☐ First aid kit/medicine
- ☐ Sunglasses
- ☐ Radio
- ☐ Camera
- ☐ Binoculars
- ☐ Flashlight
- ☐ Games, balls, bats
- ☐ Cellphones
- ☐ Tickets!

THE TAILGATER'S CHECKLIST

Before you head out the door, double-check that you have everything you need for a **BLOW-OUT BASH!**

APPETIZERS
& SNACKS

Chock-full of color and lively flavor, this salsa makes a nice appetizer paired with tortilla chips. It's great for parties because it's easy and nutritious.

chunky black bean salsa

CHRIS BEHNKE ⚐ FRUITLAND, IOWA

5 plum tomatoes, seeded and chopped
½ cup minced fresh cilantro
1 jalapeno pepper, chopped
¾ cup canned black beans, rinsed and drained
½ cup canned diced tomatoes with green chilies, drained
¼ cup chopped ripe olives
2 tablespoons chopped red onion
½ cup Italian salad dressing
Tortilla chips

1. In a bowl, combine the first eight ingredients. Toss to coat. Serve salsa with chips. Refrigerate leftovers.

YIELD: 5 cups.

EDITOR'S NOTE: When cutting or seeding hot peppers, use rubber or plastic gloves to protect your hands. Avoid touching your face.

barbecue muncher mix

MRS. DEAN HOLMES ⚑ ALTAMONT, KANSAS

*Looking for a twist on standard party mix? My family enjoys this at
Christmas and throughout the year. It also makes a nice addition to a gift basket.*

4 cups Corn Chex
4 cups Wheat Chex
2 cups cheese-flavored snack crackers
2 cups pretzel sticks
2 cups mixed nuts *or* dry roasted peanuts
½ cup butter
4 to 5 tablespoons barbecue sauce
1 tablespoon Worcestershire sauce
1 teaspoon seasoned salt

1. In a large roasting pan, combine the cereals, crackers, pretzels and nuts; set aside. In a small saucepan, melt butter; stir in the barbecue sauce, Worcestershire sauce and seasoned salt until blended. Pour over the cereal mixture and stir to coat.
2. Bake, uncovered, at 250° for 1 hour, stirring every 15 minutes. Spread on waxed paper to cool completely. Store in airtight containers.
YIELD: 14 cups.

mexican chicken wings

BARBARA MCCONAUGHEY ⚑ HOULTON, WISCONSIN

*I make these spicy appetizers for parties and football games and never have any leftovers. The hot wings
contrast nicely with the cool but zippy dip. When the wings run out, we use any extra cilantro dip on tortilla chips.*

12 whole chicken wings
   (about 2½ pounds)
⅓ cup all-purpose flour
⅓ cup cornmeal
1 tablespoon ground cumin
1½ teaspoons salt
1½ teaspoons pepper
¾ teaspoon cayenne pepper
JALAPENO CILANTRO DIP:
2½ cups (20 ounces) sour cream
3 cups fresh cilantro leaves
6 green onions, cut into 3-inch pieces
4 jalapeno peppers, seeded
3 teaspoons salt

1. Cut chicken wings into three sections; discard wing tip section. In a large resealable plastic bag, combine the flour, cornmeal, cumin, salt, pepper and cayenne. Add the chicken wings, a few at a time. Seal bag and shake to coat.
2. Transfer to a greased 13-in. x 9-in. x 2-in. baking pan. Bake, uncovered, at 375° for 25-27 minutes on each side or until juices run clear and coating is set.
3. Meanwhile, in a blender, combine dip ingredients; cover and process until blended. Refrigerate until serving. Serve with wings.
YIELD: 2 dozen (3⅔ cups dip).

EDITOR'S NOTE: 2½ pounds of uncooked chicken wing sections (wingettes) may be substituted for the whole chicken wings. Omit first step. When cutting or seeding hot peppers, use rubber or plastic gloves to protect your hands. Avoid touching your face.

crab and cream cheese dip

NADINE MCGEHEE ⚐ GREENVILLE, MISSISSIPPI

*This creamy dip is the perfect accompaniment to any party menu.
Plus, it's different than the run-of-the-mill snacks. It's so delicious on crisp crackers.*

1 package (3 ounces) cream cheese, softened
2 tablespoons mayonnaise
1½ teaspoons thinly sliced green onion
1½ teaspoons diced pimiento, drained
1½ teaspoons Worcestershire sauce
½ teaspoon prepared horseradish
⅓ cup crabmeat, drained, flaked and cartilage removed
1 tablespoon finely chopped pecans
Assorted crackers

1. In a mixing bowl, combine cream cheese and mayonnaise. Stir in the green onion, pimiento, Worcestershire sauce and horseradish; mix well. Stir in crab.

2. Place in a 1-cup serving bowl and sprinkle with pecans. Refrigerate for at least 2 hours. Serve with crackers.

YIELD: 2 servings.

kiddie crunch mix

KARA DE LA VEGA ⚐ SOMERSET, CALIFORNIA

This no-bake snack mix is a real treat for kids, and you can easily increase the amount to fit your needs. Place it in individual plastic bags or pour some into colored ice cream cones and cover with plastic wrap for a fun presentation.

1 cup animal crackers
1 cup miniature teddy bear-shaped chocolate graham crackers
1 cup miniature pretzels
1 cup salted peanuts
1 cup M&M's
1 cup chocolate *or* yogurt-covered raisins

1. In a bowl, combine all ingredients; mix well. Store in an airtight container.

YIELD: 6 cups.

I used reduced-fat items to lighten up this Parmesan and bacon dip. It is a snap to mix up the night before, and I get requests for the recipe whenever I serve it.

bacon ranch dip

PAM GARWOOD 🏁 LAKEVILLE, MINNESOTA

½ cup reduced-fat mayonnaise
½ cup reduced-fat ranch salad dressing
½ cup fat-free sour cream
½ cup shredded Parmesan cheese
¼ cup crumbled cooked bacon
Assorted fresh vegetables

1. In a bowl, combine the first five ingredients; mix well. Cover and refrigerate for at least 1 hour before serving. Serve with vegetables.
YIELD: 1½ cups.

artichoke nibbles

KAREN BROWN ☞ TRENTON, MICHIGAN

1 small onion, chopped
1 garlic clove, minced
1 teaspoon vegetable oil
2 jars (6½ ounces *each*) marinated
    artichoke hearts, drained and chopped
4 eggs
2 tablespoons minced fresh parsley
¼ teaspoon salt
⅛ teaspoon pepper
⅛ teaspoon dried oregano
⅛ teaspoon hot pepper sauce
2 cups (8 ounces) shredded cheddar cheese
⅓ cup crushed saltines
    (about 10 crackers)

1. In a small skillet, saute onion and garlic in oil until tender. Stir in artichokes. Remove from the heat; set aside. In a large bowl, whisk the eggs, parsley, salt, pepper, oregano and pepper sauce. Stir in cheese, cracker crumbs and artichoke mixture.

2. Pour into a greased 11-in. x 7-in. x 2-in. baking dish. Bake, uncovered, at 325° for 25-30 minutes or until a knife inserted near the center comes out clean. Cool for 10-15 minutes before cutting into 1-in. squares. Serve warm.

YIELD: about 6 dozen.

fruit salsa with ginger chips

CHRISTY JOHNSON ⚑ COLUMBUS, OHIO

1 can (20 ounces) unsweetened crushed pineapple

1 large mango *or* 2 medium peaches, peeled and chopped

2 medium kiwifruit, peeled and chopped

¼ cup chopped macadamia nuts

4½ teaspoons brown sugar

4½ teaspoons flaked coconut

8 flour tortillas (8 inches)

1 tablespoon water

¼ cup sugar

1 to 2 teaspoons ground ginger

1. Drain pineapple, reserving 3 tablespoons juice. In a large bowl, combine the pineapple, mango, kiwi, nuts, brown sugar, coconut and reserved juice. Cover and refrigerate for at least 1 hour.

2. For chips, lightly brush one side of each tortilla with water. Combine sugar and ginger; sprinkle over the moistened side of tortillas. Cut each into six wedges. Place in a single layer on ungreased baking sheets.

3. Bake at 400° for 5-7 minutes or until chips are golden brown and crisp. Cool on wire racks. Serve with salsa.

YIELD: 12 servings.

Pineapple, mango and kiwifruit give my fruit salsa a tropical twist. This combination of sweet salsa and crisp gingery chips is wonderful on a hot day. I like to serve this with pineapple iced tea, which I make by simply adding some of the drained pineapple juice from this recipe to a pitcher of tea.

Here's a delightful hors d'oeuvre that's excellent for any occasion. The combo of salmon, cream cheese and curry powder gives it terrific flavor.

salmon cheese spread

RAYMONDE BERNIER ST. HYACINTHE, QUEBEC

2 packages (3 ounces *each*) cream cheese, softened
3 tablespoons mayonnaise
1 tablespoon lemon juice
½ teaspoon salt
½ teaspoon curry powder
¼ teaspoon dried basil
⅛ teaspoon pepper
1 can (7½ ounces) salmon, drained, bones and skin removed
2 green onions, thinly sliced
Assorted crackers

1. In a mixing bowl, combine the cream cheese, mayonnaise and lemon juice. Add the salt, curry powder, basil and pepper; mix well. Gently stir in salmon and onions. Cover and refrigerate for at least 1 hour. Serve with crackers.

YIELD: 1½ cups.

LET SIT FOR EASIER SPREADING
Allow cheese balls, dips and spreads that contain cream cheese to stand at room temperature for 15 minutes before serving time for easier spreading and more flavor.

cucumber ham roll-ups

DEBBIE SMITH  URBANA, OHIO

*I came across this recipe while looking for a new dish to take to a party.
Everyone loves these refreshing roll-ups...even the kids!*

1 medium cucumber
1 package (8 ounces) cream cheese, softened
2 tablespoons prepared mustard
1 teaspoon dill weed
8 thin rectangular slices deli ham

1. Peel cucumber; cut in half lengthwise. Scoop out the seeds with a spoon. Cut each half lengthwise into four strips; set aside. In a small mixing bowl, combine the cream cheese, mustard and dill.
2. Spread about 2 tablespoons over each ham slice. Place a cucumber strip on the wide end; roll up tightly jelly-roll style. Cut off any cucumber that extends beyond ham slice.
3. Wrap tightly in plastic wrap and refrigerate for at least 2 hours. Cut into ¾-in. slices using a serrated knife.

YIELD: about 4 dozen.

creamy taco dip

DENISE SMITH  LUSK, WYOMING

You'll know this dip is a hit at your next gathering when you come home with an empty dish!

2 packages (8 ounces *each*) cream cheese, softened
1 cup (8 ounces) sour cream
1 jar (8 ounces) taco sauce *or* salsa
2 teaspoons ground cumin
1 can (15 ounces) refried beans
1 cup shredded lettuce
1 cup (4 ounces) shredded cheddar cheese
1 medium tomato, diced
¼ cup chopped ripe olives
¼ cup canned chopped green chilies
Tortilla chips

1. In a mixing bowl, beat cream cheese and sour cream until smooth. Stir in taco sauce and cumin; set aside. Spread the refried beans over the bottom of a serving platter or 13-in. x 9-in. x 2-in. dish.
2. Spread cream cheese mixture over the beans, leaving about 1 in. uncovered around the edges. Top with layers of lettuce, cheese, tomato, olives and chilies. Serve with tortilla chips.

YIELD: 16-20 servings.

burnt peanuts

SUE GRONHOLZ ⚑ COLUMBUS, WISCONSIN

As far as my family's concerned, I can't make this nutty treat too often. In fact, I save pint jars throughout the year as containers for this popular snack I also give as Christmas gifts.

1 cup sugar
½ cup water
1 teaspoon red food coloring, optional
2 cups raw Spanish peanuts with skins (no substitutes)

1. In a heavy saucepan, combine the sugar, water and food coloring if desired. Bring to a boil over medium heat; stir in peanuts. Cook, stirring occasionally, for 12 minutes or until peanuts are coated and no syrup remains.

2. Spread peanuts into an ungreased 15-in. x 10-in. x 1-in. baking pan; separate with a fork. Bake at 300° for 30 minutes, stirring every 10 minutes. Cool. Store peanuts in an airtight container at room temperature.

YIELD: about 4 cups.

spiced honey pretzels

MARY LOU MOON ⚑ BEAVERTON, OREGON

If your tastes run to sweet and spicy, you'll love these zesty pretzels with a twist. The coating is so yummy, you won't need a dip to enjoy them! They're great for munching, and you won't feel a bit guilty.

4 cups thin pretzel sticks
3 tablespoons honey
2 teaspoons butter, melted
1 teaspoon onion powder
1 teaspoon chili powder

1. Line a 15-in. x 10-in. x 1-in. baking pan with foil; coat the foil with nonstick cooking spray. Place pretzels in a large bowl.

2. In a small bowl, combine the honey, butter, onion powder and chili powder. Pour over pretzels; toss to coat evenly. Spread into prepared pan. Bake at 350° for 8 minutes, stirring once. Cool on a wire rack, stirring gently several times to separate.

YIELD: 8 servings.

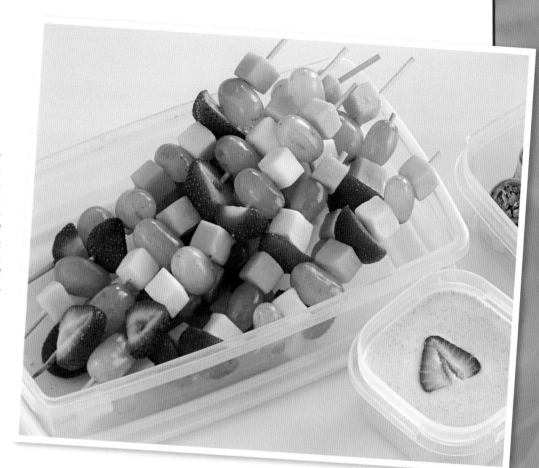

This fresh and fruity snack is easy to make ahead and carry to the ballpark, beach or playing field. The cinnamon-spiced yogurt dip adds that special touch everyone loves!

fruit 'n' cheese kabobs

TASTE OF HOME TEST KITCHEN

1 pint fresh strawberries, halved

1½ cups green grapes

1 package (8 ounces) cheddar and Monterey Jack cheese cubes

1 cup (8 ounces) vanilla yogurt

½ cup sour cream

2 tablespoons honey

½ teaspoon ground cinnamon

1. On 12 wooden skewers, alternately thread the strawberries, grapes and cheese cubes. For the dip, in a small bowl, combine the yogurt, sour cream, honey and cinnamon. Serve immediately or refrigerate.

YIELD: 12 kabobs (1½ cups dip).

PREPARE THEM AHEAD
Make appetizers ahead of serving time but store them in the refrigerator; just be sure to wrap them tightly with foil or plastic wrap.

Being from America's Dairyland, I'm always on the lookout for new ways to serve cheese. I received this delicious recipe from a friend a few years ago and am happy to share it with others.

marinated mozzarella cubes

ARLINE ROGGENBUCK ⚑ SHAWANO, WISCONSIN

1 pound part-skim mozzarella cheese, cut into 1-inch cubes

1 jar (7 ounces) roasted red peppers, drained and cut into bite-size pieces

6 fresh thyme sprigs

2 garlic cloves, minced

1¼ cups olive oil

2 tablespoons minced fresh rosemary

2 teaspoons Italian seasoning

¼ teaspoon crushed red pepper flakes

Bread *or* crackers

1. In a quart jar with a tight-fitting lid, layer a third of the cheese, peppers, thyme and garlic. Repeat layers twice. In a small bowl, combine the oil, rosemary, Italian seasoning and pepper flakes; mix well.

2. Pour into the jar; seal and turn upside down. Refrigerate overnight, turning several times. Serve with bread or crackers.

YIELD: 12-16 servings.

cheesy pecan roll

ANGIE MONK QUITMAN, TEXAS

*Years ago, I judged a local 4-H food show, where this roll won first prize
in the snack foods category. My family has also labeled it a winner!*

- 1 package (8 ounces) cream cheese, softened
- 2 teaspoons steak sauce
- ½ teaspoon salt
- ¼ teaspoon garlic powder
- ¾ cup finely chopped cooked chicken
- 2 tablespoons minced celery
- 1 tablespoon minced onion
- ½ cup ground pecans
- Assorted crackers

1. In a bowl, combine cream cheese, steak sauce, salt and garlic powder until smooth. Stir in the chicken, celery and onion. Shape into a 9-in.-long log. Roll in pecans. Cover and refrigerate until serving. Serve with crackers.

YIELD: 8-10 servings.

popcorn nut crunch

MIDGE STOLTE BLACKFALDS, ALBERTA

*For my family, it's not a party here until I make this. As long as it's kept
in a dry place, this snack will last—up to three weeks, if you seal it in a tin.*

- 2 quarts popped popcorn
- 1 cup blanched whole almonds, toasted
- 1 cup *each* pecan halves, cashews, Brazil nuts and hazelnuts, toasted
- 1½ cups sugar
- 1 cup dark corn syrup
- ½ cup butter
- 1 teaspoon vanilla extract
- ½ teaspoon ground cinnamon

1. Place the popcorn and nuts in a lightly greased 5-qt. Dutch oven. Bake at 250° for 20 minutes.
2. Meanwhile, in a medium saucepan, combine the sugar, corn syrup and butter; bring to a boil over medium heat, stirring constantly. Cook, without stirring, until a candy thermometer reads 290° (soft-crack stage). Remove from the heat; stir in the vanilla and cinnamon.
3. Pour a small amount at a time over popcorn mixture, stirring constantly until the mixture is well coated. Immediately spread on greased baking sheets. Cool; break into pieces. Store in airtight containers.

YIELD: about 4 quarts.

EDITOR'S NOTE: We recommend that you test your candy thermometer before each use by bringing water to a boil; the thermometer should read 212°. Adjust your recipe temperature up or down based on your test.

grilled greek crostini topping

STEPHANIE PROEBSTING ⚑ BARRINGTON, ILLINOIS

2 large vine-ripe tomatoes, halved and
   thinly sliced

1 package (8 ounces) feta cheese, halved
   lengthwise

3 teaspoons minced fresh oregano

3 teaspoons olive oil

Ground pepper

Sliced French bread baguette, toasted

1. Arrange a third of the tomato slices in a single layer on a double thickness of heavy-duty foil (about 12 in. square). Place half of the cheese over tomatoes; sprinkle with 1 teaspoon oregano and drizzle with 1 teaspoon oil. Sprinkle with a dash of pepper. Repeat layers.

2. Top with remaining tomato slices. Drizzle with remaining oil and sprinkle with remaining oregano and a dash of pepper. Fold foil around mixture and seal tightly.

3. Grill mixture, covered, over medium heat for 8-10 minutes or until heated through. Open foil carefully to allow steam to escape. Transfer to a serving platter; serve with toasted baguette.

YIELD: 8 servings.

I got the idea for this quick and easy appetizer while on a vacation in Greece. It's nice for summer get-togethers.

Between the flavorful sauce and colorful, crunchy slaw, these hand-held sandwiches demand attention from partygoers.

baja chicken & slaw sliders

JANET HYNES MOUNT PLEASANT, WISCONSIN

¼ cup reduced-fat sour cream
½ teaspoon grated lime peel
¼ teaspoon lime juice

SLAW:

1 cup broccoli coleslaw mix
2 tablespoons finely chopped sweet red pepper
2 tablespoons finely chopped sweet onion
2 tablespoons minced fresh cilantro
2 teaspoons finely chopped seeded jalapeno pepper
2 teaspoons lime juice
1 teaspoon sugar

SLIDERS:

4 boneless skinless chicken breast halves (4 ounces *each*)
½ teaspoon ground cumin
½ teaspoon chili powder
¼ teaspoon salt
¼ teaspoon coarsely ground pepper
8 Hawaiian sweet rolls, split
8 small lettuce leaves
8 slices tomato

1. In a small bowl, combine the sour cream, lime peel and lime juice. In another small bowl, combine the slaw ingredients. Chill the sauce and slaw until serving.

2. Cut each chicken breast in half widthwise; flatten to ½-in. thickness. Sprinkle with seasonings.

3. Moisten a paper towel with cooking oil; using long-handled tongs, lightly coat the grill rack. Grill chicken, covered, over medium heat or broil 4 in. from the heat for 4 to 7 minutes on each side or until no longer pink.

4. Grill rolls, cut sides down, for 30-60 seconds or until toasted. Serve chicken on rolls with lettuce, tomato, sauce and slaw.

YIELD: 8 servings.

EDITOR'S NOTE: Wear disposable gloves when cutting hot peppers; the oils can burn skin. Avoid touching your face.

pretzel snackers

ELISSA ARMBRUSTER ▷ MEDFORD, NEW JERSEY

I first served this treat when my husband's aunt came to visit, and she asked for the recipe. She has since reported that all her friends enjoy it as much as we do! The recipe can be doubled or tripled with great results.

2 packages (16 ounces *each*) sourdough pretzel nuggets
1 envelope ranch salad dressing mix
1½ teaspoons dried oregano
1 teaspoon lemon-pepper seasoning
1 teaspoon dill weed
½ teaspoon garlic powder
½ teaspoon onion powder
¼ cup olive oil

1. Place pretzels in a large bowl. In a small bowl, combine dressing mix, oregano, lemon-pepper, dill weed, garlic powder and onion powder. Sprinkle over pretzels; toss gently to combine. Drizzle with oil; toss until well coated.

2. Spread in a 15-in. x 10-in. x 1-in. baking pan coated with nonstick cooking spray. Bake, uncovered, at 350° for 10 minutes. Stir; bake 5 minutes longer. Cool completely. Store in airtight containers.

YIELD: 20 (½-cup) servings.

white bean dip

LINN LANDRY ▷ HONEYDEW, CALIFORNIA

My family and I enjoy eating this with tortilla chips, crackers and just about anything else we can find to dip into it—including our fingers!

1 can (15 to 16 ounces) cannellini beans *or* great northern beans, rinsed and drained
1 tablespoon lemon juice
2 tablespoons plain yogurt
2 tablespoons chopped fresh parsley
½ teaspoon freshly ground black pepper
¼ teaspoon hot pepper sauce
2 to 3 garlic cloves
Salt to taste
Pita bread, corn chips *or* fresh vegetables

1. In a food processor or blender, combine the first eight ingredients. Cover and process until smooth. Refrigerate until serving. Serve with toasted pita bread triangles, corn chips or fresh vegetables.

YIELD: 1¼ cups.

Dip into this crunchy concoction to satisfy a craving for a snack that's both sweet and salty. It's a satisfying party mix that always gets snapped up in seconds. Try it and you'll see why.

nutty popcorn party mix

ZITA WILENSKY ⚑ NORTH MIAMI BEACH, FLORIDA

3 quarts popped popcorn
1 cup unsalted dry roasted peanuts
1 jar (3½ ounces) macadamia nuts, halved
½ cup slivered almonds
¼ cup flaked coconut
¾ cup butter
1 cup sugar
½ cup packed brown sugar
¼ cup light corn syrup
¼ cup strong brewed coffee
⅛ teaspoon ground cinnamon
2 teaspoons vanilla extract

1. In a large bowl, combine popcorn, nuts and coconut. In a saucepan, combine the butter, sugars, corn syrup, coffee and cinnamon. Bring to a boil over medium heat; boil and stir for 5 minutes. Remove from the heat; stir in vanilla. Pour over popcorn mixture and stir until coated.
2. Transfer to two greased 15-in. x 10-in. x 1-in. baking pans. Bake, uncovered, at 250° for 45-55 minutes or until golden brown, stirring every 15 minutes. Spread onto waxed paper; cool completely. Store in airtight containers.

YIELD: about 12 cups.

ZIPPIER MICROWAVE POPCORN
You can spice up regular microwave popcorn by sprinkling in a bit of cayenne pepper. Then refold the bag and shake well to distribute the flavor.

In this recipe, ripe garden ingredients and subtle seasonings make a mouthwatering salsa that's a real party treat.

garden salsa

MICHELLE BERAN ☞ CLAFLIN, KANSAS

  6 medium tomatoes, finely chopped
¾ cup finely chopped green pepper
½ cup finely chopped onion
½ cup thinly sliced green onions
  6 garlic cloves, minced
  2 teaspoons cider vinegar
  2 teaspoons lemon juice
  2 teaspoons olive oil
  1 to 2 teaspoons minced jalapeno pepper
  1 to 2 teaspoons ground cumin
½ teaspoon salt
¼ to ½ teaspoon cayenne pepper
Tortilla chips

1. In a large bowl, combine the tomatoes, green pepper, onions, garlic, vinegar, lemon juice, oil, jalapeno and seasonings. Cover and refrigerate until serving. Serve with tortilla chips.

YIELD: 5 cups.

EDITOR'S NOTE: When cutting or seeding hot peppers, use rubber or plastic gloves to protect your hands. Avoid touching your face.

bacon-broccoli cheese ball

TAMARA RICKARD ⚑ BARTLETT, TENNESSEE

1 package (8 ounces) cream cheese, softened
1 cup (4 ounces) finely shredded cheddar cheese
½ teaspoon pepper
1 cup finely chopped broccoli florets
6 bacon strips, cooked and crumbled
Assorted crackers

1. In a mixing bowl, beat cream cheese, cheddar cheese and pepper until blended. Stir in the broccoli. Shape into a ball and roll in bacon. Cover and refrigerate. Remove from refrigerator 15 minutes before serving. Serve with crackers.

YIELD: 2½ cups.

SHAPING A CHEESE BALL
Keep hands and countertop clean by spooning the cheese mixture onto a piece of plastic wrap. Working from the underside of the wrap, pat the mixture into a ball. Complete recipe as directed.

I needed a quick appetizer one night when dinner was running late, so I combined a few leftovers into this easy cheese ball. For variety, you can shape it into a log, or substitute favorite herbs for the pepper.

crunchy combo

GLORIA SCHMITZ ⌦ ELKHART, INDIANA

My husband and our four sons enjoy this any time of year. I love it while wrapping holiday gifts.
What's more, the treat carries well to gatherings and makes a nice present when packaged in pretty tins.

6 cups toasted oat cereal
1½ cups miniature pretzels
1½ cups Cheetos
½ cup butter, melted
¼ cup grated Parmesan cheese
½ teaspoon garlic salt
½ teaspoon onion salt
½ teaspoon Italian seasoning, optional

1. In a large bowl, combine the cereal, pretzels and Cheetos. Combine the remaining ingredients; pour over the cereal mixture and stir to coat.
2. Spread into an ungreased 15-in. x 10-in. x 1-in. baking pan. Bake at 275° for 30 minutes, stirring every 10 minutes. Cool. Store in an airtight container.

YIELD: about 9 cups.

chili cheese popcorn

PHYLLIS SCHMALZ ⌦ KANSAS CITY, KANSAS

Pack some bags of this zesty popcorn, and your next road trip will zip by.

8 cups popped popcorn
¼ cup butter, melted
½ teaspoon chili powder
¼ teaspoon salt
½ cup grated Parmesan cheese

1. Place popcorn in a large bowl. Combine the butter, chili powder and salt; pour over the popcorn. Spread in a 15-in. x 10-in. x 1-in. baking pan; sprinkle with Parmesan cheese.
2. Broil 6 in. from the heat for 2-3 minutes or until the cheese is melted. Toss well to coat. Store in an airtight container.

YIELD: 2 quarts.

Here's a recipe that's simple but so good! This tangy cheese spread has a wonderful combination of flavors that taste even better served with crisp rye crackers. It's a fine appetizer or snack!

horseradish cheese spread

MARGIE WAMPLER ⚑ BUTLER, PENNSYLVANIA

1 **pound process cheese, cut into cubes**
1 **cup mayonnaise**
½ **cup horseradish**
Assorted crackers

1. Melt cheese in the top of a double boiler. Remove from the heat. Stir in mayonnaise and horseradish. Pour into a small crock or ceramic bowl. Refrigerate until serving. Serve with crackers. **YIELD:** about 2½ cups.

EASY APPETIZER
For an easy but delicious appetizer, grill small chunks of kielbasa and serve it with horseradish sauce for dipping.

I got this spicy recipe from a friend but altered the ingredient amounts to adjust the hotness of the sauce. Make sure everyone has extra napkins. These wings are messy to eat but oh, so good!

barbecue chicken wings

JEAN ANN HERRITT ⚑ CANTON, OHIO

3	pounds whole chicken wings
2	cups ketchup
½	cup honey
2	tablespoons lemon juice
2	tablespoons vegetable oil
2	tablespoons soy sauce
2	tablespoons Worcestershire sauce
1	tablespoon paprika
4	garlic cloves, minced
1½	teaspoons curry powder
½	teaspoon pepper
⅛	teaspoon hot pepper sauce

1. Cut chicken wings into three sections; discard wing tips. Place wings in a greased 15-in. x 10-in. x 1-in. baking pan. Bake at 350° for 35-40 minutes or until juices run clear.
2. In a large bowl, combine remaining ingredients. Pour ½ cup into a 3-qt. slow cooker. Drain the chicken wings; add to slow cooker. Drizzle with the remaining sauce. Cover and cook on low for 1 hour, basting occasionally.

YIELD: 10 servings.

EDITOR'S NOTE: 3 pounds of uncooked chicken wing sections (wingettes) may be substituted for the whole chicken wings. Omit the first step.

ranch pretzels

LOIS KERNS ⚐ HAGERSTOWN, MARYLAND

For a fast, fun snack, start with plain pretzels and add a new twist. It takes just
a few minutes to coat them with seasonings and pop them into the oven to bake.

1 package (20 ounces) large thick pretzels
1 envelope ranch salad dressing mix
¾ cup vegetable oil
1½ teaspoons dill weed
1½ teaspoons garlic powder

1. Break pretzels into bite-size pieces and place in a large bowl. Combine remaining ingredients; pour over pretzels. Stir to coat.

2. Pour into an ungreased 15-in. x 10-in. x 1-in. baking pan. Bake at 200° for 1 hour, stirring every 15 minutes.

YIELD: 12 cups.

salsa guacamole

LAUREN HEYN ⚐ OAK CREEK, WISCONSIN

I've never tasted better guacamole than this. If there's time, I make homemade tortilla chips, too.

6 small ripe avocados, halved, pitted and peeled
¼ cup lemon juice
1 cup salsa
2 green onions, finely chopped
¼ teaspoon salt
¼ teaspoon garlic powder
Tortilla chips

1. In a bowl, mash avocados with lemon juice. Stir in salsa, onions, salt and garlic powder. Serve immediately with tortilla chips.

YIELD: 4 cups.

cheesy beef taco dip

CAROL SMITH ⚑ SANFORD, NORTH CAROLINA

2 pounds ground beef

1 large onion, finely chopped

1 medium green pepper, finely chopped

1 pound process cheese (Velveeta), cubed

1 pound pepper Jack cheese, cubed

1 jar (16 ounces) taco sauce

1 can (10 ounces) diced tomatoes and green chilies, drained

1 can (4 ounces) mushroom stems and pieces, drained and chopped

1 can (2¼ ounces) sliced ripe olives, drained

Tortilla chips

1. In a large skillet, cook the beef, onion and green pepper over medium heat until meat is no longer pink; drain. Stir in the cheeses, taco sauce, tomatoes, mushrooms and olives. Cook and stir over low heat until cheese is melted. Serve warm with tortilla chips.

YIELD: 10 cups.

For a warm, hearty snack with a bit of a kick, try this recipe. It's a hit with my family, and guests rave about it, too.

favorite snack mix

CAROL ALLEN MCLEANSBORO, ILLINOIS

6 cups Crispix
1 can (10 ounces) mixed nuts
1 package (10 ounces) pretzel sticks
¾ cup butter
¾ cup packed brown sugar

1. In a large bowl, combine the cereal, nuts and pretzels. In a small saucepan over low heat, melt butter. Add brown sugar; cook and stir until dissolved. Pour over cereal mixture; stir to coat.
2. Place a third on a greased 15-in. x 10-in. x 1-in. baking pan. Bake at 325° for 8 minutes; stir and bake 6 minutes longer. Spread on waxed paper to cool. Repeat with the remaining mixture.

YIELD: about 14 cups.

My mother-in-law gave me this recipe. It's simple to make, and it tastes like the real thing!

taffy apple dip

SUE GRONHOLZ ⚑ COLUMBUS, WISCONSIN

1 package (8 ounces) cream cheese, softened
¾ cup packed brown sugar
1 tablespoon vanilla extract
½ cup chopped peanuts
6 apples, cut into wedges

1. In a small bowl, beat cream cheese, brown sugar and vanilla until smooth. Spread mixture on a small serving plate; top with nuts. Serve with apple wedges.

YIELD: 6 servings.

KEEP APPLES FROM BROWNING
To keep cut apple slices from turning brown, dip them into or sprinkle them with lemon or lime juice, or with lemon-lime soda.

frosted hazelnuts

KATHLEEN LUTZ ▷ STEWARD, ILLINOIS

These yummy nuts will be the hit of any party spread. Their sweetness is a nice counterpart to saltier snacks.

2 egg whites
1 cup sugar
2 tablespoons water
1 teaspoon salt
½ teaspoon *each* ground cloves, cinnamon and allspice
4 cups hazelnuts *or* filberts

1. In a medium bowl, lightly beat egg whites. Add sugar, water, salt and spices; mix well. Let stand 5 minutes or until sugar is dissolved. Add hazelnuts; stir gently to coat.
2. Spread into two greased 15-in. x 10-in. x 1-in. baking pans. Bake at 275° for 50-60 minutes or until crisp. Remove to waxed paper to cool. Store in airtight containers.
YIELD: 6 cups.

cinnamon popcorn

CAROLINE ROBERTS ▷ FINDLAY, OHIO

My family can't get enough of this popcorn. It's a great finger food for traveling, since it's not sticky.

2 quarts plain popped popcorn
1 egg white, lightly beaten
½ cup sugar
1 teaspoon ground cinnamon
¼ teaspoon salt

1. Place popcorn in a 15-in. x 10-in. x 1-in. baking pan. In a small bowl, mix egg white, sugar, cinnamon and salt. Pour over the popcorn and mix thoroughly. Bake at 300° for 20 minutes. Cool completely. Store in an airtight container.
YIELD: 2 quarts.

easy salsa

MIKEL CHAPMAN ⚑ HELENA, OKLAHOMA

Garden tomatoes and onions make this homemade salsa so much better than salsa from a jar.

4 medium tomatoes, chopped
1 medium onion, chopped
¼ cup chunky salsa
½ teaspoon salt
¼ teaspoon pepper
¼ cup canned chopped green chilies, optional

1. In a large bowl, combine the tomatoes, onion, salsa, salt and pepper. Add the chilies if desired. Cover and refrigerate for several hours.
YIELD: 4½ to 5 cups.

PICK FRESH PRODUCE
Fresh fruit and vegetables make a great addition to a tailgate party. Make it really easy on yourself and purchase ones that are labeled "ready to eat" or "washed."

colorful popcorn balls

MARY KAY MORRIS ⚑ COKATO, MINNESOTA

For extra fun at a sports party, choose gelatin flavors that match your team's colors.

9 cups popped popcorn
¼ cup butter
1 package (10 ounces) large marshmallows
6 tablespoons fruit-flavored gelatin (any flavor)

1. Place popcorn in a large bowl and set aside. In a saucepan, melt butter and marshmallows over low heat. Stir in gelatin until dissolved. Pour over popcorn and toss to coat. When cool enough to handle, lightly butter hands and quickly shape mixture into balls.
YIELD: 1 dozen.

There's an abundance of excellent cheeses made in our state, but sharp cheddar is our favorite. My mom used to make this for all our family gatherings, and it was popular. Now I make it for get-togethers as well. It even gets my kids to eat vegetables!

zesty vegetable dip

LAURA MILLS LIVERPOOL, NEW YORK

1 cup mayonnaise

1 cup (4 ounces) shredded sharp cheddar cheese

½ cup sour cream

1 envelope Italian salad dressing mix

1 tablespoon dried minced onion

1 tablespoon dried parsley flakes

1 tablespoon lemon juice

1 teaspoon Worcestershire sauce

Assorted fresh vegetables

1. In a small bowl, combine the mayonnaise, cheese, sour cream, dressing mix, onion, parsley flakes, lemon juice and Worcestershire sauce.

2. Cover and refrigerate for 2 hours or until chilled. Serve with vegetables.

YIELD: 2 cups.

cajun party mix

MIRIAM HERSHBERGER HOLMESVILLE, OHIO

2½ cups Corn Chex cereal
2 cups Rice Chex cereal
2 cups Crispix cereal
1 cup mini pretzels
1 cup mixed nuts
½ cup butter, melted
1 tablespoon dried parsley flakes
1 teaspoon celery salt
1 teaspoon garlic powder
¼ to ½ teaspoon cayenne pepper
¼ teaspoon hot pepper sauce

1. Combine the cereals, pretzels and nuts. Pour into an ungreased 15-in. x 10-in. x 1-in. baking pan. Mix the remaining ingredients; pour over the cereal mixture and stir to coat. Bake at 250° for 40-60 minutes, stirring every 15 minutes. Cool. Store in airtight containers.

YIELD: 8 cups.

four-tomato salsa

CONNIE SIESE ⚑ WAYNE, MICHIGAN

7 plum tomatoes, chopped

7 medium tomatoes, chopped

3 medium yellow tomatoes, chopped

3 medium orange tomatoes, chopped

1 teaspoon salt

2 tablespoons lime juice

2 tablespoons olive oil

1 medium white onion, chopped

⅔ cup chopped red onion

2 green onions, chopped

½ cup *each* chopped sweet red, orange, yellow and green peppers

3 pepperoncinis, chopped

3 pickled sweet banana wax peppers, chopped

½ cup minced fresh parsley

2 tablespoons minced fresh cilantro

1 tablespoon dried chervil

Tortilla chips

1. In a colander, combine the tomatoes and salt. Let drain for 10 minutes. Transfer to a large bowl.
2. Stir in the lime juice, oil, onions, peppers, parsley, cilantro and chervil. Serve with tortilla chips. Refrigerate or freeze the leftovers.

YIELD: 14 cups.

EDITOR'S NOTE: Look for pepperoncinis (pickled peppers) in the pickle and olive section of your grocery store.

A variety of tomatoes, onions and peppers makes this chunky salsa so good. Whenever I try to take a batch to a get-together, it's hard to keep my family from finishing it off first! It's super with tortilla chips or even as a relish with meat.

My family prefers these mild-tasting chicken wings to the more traditional hot wings. I've found they are great for any party.

grilled glazed drummies

LAURA MAHAFFEY ⌲ ANNAPOLIS, MARYLAND

  1 cup ketchup
 ⅓ cup reduced-sodium soy sauce
  4 teaspoons honey
 ¾ teaspoon ground ginger
 ½ teaspoon garlic powder
  3 pounds fresh or frozen chicken drumettes, thawed

1. In a small bowl, combine the first five ingredients. Pour 1 cup marinade into a large resealable plastic bag. Add the chicken; seal bag and turn to coat. Refrigerate for at least 4 hours or overnight. Cover and refrigerate the remaining marinade for basting.

2. Drain chicken and discard marinade. Grill, covered, over medium heat for 15-20 minutes or until juices run clear, turning and basting occasionally with reserved marinade.

YIELD: about 2 dozen.

greek garden appetizer

DEL MASON 🏴 MARTENSVILLE, SASKATCHEWAN

Here's an impressive dip that's perfect for summer gatherings. Prepared with a flavored cream cheese, feta and chopped garden veggies, it tastes great with pita pockets or wedges.

1 carton (8 ounces) spreadable garden vegetable cream cheese
2 cups (8 ounces) crumbled feta cheese
¼ cup plain yogurt
½ teaspoon minced garlic
¼ teaspoon dried oregano
¼ teaspoon pepper
1½ cups chopped cucumber
1 cup chopped seeded tomatoes
¼ cup chopped green onions
2 tablespoons sliced ripe olives
Miniature pita pockets

1. In a large bowl, combine the cream cheese, feta, yogurt, garlic, oregano and pepper. Spread into a 9-in. pie plate. Sprinkle the cucumber, tomatoes, onions and olives over the cream cheese mixture. Serve with pita bread. Refrigerate leftovers.

YIELD: 4 cups.

---

picnic stuffed eggs

REBECCA REGISTER 🏴 TALLAHASSEE, FLORIDA

My dad loves these stuffed eggs—a Southern favorite. I've been cooking since I was a teenager, and this is one of my first original recipes.

12 hard-cooked eggs
½ cup mayonnaise
¼ cup sweet pickle relish, drained
1 tablespoon honey mustard
1 teaspoon garlic salt
½ teaspoon Worcestershire sauce
¼ teaspoon pepper
Fresh parsley sprigs, optional

1. Slice eggs in half lengthwise; remove yolks and set whites aside. In a small bowl, mash yolks with a fork. Add the mayonnaise, relish, honey mustard, garlic salt, Worcestershire sauce and pepper; mix well.

2. Stuff or pipe into the egg whites. Refrigerate until serving. Garnish with parsley if desired.

YIELD: 2 dozen.

taco roll-ups

DENICE LOUK ⚑ GARNETT, KANSAS

Our friend made these roll-ups for a garden party. A sprinkling of onion soup mix makes them different.

2 packages (8 ounces *each*) cream cheese, softened
1 cup (8 ounces) sour cream
2 cups (8 ounces) finely shredded cheddar cheese
½ cup picante sauce
1 can (4½ ounces) chopped ripe olives, drained
2 tablespoons taco seasoning
1 tablespoon onion soup mix
8 flour tortillas (10 inches)

1. In a small mixing bowl, beat cream cheese and sour cream until smooth; stir in the cheddar cheese, picante sauce, olives, taco seasoning and soup mix. Spread over tortillas; roll up jelly-roll style.

2. Wrap in plastic wrap; refrigerate for at least 1 hour. Just before serving, cut into 1-in. pieces with a serrated knife.

YIELD: about 3½ dozen.

VARY YOUR VEGGIES
Try radishes, sweet red pepper strips, sugar snap peas and cherry tomatoes in addition to usual veggie dippers such as carrots, celery, broccoli and cauliflower.

tortellini appetizers

PATRICIA SCHMIDT ⚑ STERLING HEIGHTS, MICHIGAN

These kabobs will lend Italian flavor to any inside or outdoor get-together.

18 refrigerated cheese tortellini, cooked, drained and cooled
¼ cup Italian salad dressing
6 thin slices (4 ounces) provolone cheese
6 thin slices (2 ounces) Genoa salami
18 large stuffed olives

1. In a resealable plastic bag, combine the tortellini and salad dressing. Seal and refrigerate for 4 hours. Drain and discard dressing.

2. Place a cheese slice on each slice of salami; roll up tightly. Cut each into thirds. To make kabobs, thread a tortellini, salami portion and an olive onto a toothpick.

YIELD: 1½ dozen.

Dairy products make this yummy spread rich and creamy, and pecans give it a pleasant crunch.

cattleman's spread

TERESA STUTZMAN ⚑ ADAIR, OKLAHOMA

1 cup chopped pecans
2 tablespoons butter
2 packages (8 ounces *each*) cream cheese, softened
1 cup (8 ounces) sour cream
½ teaspoon garlic powder
2 packages (2½ ounces *each*) dried beef, chopped
4 teaspoons diced onion
Crackers and breadsticks

1. In a skillet, saute pecans in butter until golden; set aside. In a mixing bowl, beat cream cheese until smooth. Add sour cream and garlic powder; mix well. Stir in beef and onion.

2. Spread into a greased 13-in. x 9-in. x 2-in. baking dish. Top with the pecans. Bake, uncovered, at 350° for 20 minutes or until heated through. Serve with crackers and breadsticks.

YIELD: 3½ cups.

I tend to make these only for special occasions because I cannot keep my husband and son (and myself!) away from them. They never last long, so you might want to make a double batch.

sugared peanuts

POLLY HALL ☞ ROCKFORD, MICHIGAN

5 **cups unsalted peanuts**
1 **cup sugar**
1 **cup water**
¼ **teaspoon salt**

1. In a large heavy saucepan, combine the peanuts, sugar and water. Bring to a boil; cook until syrup has evaporated, about 10 minutes.
2. Spread mixture into a greased 15-in. x 10-in. x 1-in. baking pan; sprinkle with salt.
3. Bake at 300° for 30-35 minutes or until dry and lightly browned. Cool completely. Store in an airtight container.
YIELD: 5 cups.

slow-cooked smokies

SUNDRA HAUCK ⚑ BOGALUSA, LOUISIANA

*I like to include these little sausages smothered in barbecue sauce
on all my party and picnic menus. They're popular with children and adults.*

1 package (1 pound) miniature smoked
  sausages
1 bottle (28 ounces) barbecue sauce
1¼ cups water
3 tablespoons Worcestershire sauce
3 tablespoons steak sauce
½ teaspoon pepper

1. In a 3-qt. slow cooker, combine all ingredients. Cover and cook on low for 5-6 hours or until heated through. Serve with a slotted spoon.
YIELD: 8 servings.

grilled steak appetizers with stilton sauce

RADELLE KNAPPENBERGER ⚑ OVIEDO, FLORIDA

*Here's a hearty appetizer that'll get any gathering off to a delicious start.
The rich, creamy cheese sauce complements the grilled steak to perfection.*

2 boneless beef top loin steaks
  (8 ounces *each*)
¼ teaspoon salt
¼ teaspoon pepper
½ cup white wine
⅓ cup heavy whipping cream
3 tablespoons sour cream
2 ounces Stilton cheese, cubed

1. Sprinkle steaks with salt and pepper. Grill steaks, covered, over medium heat for 4-6 minutes on each side or until meat reaches desired doneness (for medium-rare, a thermometer should read 145°; medium, 160°; well-done, 170°). Remove meat to a cutting board and keep warm.
2. In a small saucepan, bring wine to a boil; cook until reduced by half. Add cream. Bring to a gentle boil. Reduce heat; simmer, uncovered, until thickened, stirring occasionally. Remove from the heat. Add sour cream and cheese; stir until cheese is melted.
3. Cut the steaks into 1-in. cubes; skewer with toothpicks. Serve with sauce.
YIELD: 20 appetizers (¾ cup sauce).

EDITOR'S NOTE: Top loin steak may be labeled as strip steak, Kansas City steak, New York strip steak, ambassador steak or boneless club steak in your region. You may substitute ⅓ cup crumbled blue cheese for the Stilton cheese.

cranberry meatballs and sausage

MARYBELL LINTOTT ☞ VERNON, BRITISH COLUMBIA

- 1 egg, beaten
- 1 small onion, finely chopped
- ¾ cup dry bread crumbs
- 1 tablespoon dried parsley flakes
- 1 tablespoon Worcestershire sauce
- ¼ teaspoon salt
- 1 pound bulk pork sausage
- 1 can (16 ounces) jellied cranberry sauce
- 3 tablespoons cider vinegar
- 2 tablespoons brown sugar
- 1 tablespoon prepared mustard
- 1 package (1 pound) miniature smoked sausage links

1. In a large bowl, combine the first six ingredients. Crumble bulk sausage over the mixture and mix well. Shape into 1-in. balls. In a large skillet, cook meatballs over medium heat until browned on all sides; drain.
2. In a large saucepan, combine the cranberry sauce, vinegar, brown sugar and mustard. Cook and stir over medium heat until cranberry sauce is melted.
3. Add the meatballs and sausage links. Bring to a boil. Reduce heat; simmer, uncovered, for 10-15 minutes or until meatballs are no longer pink and sauce is slightly thickened.

YIELD: 14-16 servings.

Years ago, I found a version of this recipe in a cookbook. At first taste, my family judged it a keeper. The tangy, saucy meatballs are requested by our friends whenever I host a party. We also take the yummy dish on camping trips.

This attractive dip is guaranteed to disappear in a hurry whenever it's served.

avocado taco dip

RUTH ANN STELFOX ⚑ RAYMOND, ALBERTA

1 can (16 ounces) refried beans

1 cup (8 ounces) sour cream

⅔ cup mayonnaise

1 envelope taco seasoning

1 can (4 ounces) chopped green chilies, drained

4 medium ripe avocados, halved, pitted and peeled

2 teaspoons lime juice

¼ teaspoon salt

¼ teaspoon garlic powder

1 cup (4 ounces) shredded sharp cheddar cheese

½ cup thinly sliced green onions

½ cup chopped fresh tomato

1 can (2¼ ounces) sliced ripe olives, drained

Tortilla chips

1. Spread beans in a shallow 2½-qt. dish. In a bowl, combine sour cream, mayonnaise and taco seasoning; spread over beans. Sprinkle with green chilies.

2. In a bowl, mash avocados with lime juice, salt and garlic powder. Spread over the chilies. Sprinkle with the cheese, onions, tomato and olives. Cover and refrigerate until serving. Serve with tortilla chips.

YIELD: 12-14 servings.

antipasto appetizer salad

TAMRA DUNCAN ⚑ LINCOLN, ARKANSAS

*Serve this with a slotted spoon as an appetizer or over torn
Romaine lettuce as a salad. I like it with toasted baguette slices on the side.*

- 1 jar (16 ounces) roasted sweet red pepper strips, drained
- ½ pound part-skim mozzarella cheese, cubed
- 1 cup grape tomatoes
- 1 jar (7½ ounces) marinated quartered artichoke hearts, undrained
- 1 jar (7 ounces) pimiento-stuffed olives, drained
- 1 can (6 ounces) pitted ripe olives, drained
- 1 teaspoon dried basil
- 1 teaspoon dried parsley flakes

Pepper to taste

Toasted baguette slices *or* Romaine lettuce, torn

1. In a large bowl, combine the first nine ingredients; toss to coat. Cover and refrigerate for at least 4 hours before serving.
2. Serve with baguette slices or over lettuce.

YIELD: 6 cups.

EDITOR'S NOTE: This recipe was tested with Vlasic roasted red pepper strips.

beary good snack mix

DORIS WEDIGE ⚑ ELKHORN, WISCONSIN

*My family loves to hike and spend time outdoors, and we take this snack mix
along for a boost of energy. Kids love the fun colors and shapes.*

- 1 package (10 ounces) honey bear-shaped crackers (about 4 cups)
- 1 package (7 ounces) dried banana chips (about 2 cups)
- 2 cups M&M's
- 1 cup salted peanuts
- 1 cup dried cranberries

1. In a large bowl, combine all the ingredients. Store in an airtight container.

YIELD: 10 cups.

STORING NUTS
Raw peanuts—those that have not been roasted—can be frozen in resealable plastic freezer bags or airtight freezer containers for up to one year.

I brought this snappy recipe to work for a potluck. I started cooking the meatballs in the morning, and by lunchtime they were ready. They disappeared fast!

marmalade meatballs

JEANNE KISS ⚑ GREENSBURG, PENNSYLVANIA

1 bottle (16 ounces) Catalina salad dressing

1 cup orange marmalade

3 tablespoons Worcestershire sauce

½ teaspoon crushed red pepper flakes

1 package (32 ounces) frozen fully cooked homestyle meatballs, thawed

1. In a 3-qt. slow cooker, combine salad dressing, marmalade, Worcestershire sauce and pepper flakes. Stir in meatballs. Cover and cook on low for 4-5 hours or until heated through.

YIELD: about 5 dozen.

Colorful corn salsa is sure to be a hit with family and friends. It's an easy accompaniment to an outdoor cookout and adds a kick of flavor to whatever's on the grill.

corn salsa

SHIRLEY GLAAB ➢ HATTIESBURG, MISSISSIPPI

3 cups frozen corn, thawed
1 can (15 ounces) black beans, rinsed and drained
5 green onions, thinly sliced
1 medium sweet red pepper, finely chopped
1 jalapeno pepper, finely chopped
⅓ cup rice vinegar
1 tablespoon olive oil
1 tablespoon Dijon mustard
½ teaspoon salt
¼ to ½ teaspoon hot pepper sauce
¼ teaspoon pepper
Dash cayenne pepper
⅔ cup minced fresh cilantro

1. In a large bowl, combine the first five ingredients. In another bowl, whisk the vinegar, oil, mustard, salt, pepper sauce, pepper and cayenne. Stir in cilantro. Drizzle over corn mixture and toss to coat.
2. Chill until serving. Serve with your favorite snack chips or grilled meats.

YIELD: 5 cups.

EDITOR'S NOTE: Wear disposable gloves when cutting hot peppers; the oils can burn skin. Avoid touching your face.

garlic-onion cheese spread

MICHELLE DEFRIEZ 🏴 GRAND BLANC, MICHIGAN

2 packages (8 ounces *each*) cream cheese, softened

2 to 3 tablespoons apricot preserves

3 green onions (green portion only), chopped

3 tablespoons crumbled cooked bacon

½ to 1 teaspoon minced garlic

Dash pepper

Assorted crackers

1. In a small bowl, beat cream cheese and preserves until blended. Stir in the onions, bacon, garlic and pepper. Refrigerate until serving. Serve the spread with crackers.

YIELD: 2¼ cups.

Whenever there's an event at church, my friends always remind me to bring this cheese spread. It's irresistible on crackers!

trail mix

SANDRA THORN ⚑ SONORA, CALIFORNIA

With nuts, raisins, M&M's and coconut, this is a super party mix. It's also a tasty treat anytime.

- 2 **pounds dry roasted peanuts**
- 2 **pounds cashews**
- 1 **pound raisins**
- 1 **pound M&M's**
- ½ **pound flaked coconut**

1. Combine all ingredients in a large bowl. Store in an airtight container.

YIELD: 6 quarts.

italian nut medley

KAREN RIORDAN ⚑ FERN CREEK, KENTUCKY

Italian salad dressing is the easy secret ingredient—it adds just the right zip to plain mixed nuts.

- 2 **tablespoons butter**
- 4 **cups mixed nuts**
- 1 **tablespoon soy sauce**
- 1 **envelope Italian salad dressing mix**

1. In a skillet, melt the butter over medium heat. Add nuts; cook and stir constantly for 2 minutes. Stir in soy sauce. Sprinkle with salad dressing mix; stir to coat.

2. Immediately transfer to a greased baking pan and spread in a single layer. Cool. Store in an airtight container.

YIELD: 4 cups.

BEVERAGES

You can have this juice plain or use it in any recipe that calls for vegetable juice as an ingredient.

spicy tomato juice

KATHLEEN GILL ☞ BUTTE, MONTANA

13 pounds ripe tomatoes
    (about 40 medium)
 2 celery ribs, coarsely chopped
 3 medium onions, coarsely chopped
 1 medium green pepper, coarsely chopped
1½ cups chopped fresh parsley
 ½ cup sugar
 1 tablespoon Worcestershire sauce
 4 teaspoons salt
 ¼ teaspoon hot pepper sauce
 ¼ teaspoon cayenne pepper
 ¼ teaspoon pepper

1. Quarter tomatoes; place in a 6-qt. kettle. Add the celery, onions, green pepper and parsley. Simmer, uncovered, until vegetables are tender, about 45 minutes, stirring occasionally. Cool slightly; put through a sieve or food mill. Return to kettle. Add remaining ingredients; mix well.

2. Bring to a boil. Remove from heat; cool. Pour into freezer containers, leaving ½-in. headspace. Freeze for up to 12 months.

YIELD: about 5 quarts.

golden punch

NANCY JOHNSON ⚑ LAVERNE, OKLAHOMA

For a super addition to any celebration, you can't go wrong with this. The juices lend a terrific tropical taste! It's great for baby showers, weddings, outdoor parties or any time you need to serve a crowd. You can make it ahead of time and add the soda at the last minute.

6 cups water
4 cups sugar
1 can (46 ounces) pineapple juice
1 can (12 ounces) frozen orange juice concentrate
1 can (6 ounces) frozen lemonade concentrate
½ teaspoon almond *or* vanilla extract
1 bottle (2 liters) lemon-lime soda

1. In a large saucepan, bring the water and sugar to a boil; cook and stir for 2 minutes. Pour into a large container; add pineapple juice, concentrates and extract. Cover and freeze.
2. Remove from freezer 1-2 hours before serving. Just before serving, mash the mixture with a potato masher and stir in soda.

YIELD: 32 (¾-cup) servings.

CAN'T BEAT BLENDED DRINKS!
You can enjoy blended drinks while tailgating with hand- or gas-powered blenders. Simply mix any flavor of juice with fresh fruit, blend, and your guests will be delighted!

lemon-orange iced tea

DAWN LOWENSTEIN ⚑ HATBORO, PENNSYLVANIA

I finally found a recipe for iced tea that doesn't have the aftertaste of artificial sweetener. This is perfect for folks who need to monitor their sugar intake.

2 quarts cold water, *divided*
6 individual tea bags
2 sprigs fresh mint
1 tub sugar-free lemonade soft drink mix
2 cups orange juice

1. In a saucepan, bring 1 qt. of water to a boil. Remove from heat. Add tea bags and mint; let stand for 10 minutes. Discard tea bags and mint.
2. Pour tea into a large pitcher. Add lemonade drink mix, orange juice and remaining water; stir well. Refrigerate until chilled. Serve over ice.

YIELD: 10 servings.

cherry punch

DAVLYN JONES ⚐ SAN JOSE, CALIFORNIA

*This punch is not too sweet, so it really satisfies. My family and friends
have sipped it at countless gatherings, from picnics to the holidays, over the years.*

1 can (6 ounces) frozen lemonade
   concentrate, thawed
1 can (6 ounces) frozen limeade
   concentrate, thawed
1 can (20 ounces) pineapple chunks,
   undrained
2 cups water
2 liters cherry soda, chilled
2 liters ginger ale, chilled
Lemon and lime slices, optional

1. In a blender, combine the concentrates and pineapple; cover and blend until smooth. Pour into a gallon container; stir in water. Store in the refrigerator.

2. To serve, pour the mixture into a punch bowl; add the cherry soda and ginger ale. Garnish with the lemon and lime slices if desired.

YIELD: about 6 quarts.

raspberry cider

PAT MCILRATH ⚐ GRINNELL, IOWA

Here's a refreshing cooler for a late-summer afternoon. The cider is so pretty in a clear sparkling glass!

1 pint (2 cups) fresh *or* frozen raspberries
4 cups apple cider
Mint sprigs, optional

1. In a bowl, crush berries. Add the cider and mix well. Strain through a fine sieve or cheesecloth. Chill. Garnish with the mint sprigs if desired.

YIELD: about 5 cups.

My sister and I spent a week each summer with Aunt Frances, who always had this thirst-quenching lemonade in a stoneware crock in the refrigerator. It's an absolutely delicious drink after a hot day of running around.

aunt frances' lemonade

DEBBIE BLACKBURN ⚑ CAMP HILL, PENNSYLVANIA

5 *each* lemons, limes and oranges
3 quarts water
1½ to 2 cups sugar

1. Squeeze the juice from four of the lemons, limes and oranges; pour into a gallon container. Thinly slice the remaining fruit and set aside for garnish. Add water and sugar to juices; mix well. Store in the refrigerator. Serve on ice with fruit slices.
YIELD: 12-16 servings (1 gallon).

lemon cider

ANNETTE ENGELBERT ⚑ BRUCE CROSSING, MICHIGAN

1 gallon apple cider
  1 can (12 ounces) frozen lemonade concentrate, thawed
  1 lemon, thinly sliced or cinnamon sticks

1. In a punch bowl, combine cider and lemonade concentrate; mix well. Float lemon slices on top. Or, to serve warm, heat cider and lemonade concentrate; garnish individual servings with cinnamon sticks.

YIELD: 4½ quarts.

pineapple iced tea

KATHY KITTELL ⚑ LENEXA, KANSAS

1 quart water

7 individual tea bags

1 cup unsweetened pineapple juice

⅓ cup lemon juice

2 tablespoons sugar

1. In a saucepan, bring water to a boil. Remove from the heat. Add tea bags; cover and steep for 3-5 minutes. Discard tea bags.

2. Stir in the pineapple juice, lemon juice and sugar until sugar is dissolved. Refrigerate overnight for the flavors to blend. Serve over ice.

YIELD: 5 servings.

This thirst-quenching tea is easy to mix up and has a sparkling flavor we all enjoy.

Everyone who tastes this slightly sweet punch wants seconds, and then they ask for the recipe. It's great with a game day breakfast or brunch, but also good just by itself as a thirst-quencher. When covered, it'll keep in the fridge for several days.

pink grapefruit punch

TERRY TAYLOR-HESKETT ⚑ GOLIAD, TEXAS

4 cups water, *divided*

2 tablespoons confectioners' sugar

2 cups pink grapefruit juice

1 can (12 ounces) frozen pink lemonade concentrate, thawed

3 tablespoons maraschino cherry juice

Orange *or* lemon slices and maraschino cherries, optional

1. Combine ¼ cup water and sugar in a small microwave-safe bowl. Microwave on high for 30 seconds or until the sugar dissolves; cool. In a large pitcher, combine the grapefruit juice, lemonade concentrate, cherry juice, sugar mixture and remaining water. Chill. Serve over ice. Garnish with orange or lemon slices and cherries if desired.

YIELD: 8-10 servings (1¾ quarts).

TIMING IS EVERYTHING
Get there early! You'll want to arrive three to four hours before game time to beat the crowd and claim your turf. And plan to stay late so you don't miss a moment of the postgame action.

mulled dr pepper

BERNICE MORRIS ⚑ MARSHFIELD, MISSOURI

When neighbors or friends visit us on cool evenings, I serve this warm beverage with ham sandwiches and deviled eggs.

- 8 cups Dr Pepper
- ¼ cup packed brown sugar
- ¼ cup lemon juice
- ½ teaspoon ground allspice
- ½ teaspoon whole cloves
- ¼ teaspoon salt
- ¼ teaspoon ground nutmeg
- 3 cinnamon sticks (3 inches)

Additional cinnamon sticks, optional

1. In a 3-qt. slow cooker, combine the first eight ingredients; mix well. Cover and cook on low for 2 hours or until desired temperature is reached. Discard cloves and cinnamon sticks before serving. Garnish each mugful with a cinnamon stick if desired.

YIELD: 8-10 servings.

orange juice spritzer

MICHELLE KRZMARZICK ⚑ REDONDO BEACH, CALIFORNIA

This is a tasty twist on regular orange juice. Ginger ale adds a nice amount of fizz.

- 1 quart orange juice
- 1 liter ginger ale, chilled
- ¼ cup maraschino cherry juice

Orange wedges and maraschino cherries, optional

1. In a 2-qt. container, combine the orange juice, ginger ale and cherry juice; stir well. Serve over ice. Garnish each glass with an orange wedge and cherry if desired.

YIELD: 2 quarts.

strawberry cooler

JUDY ROBERTSON RUSSELL SPRINGS, KENTUCKY

3 cups water
5 cups sliced fresh strawberries
¾ to 1 cup sugar
¼ cup lemon juice
2 teaspoons grated lemon peel
1 cup ginger ale
Crushed ice
Whole strawberries, optional

1. In a blender, process the water, strawberries, sugar, lemon juice and peel in batches until smooth. Strain the berry seeds if desired. Pour into a pitcher; stir in the ginger ale. Serve over ice. Garnish with whole berries if desired.
YIELD: 8 servings.

peachy spiced cider

ROSE HARMAN ⚑ HAYS, KANSAS

I served this at a party once and received so many compliments, I've been making it often since.

- 4 cans (5½ ounces *each*) peach nectar *or* apricot nectar
- 2 cups apple juice
- ¼ to ½ teaspoon ground ginger
- ¼ teaspoon ground cinnamon
- ¼ teaspoon ground nutmeg
- 4 fresh orange slices (¼ inch thick), halved

1. Combine the first five ingredients in a slow cooker. Top with the orange slices. Cover and cook on low for 4-6 hours or until heated through. Stir before serving.

YIELD: about 1 quart.

spiced coffee

JOANNE HOLT ⚑ BOWLING GREEN, OHIO

Even those who usually don't drink coffee will find this special blend with a hint of chocolate appealing. I keep a big batch simmering at a brunch or open house.

- 8 cups brewed coffee
- ⅓ cup sugar
- ¼ cup chocolate syrup
- ½ teaspoon anise extract
- 4 cinnamon sticks (3 inches)
- 1½ teaspoons whole cloves

Additional cinnamon sticks, optional

1. In a 3-qt. slow cooker, combine the coffee, sugar, chocolate syrup and anise extract. Place cinnamon sticks and cloves in a double thickness of cheesecloth; bring up corners of cloth and tie with string to form a bag. Add to slow cooker. Cover and cook on low for 2-3 hours.

2. Discard spice bag. Ladle coffee into mugs; garnish each with a cinnamon stick if desired

YIELD: 8 cups.

tropical punch

RUTH SEITZ ▷ COLUMBUS JUNCTION, IOWA

Bananas give this punch a deliciously different twist. The recipe serves 40, so it's perfect for parties.

3 cups water
¾ cup sugar
3 ripe bananas
1 can (46 ounces) pineapple juice, chilled
1½ cups orange juice
¼ cup lemon juice
1 bottle (2 liters) ginger ale, chilled

1. In a blender, blend water, sugar and bananas until smooth and sugar is dissolved. Pour into a large bowl; stir in the remaining ingredients. Serve immediately.

YIELD: 40 (½-cup) servings.

CHOOSE INSULATED CUPS
Insulated cups are good for tailgating because they keep cold beverages cold and warm beverages warm. Some cups may not be safe for hot drinks—check the package label before purchasing.

hot cranberry punch

LAURA BURGESS ▷ BALLWIN, MISSOURI

I serve this rosy spiced beverage at parties and family gatherings during the winter. Friends like the tangy flavor it gets from Red Hots. It's a nice change from the usual hot chocolate.

8 cups hot water
1½ cups sugar
4 cups cranberry juice
¾ cup orange juice
¼ cup lemon juice
12 whole cloves, optional
½ cup Red Hot candies

1. In a 5-qt. slow cooker, combine water, sugar and juices; stir until sugar is dissolved. If desired, place cloves in a double thickness of cheesecloth; bring up corners of cloth and tie with string to form a bag.
2. Add spice bag and Red Hots to slow cooker. Cover and cook on low for 2-3 hours or until heated through. Before serving, discard spice bag and stir punch.

YIELD: 3½ quarts.

raspberry mint cooler

PATTY KILE GREENTOWN, PENNSYLVANIA

9 cups water, *divided*

1 to 1½ cups coarsely chopped fresh mint

½ cup sugar

3 packages (10 ounces *each*) frozen sweetened raspberries

2¼ cups lemonade concentrate, undiluted (18 ounces)

Ice cubes

1. In a large saucepan, bring 3 cups water, mint and sugar to a boil. Reduce heat; simmer, uncovered, for 10-15 minutes. Stir in the raspberries, lemonade concentrate and remaining water. Refrigerate overnight.

2. Strain raspberry mixture, reserving liquid. Press berries and mint through a sieve; discard seeds and mint. Combine raspberry juice with the reserved liquid. Serve over ice.

YIELD: 11 servings.

This lovely punch is so convenient because you can make it ahead of time and add the ginger ale just before serving.

pretty pink punch
TASTE OF HOME TEST KITCHEN

2 tablespoons sugar

3 cups cold water

2 bottles (64 ounces *each*) cranberry-raspberry drink, chilled

1 can (46 ounces) pineapple juice, chilled

1 can (12 ounces) frozen pink lemonade concentrate, thawed

1 liter ginger ale, chilled

Decorative ice mold, optional

1. In a punch bowl, dissolve sugar in water. Add juices and lemonade concentrate; mix well. Stir in ginger ale. Top with an ice mold if desired and serve immediately.

YIELD: 40 (3/4-cup) servings.

lemon grape cooler

DELORES GEORGE 🚩 ST. LOUIS, MISSOURI

*While on vacation, we sampled this tasty grape beverage that has
hints of lemon and tea. We enjoyed it so much, I had to ask for the recipe.*

1½ cups sugar
1 cup lemon juice
1 cup white grape juice
2 tablespoons unsweetened instant tea
Water

1. In a gallon container, combine the sugar, juices and tea. Add water to measure 1 gallon. Cover and refrigerate until chilled.
YIELD: 16 servings (1 gallon).

fresh lemonade syrup

KATHY KITTELL 🚩 LENEXA, KANSAS

*This is a refreshing drink to enjoy on those lazy dog days of summer. With the
simple syrup in the fridge, it's a breeze to stir up this cooler by the glass or pitcher.*

3 cups sugar
1 cup boiling water
3 cups lemon juice (about 16 lemons)
2 tablespoons grated lemon peel

1. In a 1½-qt. heatproof container, dissolve sugar
in boiling water. Cool. Add lemon juice and peel;
mix well. Cover and store in the refrigerator for
up to 1 week. Mix with water to taste.
YIELD: 5½ cups syrup (number of batches varies
depending on concentration of lemonade).

sparkling grape punch

ARLYN KRAMER 🏴 DUMAS, ARKANSAS

This lovely mauve-colored punch is both bubbly and fruity...plus, it's simple to fix for a crowd.

2 cups water
1 cup sugar
2 cups grape juice, chilled
1 cup orange juice, chilled
2 liters ginger ale, chilled

1. In a saucepan, combine water and sugar. Bring to a boil; boil for 3 minutes. Cool. Stir in juices. Stir in ginger ale just before serving.
YIELD: about 5½ quarts.

LOCATION, LOCATION, LOCATION
Find a good spot to park, such as near a grassy area or at the end of the parking row. This gives you more room for serious tailgating!

creamy hot chocolate

FLO SNODDERLY 🏴 NORTH VERNON, INDIANA

I just need a few basic ingredients to stir up this drink. It's smooth and not too sweet, making it just right for cozy winter days.

½ cup baking cocoa
1 can (14 ounces) sweetened condensed milk
⅛ teaspoon salt
6½ cups water
1½ teaspoons vanilla extract
Miniature marshmallows, optional

1. In a large saucepan, combine the cocoa, milk and salt. Cook and stir over medium heat. Gradually add water; cook and stir until heated through. Stir in vanilla. Top each serving with marshmallows if desired.
YIELD: 8 servings.

sweet citrus iced tea

DIANE KIRKPATRICK ⚑ TERRE HILL, PENNSYLVANIA

My family has been making iced tea this way since I was a child. It's perfect for potlucks and parties. It's so delicious, everyone will want to know how you made it.

14½ cups water, *divided*
10 individual tea bags
1½ cups sugar
⅔ cup lemon juice
¼ cup thawed orange juice concentrate
Ice cubes

1. In a large saucepan, bring 4 cups of water just to a boil. Remove from the heat. Add tea bags; let stand for 10 minutes. Discard tea bags.
2. Pour the tea into a large container. Stir in the sugar, lemon juice, orange juice concentrate and remaining water. Refrigerate until chilled. Serve tea over ice.

YIELD: 1 gallon.

beer margaritas

TASTE OF HOME TEST KITCHEN

There's nothing more refreshing than this cool combination of two popular drinks, beer and margaritas.

¾ cup thawed limeade concentrate
1 bottle (12 ounces) beer
¾ cup vodka
¾ cup water
Ice cubes, optional
GARNISH:
Lime slices

1. In a pitcher, combine the limeade concentrate, beer, vodka and water. Serve over ice if desired in pilsner or highball glasses. Garnish as desired.

YIELD: 4 servings.

EDITOR'S NOTE: This recipe was tested with Corona beer.

picnic fruit punch

MARION LOWERY ⚑ MEDFORD, OREGON

2 quarts cranberry juice
3 cups pineapple juice
3 cups orange juice
¼ cup lemon juice
1 liter ginger ale, chilled
1 medium navel orange, sliced

1. Combine the juices in a large container. Refrigerate. Just before serving, stir in ginger ale and orange slices.

YIELD: 5 quarts.

six-vegetable juice

DEBORAH MOYER ⚑ LIBERTY, PENNSYLVANIA

5 pounds ripe tomatoes, peeled and chopped
½ cup water
¼ cup chopped green pepper
¼ cup chopped carrot
¼ cup chopped celery
¼ cup lemon juice
2 tablespoons chopped onion
1 tablespoon salt
1 to 1½ small serrano peppers

1. In a large Dutch oven or soup kettle, combine the first eight ingredients. Remove the stems and seeds, if desired, from peppers; add to tomato mixture. Bring to a boil; reduce heat.
2. Cover and simmer for 30 minutes or until vegetables are tender. Cool. Press mixture through a food mill or fine sieve.
3. Refrigerate or freeze. Shake or stir the juice well before serving.

YIELD: 2 quarts.

EDITOR'S NOTE: When cutting or seeding hot peppers, use rubber or plastic gloves to protect your hands. Avoid touching your face.

Our family and friends enjoy my vegetable garden by the glassful. My husband likes spicy foods, and after one sip, he proclaimed this juice perfect. For more delicate palates, you may leave out the hot peppers.

This juice is a favorite at our place. I'll often double the batch and send a jar next door to my mother-in-law! I was looking for a way to sweeten lemonade without using more sugar when I came up with the recipe.

orange lemonade

WENDY MASTERS ✍ GRAND VALLEY, ONTARIO

1¾ **cups sugar**
2½ **cups water**
1½ **cups fresh lemon juice (about 8 lemons)**
1½ **cups fresh orange juice (about 5 oranges)**
2 **tablespoons grated lemon peel**
2 **tablespoons grated orange peel**
Water

1. In a medium saucepan, combine sugar and water. Cook over medium heat, stirring occasionally, until sugar dissolves. Cool. Add juices and peel to cooled sugar syrup.
2. Cover and let stand at room temperature 1 hour. Strain the syrup, cover and refrigerate. To serve, fill glasses or pitcher with equal amounts of the fruit syrup and water. Add ice and serve.

YIELD: 12 servings.

apple grape drink

DEBORAH BUTTS ⚑ UNION BRIDGE, MARYLAND

*Why settle for plain juice at brunch when you can sip this fizzy morning beverage
by stirring together just four ingredients? Everyone loves the taste of this sweet punch.*

6 cups apple juice, chilled

3 cups white grape juice, chilled

1 can (12 ounces) frozen lemonade
concentrate, thawed

1 liter club soda, chilled

1. In a large container, combine the juices and lemonade concentrate. Stir in club soda. Serve immediately.
YIELD: 3¾ quarts.

tangy fruit punch

ANN COUSIN ⚑ NEW BRAUNFELS, TEXAS

*Fruity tastes mingle wonderfully in this rosy punch. It's a popular beverage,
since its versatile sweet-tart tang goes well with all kinds of foods.*

1 can (46 ounces) pineapple juice

1 can (12 ounces) frozen orange juice
concentrate, thawed

¾ cup lemonade concentrate

1 cup water, *divided*

½ cup sugar

2 large ripe bananas

1 package (20 ounces) frozen
unsweetened whole strawberries, thawed

2 liters ginger ale, chilled

1. In a punch bowl or large container, combine pineapple juice, orange juice concentrate, lemonade concentrate, ½ cup water and sugar.
2. Place bananas, strawberries and remaining water in a blender; cover and process until smooth. Stir into the juice mixture. Cover and refrigerate. Just before serving, stir in ginger ale.
YIELD: 25-30 servings (about 5 quarts).

instant spiced tea

SHIRLEY HESTON ☞ PICKERINGTON, OHIO

Here's a warming sweet and tangy drink the whole gang will love. It also makes a great holiday hostess gift.

2 cups orange breakfast drink mix
1 cup unsweetened instant tea
⅓ cup sweetened lemonade drink mix
2 tablespoons sugar
1 teaspoon ground cinnamon
1 teaspoon ground cloves

1. In a large bowl, combine all of the ingredients. Store in an airtight container.
2. For each serving, pour 1 cup boiling water into a mug; stir in 1 tablespoon mix until dissolved.

YIELD: 48 servings (3 cups mix).

blackberry lemonade

RICH MURRAY ☞ NEVADA, MISSOURI

My lemonade is perfect for when blackberries are in season. It has a tangy, refreshing flavor.

4 cups water, *divided*
1 cup sugar
1 cup lemon juice
1 tablespoon grated lemon peel
1 cup blackberries
1 to 2 drops blue food coloring, optional

1. In a large saucepan, bring 2 cups water and sugar to a boil. Boil for 2 minutes, stirring occasionally. Remove from the heat. Stir in the lemon juice, lemon peel and remaining water; cool slightly.
2. In a blender, combine 1 cup of lemon mixture and the blackberries; cover and process until blended. Strain and discard seeds. Pour blackberry mixture and remaining lemon mixture into a pitcher; stir well. Add food coloring if desired. Refrigerate until chilled. Serve in chilled glasses over ice.

YIELD: about 1½ quarts.

topsy-turvy sangria

TRACY FIELD ⚑ BREMERTON, WASHINGTON

1 bottle (750 milliliters) merlot
1 cup sugar
1 cup orange liqueur
½ to 1 cup brandy
3 cups lemon-lime soda, chilled
1 cup sliced fresh strawberries
1 medium lemon, sliced
1 medium orange, sliced
1 medium peach, sliced
Ice cubes

1. In a pitcher, stir the wine, sugar, orange liqueur and brandy until sugar is dissolved. Stir in soda and fruit. Serve over ice.

YIELD: 10 servings (¾ cup each).

hot buttered coffee

TASTE OF HOME TEST KITCHEN

¼ cup butter, softened
1 cup packed brown sugar
1 teaspoon vanilla extract
½ teaspoon ground cinnamon
¼ teaspoon ground nutmeg
¼ teaspoon ground allspice
⅛ teaspoon ground cloves

EACH SERVING:

1 cup hot brewed coffee (French *or* other dark roast)

Cinnamon sticks and whipped cream, optional

1. In a small bowl, beat butter and brown sugar until crumbly, about 2 minutes. Beat in vanilla and spices.
2. For each serving, stir 1 tablespoon of the butter mixture into 1 cup coffee. Garnish with cinnamon stick and whipped cream if desired.
3. Cover and refrigerate leftover butter mixture for up to 2 weeks.

YIELD: 20 servings (1¼ cups mix).

Rich and rewarding, this coffee is sure to warm spirits. To save time when entertaining, serve the butter mixture with a small scoop and let guests mix their own beverages.

hot spiced cider

KIM WALLACE ⚑ DOVER, OHIO

*Next time you're tailgating during chilly weather, make a batch of this
nicely spiced cider. The wonderful aroma will warm up everyone.*

1 gallon apple cider *or* apple juice
1 cup orange juice
¼ cup maple syrup
½ teaspoon orange extract
½ teaspoon lemon extract
4 cinnamon sticks
2 teaspoons whole cloves
1 teaspoon whole allspice

1. In a Dutch oven, combine first five ingredients.
Place the cinnamon sticks, cloves and allspice
on a double thickness of cheesecloth; bring up
corners of cloth and tie with string to form a bag.
Add to the pan.
2. Cook cider, uncovered, over medium heat for
10-15 minutes or until flavors are blended (do
not boil). Discard spice bag.
YIELD: 4½ quarts.

golden fruit punch

MARGARET WAGNER ALLEN ⚑ ABINGDON, VIRGINIA

*This light, fruity punch is a breeze to serve. Since it calls for canned fruit,
there's no time-consuming peeling or chopping. I make it ahead and store it in the freezer.*

1 can (30 ounces) fruit cocktail, undrained
1 can (29 ounces) peaches, undrained
1 can (20 ounces) crushed pineapple,
undrained
4 medium bananas
2 cups sugar
2 cups water
1 can (12 ounces) frozen orange juice
concentrate, thawed
2 tablespoons lemon juice
Lemon-lime soda, chilled

1. Place fruit cocktail in a blender; cover and
process until smooth. Pour into a large freezer
container. Repeat with peaches and pineapple.
2. Place bananas, sugar and water in the blender;
process until smooth. Add to pureed fruit with
orange juice concentrate and lemon juice; mix
well. Cover and freeze.
3. Remove from the freezer 2 hours before serving.
Just before serving, break apart with a large
spoon. For each serving, in a chilled glass,
combine ¼ cup fruit slush with ¾ cup soda
YIELD: 64 (1-cup) servings.

ginger apple fizz

KIMBERLY WOOD ⚑ CADDO MILLS, TEXAS

This refreshing hot-weather drink is a nice change of pace. It's not as sweet as regular sodas.

¼ cup apple juice concentrate
⅛ teaspoon ground ginger
2 cups chilled club soda
Ice cubes

1. In a pitcher, combine apple juice concentrate and ginger. Slowly stir in soda. Serve in chilled glasses over ice.

YIELD: 2 servings.

> **MAKE ICE LOOK NICE**
> Place fresh raspberries, strawberries or other berries and fresh mint leaves in ice cube trays and fill partway with water. Freeze and use as ice cubes.

frosty fruit slush

DEBRA CORNELIUS ⚑ GRANT, NEBRASKA

This yummy slush sports a sunny citrus flavor. It's especially good on a warm day, but I make it year-round as an after-school snack.

2 cans (8 ounces *each*) crushed pineapple, drained
1 can (11 ounces) mandarin oranges, drained
5 large ripe bananas, sliced
2 cups sliced fresh strawberries
2 cups water
1 can (12 ounces) frozen lemonade concentrate, thawed
1 can (12 ounces) frozen orange juice concentrate, thawed
1 cup lemon-lime soda

1. In a blender or food processor, place half of the pineapple, oranges, bananas and strawberries; cover and process until smooth. Pour into a large bowl. Repeat.
2. Stir in the remaining ingredients; mix well. Pour or spoon ½ cup each into 24 glass or plastic cups. Cover and freeze for at least 2 hours. Remove from the freezer 15 minutes before serving. May be frozen for up to 1 month.

YIELD: 24 servings.

You only need a handful of ingredients to stir together this refreshing sipper. Its brilliant color and refreshing, not-too-sweet flavor will make it popular as the weather turns warm.

raspberry sweet tea

TASTE OF HOME TEST KITCHEN

    4 **quarts water,** *divided*

Sugar substitute equivalent to 1 cup sugar

  10 **individual tea bags**

    1 **package (12 ounces) frozen unsweetened raspberries, thawed and undrained**

    3 **tablespoons lime juice**

1. In a large saucepan, bring 2 qts. of water to a boil. Stir in sugar substitute until dissolved. Remove from the heat.

2. Add tea bags; steep for 5-8 minutes. Discard the tea bags.

3. In another saucepan, bring raspberries and remaining water to a boil. Reduce heat; simmer, uncovered, for 3 minutes. Strain and discard pulp. Add raspberry juice and lime juice to tea.

4. Transfer the tea to a large pitcher. Refrigerate until chilled.

YIELD: 15 servings.

EDITOR'S NOTE: This recipe was tested with Splenda no-calorie sweetener.

FROZEN BERRIES
Frozen rasberries are available year-round, often at a fraction of the price of fresh. They are convenient and economical in beverage recipes. And, when making smoothies, they carry the added benefit of producing a cold drink!

hot cocoa mix

RUBY GIBSON ⚐ NEWTON, NORTH CAROLINA

*I first sampled this delightful homemade hot cocoa on a camping trip
in the mountains. It was a wonderful treat on crisp mornings.*

6⅔ cups nonfat dry milk powder
1 cup instant chocolate drink mix
1 package (5 ounces) cook-and-serve
chocolate pudding mix
½ cup confectioners' sugar
½ cup powdered nondairy creamer
½ cup baking cocoa
EACH SERVING:
1 cup boiling water
Miniature marshmallows, optional

1. In a large bowl, combine the first six ingredients. Store in an airtight container in a cool dry place for up to 3 months.

2. For each serving, dissolve ⅓ cup cocoa mix in boiling water. Top with miniature marshmallows if desired.
YIELD: 21 servings (7 cups mix).

spiked lemonade

TASTE OF HOME TEST KITCHEN

Rum gives a tropical addition to this fabulous homemade lemonade. For a variation, substitute vodka for the rum.

2¼ cups sugar
5 cups water, *divided*
1 tablespoon grated lemon peel
1¾ cups lemon juice
1 cup light rum *or* vodka
6 to 8 cups ice cubes
GARNISH:
Lemon slices

1. In a large saucepan, combine the sugar, 1 cup water and lemon peel. Cook and stir over medium heat until sugar is dissolved, about 4 minutes. Remove from the heat. Stir in lemon juice and remaining water. Pour into a 2-qt. pitcher; refrigerate until chilled.

2. Stir in rum. For each serving, place ¾ to 1 cup ice in a Collins or highball glass. Pour lemonade mixture into the glass. Garnish with lemon slices as desired.
YIELD: 8 servings (about 2 quarts).

GRILLING
GREATS

These are no ordinary pork chops! I dress them up with picante sauce and a hint of orange juice. Grilling brings out the natural sweetness of the chops. They're delightful with rice or picnic salads.

orange picante pork chops

LADONNA REED 🏳 PONCA CITY, OKLAHOMA

1 cup picante sauce
⅓ cup orange juice
2 garlic cloves, minced
2 boneless pork loin chops
  (½ inch thick and 5 ounces *each*)
Hot cooked rice, optional

1. In a small bowl, combine the picante sauce, orange juice and garlic. Pour 1 cup of marinade into a large resealable plastic bag; add the pork chops. Seal bag and turn to coat; refrigerate for 4 hours or overnight. Cover and refrigerate remaining marinade.

2. Drain and discard marinade. Moisten a paper towel with cooking oil; using long-handled tongs, lightly coat the grill rack. Grill the pork chops, covered, over medium heat or broil 4-5 in. from the heat for 4-5 minutes on each side or until a thermometer reads 145°. Let stand for 5 minutes before serving.

3. Meanwhile, in a small saucepan, bring reserved marinade to a boil. Reduce heat; simmer, uncovered, for 5-7 minutes or until heated through. Serve the chops with sauce and rice if desired.

YIELD: 2 servings.

GREAT GRILLING TIPS
Trim excess fat from meats to reduce flare-ups. Use tongs instead of a meat fork to turn foods to avoid piercing and losing juices. Keep the grill covered for more efficient cooking.

beer-can chicken

STEVE BATH 🏴 LINCOLN, NEBRASKA

To add color and flavor to my chicken, I spray it with a mixture of 2 cups apple cider and 1 tablespoon balsamic vinegar as it cooks. If you're frequently opening up the grill, you may need to increase the cooking time a bit.

1 tablespoon kosher salt
1 teaspoon sugar
1 teaspoon onion powder
1 teaspoon garlic powder
1 teaspoon cayenne pepper
1 teaspoon paprika
1 teaspoon ground mustard
1 broiler/fryer chicken (3½ to 4 pounds)
1 can (12 ounces) beer

1. In a small bowl, combine the first seven ingredients. Loosen skin from around the chicken breast, thighs and legs. Rub the spice mixture onto and under skin. Tuck wing tips behind the back. Refrigerate for 1 hour.
2. Prepare grill for indirect grilling, using a drip pan. Pour out half of the beer, reserving for another use. Poke additional holes in top of the can with a can opener. Holding the chicken with legs pointed down, lower chicken over the can so it fills the body cavity.
3. Place chicken over drip pan; grill, covered, over indirect medium heat for 1¼ to 1½ hours or until meat juices run clear. Remove chicken from grill; cover and let stand for 10 minutes. Remove chicken from can.

YIELD: 6 servings.

healthy turkey burgers

CATHERINE VANSTEENKISTE 🏴 RAY, MICHIGAN

Savory and sweet, these easy and delicious burgers will lure you away from your pub favorite with just one bite. My father loves these!

¼ cup egg substitute
¼ cup seasoned bread crumbs
¼ cup dried cranberries *or* cherries
3 tablespoons crumbled feta cheese
1 pound lean ground turkey
4 whole wheat hamburger buns, split

1. In a large bowl, combine the egg substitute, bread crumbs, cranberries and feta cheese. Crumble turkey over mixture and mix well. Shape into four patties.
2. Moisten a paper towel with cooking oil; using long-handled tongs, lightly coat the grill rack. Grill, covered, over medium heat or broil 4 in. from the heat for 5-7 minutes on each side or until a thermometer reads 165° and juices run clear. Serve on buns.

YIELD: 4 servings.

walleye delight

CONNIE REILLY ⚑ STANCHFIELD, MINNESOTA

Grilling is one of the most delicious ways to make fish. Lemon juice, basil and lemon-pepper seasoning are a fantastic combination.

1 pound walleye, pike, perch *or* trout fillets
2 teaspoons butter, softened
1 tablespoon lemon juice
1 tablespoon snipped fresh basil *or* ½ to 1 teaspoon dried basil
1 teaspoon lemon-pepper seasoning
½ teaspoon garlic salt
4 ounces fresh mushrooms, sliced

1. Coat an 18-in. x 18-in. piece of heavy-duty foil with nonstick cooking spray. Place fillet on foil. Spread with butter. Sprinkle with lemon juice, basil, lemon pepper and garlic salt. Top with mushrooms.
2. Bring opposite edges of foil together; fold down several times. Fold remaining edges toward fish and seal tightly. Grill, covered, over hot heat for 10-14 minutes, turning once, or until fish flakes easily with a fork.
YIELD: 4 servings.

chili dogs

LINDA RAINEY ⚑ MONAHANS, TEXAS

Enjoy these classic dogs at home or on the go! Just make the chili ahead of time, keep it warm and then use it to top freshly grilled hot dogs at the game.

1 pound ground beef
1 garlic clove, minced
1 cup tomato juice
1 can (6 ounces) tomato paste
2 tablespoons chili powder
1 teaspoon hot pepper sauce
1 teaspoon salt
¼ teaspoon pepper
8 hot dogs
8 hot dog buns, split
Chopped onion and shredded cheddar cheese, optional

1. In a large skillet, cook the beef and garlic until meat is no longer pink; drain. Stir in the tomato juice, tomato paste, chili powder, pepper sauce, salt and pepper. Bring to a boil. Reduce heat; simmer, uncovered, for 20 minutes. Keep hot until serving.
2. Grill or broil hot dogs until heated through. Place on buns; top with chili. Sprinkle with onion and cheese if desired.
YIELD: 8 servings.

The tender beef, tangy sauce, sweet pineapple and flavorful vegetables make this main dish a memorable one. A friend of Mother's gave her this wonderful recipe. We ate the delicious warm-weather dish often, and now I prepare it for my family.

teriyaki shish kabobs

SUZANNE PELEGRIN 🏳 OCALA, FLORIDA

1 cup ketchup

1 cup sugar

1 cup soy sauce

2 teaspoons garlic powder

2 teaspoons ground ginger

2 pounds boneless beef sirloin steak (1½ inches thick), cut into 1½-inch cubes

½ fresh pineapple, trimmed and cut into 1-inch chunks

2 to 3 small zucchini, cut into 1-inch chunks

½ pound whole fresh mushrooms (medium size work best)

½ pound pearl onions

1 large green *or* sweet red pepper, cut into 1-inch pieces

1. Combine the first five ingredients in a large resealable plastic bag; reserve half of marinade. Add beef to bag. Seal the bag and turn to coat; refrigerate overnight. Cover and refrigerate the reserved marinade.

2. Drain beef and discard marinade. Thread meat, pineapple and vegetables alternately on metal or soaked wooden skewers.

3. Grill over hot heat for 15-20 minutes, turning often, or until meat reaches desired doneness and vegetables are tender.

4. In a saucepan, bring reserved marinade to a boil; boil for 1 minute. Remove the meat and vegetables from skewers; serve with marinade.

YIELD: 6-8 servings.

"More, please!" is what I hear when I serve these zippy, finger-licking ribs to family or guests. The first time my husband and I tried them, we pronounced them the best ever. The recipe has its roots in the Calgary Stampede, an annual event in our province.

calgary stampede ribs

MARIAN MISIK ⚐ SHERWOOD PARK, ALBERTA

4 pounds pork back ribs, cut into serving-size pieces

3 garlic cloves, minced

1 tablespoon sugar

1 tablespoon paprika

2 teaspoons *each* salt, pepper, chili powder and ground cumin

BARBECUE SAUCE:

1 small onion, finely chopped

2 tablespoons butter

1 cup ketchup

¼ cup packed brown sugar

3 tablespoons lemon juice

3 tablespoons Worcestershire sauce

2 tablespoons cider vinegar

1½ teaspoons ground mustard

1 teaspoon celery seed

⅛ teaspoon cayenne pepper

1. Rub ribs with garlic; place in a shallow roasting pan. Cover and bake at 325° for 2 hours. Cool slightly. Combine seasonings and rub over ribs. Cover and refrigerate for 8 hours or overnight.

2. In a small saucepan, saute onion in butter until tender. Stir in the remaining ingredients. Bring to a boil. Reduce heat; cook and stir until thickened, about 10 minutes. Remove from the heat; set aside ¾ cup. Brush ribs with some of the remaining sauce.

3. Grill, covered, over medium heat for 12 minutes, turning and basting with sauce. Serve with reserved sauce. **YIELD:** 4 servings.

grilled parmesan potatoes
TASTE OF HOME TEST KITCHEN

Take a break from usual baked potatoes by cooking these spectacular spuds on the grill. Since there's no need to boil the potatoes ahead of time, this tasty, no-fuss dish is sure to become an outdoor party favorite.

1 pound small red potatoes
¼ cup chopped green onions
2 teaspoons canola oil
1 tablespoon grated Parmesan cheese
1 teaspoon dried oregano
½ teaspoon garlic salt
¼ teaspoon pepper

1. Cut potatoes into ½-in. cubes; place in a large bowl. Add onions and oil; toss to coat. Spoon into the center of a large piece of heavy-duty foil (about 18 in. x 12 in.).
2. Combine the Parmesan cheese, oregano, garlic salt and pepper; sprinkle over potato mixture. Fold foil into a pouch and seal tightly.
3. Grill, uncovered, over medium-hot heat for 18-20 minutes or until potatoes are tender. Open foil carefully to allow steam to escape.

YIELD: 4 servings.

tender turkey burgers
SHERRY HULSMAN ▷ ELKTON, FLORIDA

These juicy, tender patties on whole wheat buns make wholesome, satisfying sandwiches. We especially like to grill them for get-togethers.

⅔ cup soft whole wheat bread crumbs
½ cup finely chopped celery
¼ cup finely chopped onion
¼ cup egg substitute
1 tablespoon minced fresh parsley
1 teaspoon Worcestershire sauce
1 teaspoon dried oregano
½ teaspoon salt
¼ teaspoon pepper
1¼ pounds lean ground turkey
6 whole wheat hamburger buns, split

1. In a bowl, combine the first nine ingredients. Crumble turkey over mixture and mix well. Shape into six patties; grill, pan-fry or broil until no longer pink. Serve on buns.

YIELD: 6 servings.

flank steak pitas

TAMMY KAMINSKI ⚑ STANWOOD, WASHINGTON

*The marinade in this yummy steak sandwich packs so much flavor,
you won't even miss fatty ingredients like cheese or mayo.*

¼ cup balsamic vinegar
2 tablespoons water
2 tablespoons reduced-sodium soy sauce
1 tablespoon hoisin sauce
2 garlic cloves, minced
1 teaspoon Thai chili sauce
¾ teaspoon pepper
½ teaspoon sesame oil
1 beef flank steak (1 pound)
4 whole pita breads
4 pieces leaf lettuce, torn
¼ teaspoon sesame seeds

1. In a small bowl, combine first eight ingredients. Pour ¼ cup marinade into a large resealable plastic bag; add the beef. Seal bag and turn to coat. Refrigerate for at least 8 hours or overnight. Cover and refrigerate remaining marinade.

2. Drain and discard marinade. Grill, covered, over medium heat for 6-8 minutes on each side or until meat reaches desired doneness (for medium-rare, a thermometer should read 145°; medium, 160°; well-done, 170°). Let stand for 10 minutes.

3. Meanwhile, grill pitas, uncovered, over medium heat for 1-2 minutes on each side or until warm. Thinly slice beef across the grain. In a large bowl, toss the beef, lettuce and reserved marinade. Serve in pitas; sprinkle with sesame seeds.

YIELD: 4 servings.

italian sausage subs

MARIELA PETROSKI ⚑ HELENA, MONTANA

Perfect for the summer grilling season, this hearty sandwich will be a picnic favorite for sure!

6 Italian sausage links (4 ounces *each*)
1 bottle (14.9 ounces) dark beer *or* nonalcoholic beer
2 cups julienned green peppers
1 cup sliced onion
2 tablespoons olive oil
2 teaspoons minced garlic
½ cup chopped fresh tomato
¾ teaspoon salt
½ teaspoon pepper
6 brat buns, split
6 slices provolone cheese, halved

1. Place sausages in a large saucepan; add beer. Bring to a boil. Reduce heat; cover and simmer for 8-10 minutes or until meat is no longer pink.

2. Meanwhile, in a large skillet, saute green peppers and onion in oil until tender. Add garlic, cook 1 minute longer. Add the tomato, salt and pepper; heat through.

3. Drain and discard beer. Grill sausages, covered, over direct medium heat for 4-5 minutes or until browned, turning occasionally. Serve on buns with the green pepper mixture and cheese.

YIELD: 6 servings.

honey-glazed chicken kabobs

TRACEY MILLER ⚑ AIKEN, SOUTH CAROLINA

⅔ cup reduced-sodium soy sauce

⅔ cup honey

½ cup canola oil

1 tablespoon prepared horseradish

2 teaspoons steak seasoning

2 garlic cloves, minced

2 pounds boneless skinless chicken breasts, cut into 1½-inch cubes

1 large sweet red pepper, cut into 1½-inch chunks

1 large green pepper, cut into 1½-inch chunks

1 large onion, cut into 1½-inch wedges

1. In a small bowl, combine the first six ingredients. Pour 1 cup marinade into a large resealable plastic bag; add the chicken. Seal bag and turn to coat; refrigerate for 5-6 hours. Cover and refrigerate remaining marinade.

2. Drain and discard marinade. On six metal or soaked wooden skewers, alternately thread chicken and vegetables. Grill, covered, over medium heat for 5-7 minutes on each side or until chicken juices run clear, basting frequently with reserved marinade.

YIELD: 6 servings.

EDITOR'S NOTE: This recipe was tested with McCormick's Montreal Steak Seasoning. Look for it in the spice aisle.

What do folks eat at a ball game? Hot dogs, of course! For our baseball theme party, I jazzed them up with an easy homemade barbecue sauce and a tangy relish that's become a family tradition.

dugout hot dogs

SUE GRONHOLZ COLUMBUS, WISCONSIN

2½ cups chopped zucchini
1 medium onion, chopped
½ cup chopped green pepper
1¼ teaspoons salt
1 cup sugar
½ cup plus 2 tablespoons white vinegar
1½ teaspoons celery seed
¼ teaspoon ground mustard
⅛ teaspoon ground turmeric
1 teaspoon cornstarch
1 tablespoon water
10 hot dogs
10 hot dog buns, split

1. For zucchini relish, in a large bowl, combine the zucchini, onion, green pepper and salt; cover and refrigerate overnight. Rinse and drain well; set aside.

2. In a large saucepan, combine the sugar, vinegar, celery seed, mustard and turmeric; bring to a boil. Add zucchini mixture; return to a boil. Reduce heat and simmer, uncovered, for 15 minutes or until crisp-tender, stirring occasionally. Combine cornstarch and water until smooth; stir into saucepan. Bring to a boil. Reduce heat; cook and stir for 3-5 minutes or until thickened. Cool. Cover and refrigerate until chilled.

3. Grill or broil hot dogs until heated through. Place on buns and top with the relish.

YIELD: 10 servings (2 cups relish).

basil burgers

JENNIE WILBURN ⚑ LONG CREEK, OREGON

½ cup loosely packed basil leaves, minced

¼ cup minced red onion

¼ cup Italian bread crumbs

¼ cup dry red wine

1 to 2 teaspoons garlic salt

2 pounds lean ground beef

8 slices Monterey Jack cheese, optional

8 hamburger buns, split

1. In a large bowl, combine the basil, onion, bread crumbs, wine and garlic salt. Crumble beef over mixture and mix well. Shape into eight patties.

2. Grill, covered, over medium heat for 5-7 minutes on each side or until a thermometer reads 160°. Top with cheese if desired. Serve on buns.

YIELD: 8 servings.

Basil is one of my favorite herbs, and that's why these burgers are chock-full of the garden darling. It gives them a savory flavor that can't be beat.

During the summer months, our kids keep me busy. So it's a welcome relief when my husband volunteers to cook out. This is his specialty.

honey-citrus chicken sandwiches

CLAIRE BATHERSON ⚑ WESTCHESTER, ILLINOIS

6 boneless skinless chicken breast halves (4 ounces *each*)
¼ cup orange juice
¼ cup lemon juice
¼ cup honey
2 tablespoons canola oil
1 tablespoon prepared mustard
¼ teaspoon poultry seasoning
⅛ to ¼ teaspoon cayenne pepper
6 slices Monterey Jack *or* Muenster cheese, optional
6 kaiser rolls, split
6 thin tomato slices
6 red onion slices
Shredded lettuce

1. Flatten chicken breasts evenly to ¼-in. thickness; set aside. In a large resealable plastic bag, combine the orange and lemon juices, honey, oil, mustard, poultry seasoning and cayenne pepper. Add the chicken breasts; seal bag and turn to coat. Refrigerate for 6-8 hours or overnight.

2. Drain and discard marinade. Grill, uncovered, over medium-low heat, turning occasionally, for 10-12 minutes or until juices run clear. If desired, top each chicken breast with a slice of cheese and grill 1-2 minutes longer or until cheese begins to melt. Serve on rolls with tomato, onion and lettuce.

YIELD: 6 servings.

steak teriyaki quesadillas

LISA HUFF WILTON, CONNECTICUT

These gently charred quesadillas embody the definition of cheesy deliciousness.
The slight smoky flavor pairs perfectly with sweet pineapple and savory steak.

⅓ cup reduced-sodium soy sauce
⅓ cup reduced-sodium chicken broth
1 tablespoon brown sugar
1 teaspoon minced fresh gingerroot
½ teaspoon onion powder
1 garlic clove, minced
1 beef top sirloin steak
  (1 inch thick and ¾ pound)
½ cup finely chopped fresh pineapple
½ cup finely chopped red onion
½ cup finely chopped green pepper
2 cups (8 ounces) shredded part-skim
  mozzarella cheese
6 flour tortillas (8 inches)

1. In a small bowl, combine the first six ingredients; set aside 3 tablespoons for filling. Pour remaining mixture into a large resealable plastic bag. Add the steak; seal bag and turn to coat. Refrigerate for 2 hours.
2. Drain steak and discard marinade. Grill steak, covered, over medium heat or broil 4 in. from the heat for 8-11 minutes on each side or until meat reaches desired doneness (for medium-rare, a thermometer should read 145°; medium, 160°; well-done, 170°).
3. Remove steak from the grill and cool slightly; cut into bite-size pieces. In a large bowl, combine the pineapple, red onion, green pepper and beef.
4. Sprinkle half of the cheese over three tortillas. Using a slotted spoon, top with beef mixture. Drizzle with reserved soy mixture. Sprinkle with remaining cheese; top with remaining tortillas.
5. Grill over medium heat for 1-2 minutes on each side or until cheese is melted. Cut each into wedges; serve immediately.

YIELD: 6 servings.

grilled cheese loaf

DEBBI BAKER GREEN SPRINGS, OHIO

I often serve buttery grilled bread with steak and a salad.
It's so quick to make, it's easy to add to whatever else you have on the grill.

1 package (3 ounces) cream cheese, softened
2 tablespoons butter, softened
1 cup (4 ounces) shredded mozzarella cheese
¼ cup chopped green onions
½ teaspoon garlic salt
1 loaf (1 pound) French bread, sliced

1. In a small bowl, beat cream cheese and butter. Add cheese, onions and garlic salt; mix well. Spread on both sides of each slice of bread.
2. Wrap loaf in a large piece of heavy-duty foil (about 28 in. x 18 in.); seal tightly. Grill, covered, over medium heat for 8-10 minutes, turning once. Open foil carefully to allow steam to escape; grill 5 minutes longer.

YIELD: 10-12 servings.

ham & cheese sandwich loaf

PAT STEVENS ⚑ GRANBURY, TEXAS

Here's a big, impressive sandwich that's hot off the grill. Sourdough bread is filled with melted cheese, crisp veggies and tender ham. It's sure to be a party favorite!

1 loaf sourdough bread (1 pound)
1 cup sliced fresh mushrooms
1 medium green pepper, cut into strips
1 medium sweet red pepper, cut into strips
1 celery rib, sliced
3 green onions, sliced
2 tablespoons olive oil
½ cup mayonnaise
2 teaspoons Italian seasoning
½ teaspoon pepper
1 pound shaved deli ham
1 cup (4 ounces) shredded Colby cheese
½ cup shredded part-skim mozzarella cheese

1. Cut bread in half horizontally. Hollow out top and bottom halves, leaving ½-in. shells. (Discard removed bread or save for another use.)
2. In a large skillet, saute the mushrooms, peppers, celery and onions in oil until tender. Remove from the heat; set aside.
3. Combine the mayonnaise, Italian seasoning and pepper; spread over bread. On the bread bottom, layer half of the ham, vegetable mixture and cheeses. Repeat layers, gently pressing down if needed. Replace bread top.
4. Wrap tightly in heavy-duty foil. Bake at 400° or grill, covered, over medium heat for 30-35 minutes or until heated through. Cut into wedges with a serrated knife.

YIELD: 8 servings.

honey-mustard brats

LILY JULOW ⚑ GAINESVILLE, FLORIDA

The flavor of these brats is enhanced by a sweet mustard glaze, which gives them a unique taste. Everyone loves them and declares them delicious!

¼ cup Dijon mustard
¼ cup honey
2 tablespoons mayonnaise
1 teaspoon steak sauce
4 uncooked bratwurst links
4 brat buns

1. In a small bowl, combine the mustard, honey, mayonnaise and steak sauce. Grill bratwurst, covered, over medium heat for 15-20 minutes or until a thermometer reads 160°, turning and basting frequently with mustard mixture. Serve on buns.

YIELD: 4 servings.

This delicious recipe came from a friend. The marinade really gives the fish a wonderful flavor. Even those who aren't that fond of fish will like it prepared this way.

barbecued trout

VIVIAN WOLFRAM ⚑ MOUNTAIN HOME, ARKANSAS

6 pan-dressed trout
⅔ cup soy sauce
½ cup ketchup
2 tablespoons lemon juice
2 tablespoons canola oil
1 teaspoon crushed dried rosemary
Lemon wedges, optional

1. Place trout in a single layer in a large resealable plastic bag. Combine soy sauce, ketchup, lemon juice, oil and rosemary; pour two-thirds of marinade into bag. Close bag and let stand for 1 hour, turning once. Set aside remaining marinade for basting.

2. Discard marinade from fish. Place the fish in a single layer in a well-greased hinged wire grill basket. Grill, covered, over medium heat for 8-10 minutes or until the fish is browned on bottom. Turn and baste with the reserved marinade; grill 5-7 minutes longer or until the fish flakes easily with a fork. Serve with lemon if desired.

YIELD: 6 servings.

I just love these burgers! They're a big hit with kids and adults. I serve them with sliced green peppers, tomato and onion slices and a jar of crushed red pepper on the side for adults. Kids enjoy them best "as-is."

grilled italian meatball burgers

PRISCILLA GILBERT ⚑ INDIAN HARBOUR BEACH, FLORIDA

  1 egg, lightly beaten
⅓ cup seasoned bread crumbs
  3 garlic cloves, minced
  1 teaspoon dried oregano
  1 teaspoon dried basil
¼ teaspoon salt
¼ teaspoon dried thyme
1½ pounds lean ground beef (90% lean)
½ pound Italian turkey sausage links, casings removed
¾ cup shredded part-skim mozzarella cheese
  8 kaiser rolls, split
  1 cup roasted garlic Parmesan spaghetti sauce, warmed

1. In a large bowl, combine the first seven ingredients. Crumble beef and sausage over mixture and mix well. Shape into eight burgers.

2. Moisten a paper towel with cooking oil; using long-handled tongs, lightly coat the grill rack. Grill burgers, covered, over medium heat or broil 4 in. from the heat for 5-7 minutes on each side or until a thermometer reads 165° and juices run clear.

3. Sprinkle burgers with cheese; cook 2-3 minutes longer or until cheese is melted. Remove and keep warm.

4. Grill or broil rolls for 1-2 minutes or until toasted. Serve burgers on rolls with spaghetti sauce.

YIELD: 8 servings.

skewered ginger beef

JEAN GAINES ⚑ RUSSELLVILLE, KENTUCKY

I always prepare several servings of this dish, freezing extras for future events. Not only do these tender slices of beef make a quick and easy dinner, but they make impressive party appetizers, too.

- 1 cup sugar
- 1 cup soy sauce
- ½ cup canola oil
- 1 bunch green onions, sliced
- 6 garlic cloves, minced
- ¼ cup sesame seeds, toasted
- ¾ teaspoon ground ginger *or* 2 teaspoons grated fresh gingerroot
- 2 teaspoons pepper
- 2 pounds beef sirloin steak, cut into ¼-inch strips

1. In a large resealable plastic bag, combine the first eight ingredients; add steak. Seal bag and turn to coat; refrigerate for 8 hours or overnight. Drain and discard marinade. Thread steak onto metal or soaked wooden skewers.

2. Grill, covered, over indirect medium heat for 15 minutes or until meat is no longer pink, turning occasionally.

YIELD: 8 servings.

COOKING WITH SKEWERS
Soak wooden skewers for at least 15 minutes in cold water before using to prevent them from burning. Leave a little space between pieces of food as you thread them onto the skewer to promote thorough cooking.

country pork ribs

BRIAN JOHNSON ⚑ LAGRANGE, GEORGIA

These hearty ribs feature a lip-smacking sauce that's tangy with just the right hint of sweetness.

- 1 cup grapefruit *or* orange juice
- 1 cup ketchup
- ½ cup cider vinegar
- ¼ cup soy sauce
- ¼ cup Worcestershire sauce
- 2 tablespoons prepared horseradish
- 2 tablespoons prepared mustard
- 2 teaspoons ground ginger
- 1 to 2 teaspoons hot pepper sauce
- ½ teaspoon garlic powder
- 4 to 5 pounds country-style pork ribs
- ¼ cup honey
- 2 tablespoons brown sugar

1. In a bowl, combine the first 10 ingredients; mix well. Pour 1½ cups marinade into a large resealable plastic bag; add ribs. Seal and turn to coat; refrigerate at least 4 hours. Cover and refrigerate remaining marinade.

2. Drain and discard marinade from the ribs. Grill, covered, over indirect medium heat for 20 minutes on each side. Meanwhile, in a saucepan, combine honey, brown sugar and reserved marinade. Bring to a boil; cook and stir for 2 minutes or until slightly thickened.

3. Baste ribs with some of the sauce. Grill 15-20 minutes longer or until a thermometer reads 160°, turning and basting occasionally. Serve with remaining sauce.

YIELD: 8 servings.

coffee marinated steak

JULIE WAL ⚑ TYRONE, PENNSYLVANIA

2 tablespoons sesame seeds
6 tablespoons butter
1 medium onion, chopped
4 garlic cloves, minced
1 cup strong brewed coffee
1 cup soy sauce
2 tablespoons white vinegar
2 tablespoons Worcestershire sauce
2 pounds boneless beef top sirloin steak
(1 inch thick)

1. In a skillet, toast the sesame seeds in butter. Add onion and garlic; saute until tender. In a bowl, combine the coffee, soy sauce, vinegar, Worcestershire sauce and sesame seed mixture. Pour half into a large resealable plastic bag; add steak. Seal bag and turn to coat; refrigerate for 8 hours or overnight, turning occasionally. Cover and refrigerate remaining marinade.

2. Drain and discard marinade from steak. Grill steak, covered, over medium-hot heat for 6-10 minutes on each side or until meat reaches desired doneness (for medium-rare, a thermometer should read 145°; medium, 160°; well-done, 170°). Warm reserved marinade and serve with steak.

YIELD: 6 servings.

My dad—a big steak lover—got this recipe from a friend, and now we never eat steak without using this marinade. It makes the meat so juicy and adds a great flavor.

low country grill

ALAINA SHOWALTER ⚑ CLOVER, SOUTH CAROLINA

2 tablespoons olive oil
1 teaspoon salt, *divided*
1 teaspoon garlic powder, *divided*
1 teaspoon seafood seasoning, *divided*
12 small red potatoes, quartered
⅓ cup butter, melted
1 pound smoked kielbasa *or* Polish sausage
3 medium ears sweet corn, cut in half
1½ pounds uncooked medium shrimp, peeled and deveined

1. In a large bowl, combine oil with ¼ teaspoon each of salt, garlic powder and seafood seasoning. Add the potatoes and toss to coat. Spoon onto a greased double thickness of heavy-duty foil (about 18 in. square).

2. Fold foil around potatoes and seal tightly. Grill, covered, over medium heat for 30-35 minutes or until tender, turning once. Set aside and keep warm.

3. In a small bowl, combine the butter with remaining salt, garlic powder and seafood seasoning. Grill kielbasa and corn, covered, over medium heat for 10-12 minutes or until kielbasa is heated through and corn is tender, turning occasionally and basting corn with half of the butter mixture. Keep warm.

4. Thread shrimp onto six metal or soaked wooden skewers; grill, covered, over medium heat for 3-4 minutes on each side or until shrimp turn pink, basting with remaining butter mixture. Slice kielbasa into six pieces before serving. Carefully open the potato packet to allow steam to escape.

YIELD: 6 servings.

Salmon is readily available cut into skinless and boneless fillets or into steaks. You can use either in this recipe.

salmon with fruit salsa
TASTE OF HOME TEST KITCHEN

2 cups chopped seedless watermelon
1½ cups cubed fresh pineapple
⅓ cup chopped sweet red pepper
¼ cup chopped green onions
¼ cup minced fresh cilantro
¼ cup orange juice
¼ cup lime juice
1 teaspoon chopped jalapeno pepper
½ teaspoon salt, *divided*
¼ teaspoon pepper, *divided*
4 salmon fillets (6 ounces *each*)

1. In a large bowl, combine the first eight ingredients; add ¼ teaspoon salt and ⅛ teaspoon pepper. Let stand at room temperature for at least 30 minutes.

2. Coat grill rack with nonstick cooking spray before starting the grill. Sprinkle salmon with remaining salt and pepper. Place on grill rack. Grill, covered, over medium heat for 6-9 minutes on each side or until fish flakes easily with a fork. Serve the salsa with a slotted spoon with salmon.

YIELD: 4 servings.

EDITOR'S NOTE: When cutting or seeding hot peppers, use rubber or plastic gloves to protect your hands. Avoid touching your face.

jamaican pork tenderloin

ROSETTA HOCKETT ⚑ COLORADO SPRINGS, COLORADO

⅓ cup orange juice

⅓ cup soy sauce

3 tablespoons lemon juice

2 tablespoons olive oil

1 large onion, chopped

1 cup chopped green onions

1 jalapeno pepper

3 tablespoons minced fresh thyme *or*
2 teaspoons dried thyme

¾ teaspoon salt

¾ teaspoon *each* ground allspice, cinnamon
and nutmeg

¼ teaspoon ground ginger *or* 2 teaspoons
minced fresh gingerroot

¼ teaspoon pepper

2 pork tenderloins (1 pound *each*)

1. In a food processor, combine the orange juice, soy sauce, lemon juice, oil, onion, green onions, jalapeno, thyme, salt, allspice, cinnamon, nutmeg, ginger and pepper. Cover and process until smooth. Pour into a large resealable plastic bag; add the pork. Seal bag and turn to coat; refrigerate overnight.

2. Coat grill rack with nonstick cooking spray before starting the grill. Drain and discard marinade from pork. Grill, covered, over indirect medium heat for 20-25 minutes or until a thermometer reads 160°. Let stand for 5 minutes before slicing.

YIELD: 6 servings.

EDITOR'S NOTE: When cutting or seeding hot peppers, use rubber or plastic gloves to protect your hands. Avoid touching your face.

This recipe is perfect for barbecues and parties! A spicy citrus marinade adds plenty of flavor to the tenderloin. Then you can cook the meat in just minutes the next day.

grilled veggie sandwiches

MELISSA WILBANKS ⚑ MEMPHIS, TENNESSEE

Get a grip on lunch! Here's a fun recipe for using up those summer garden veggies.
Carnivores won't even miss the meat in these fresh-tasting grilled sandwiches.

1 small zucchini
1 small yellow summer squash
1 small eggplant
Cooking spray
1 medium onion, sliced
1 large sweet red pepper, cut into rings
4 whole wheat hamburger buns, split
3 ounces fat-free cream cheese
¼ cup crumbled goat cheese
1 garlic clove, minced
⅛ teaspoon salt
⅛ teaspoon pepper

1. Cut the zucchini, squash and eggplant into ¼-in.-thick strips; spritz with cooking spray. Spritz onion and red pepper with cooking spray.
2. Grill vegetables, covered, over medium heat for 4-5 minutes on each side or until crisp-tender. Remove and keep warm. Grill buns, cut side down, over medium heat for 30-60 seconds or until toasted.
3. In a small bowl, combine the cheeses, garlic, salt and pepper; spread over bun bottoms. Top with vegetables. Replace bun tops.
YIELD: 4 servings.

firecracker burgers

KELLY WILLIAMS ⚑ FORKED RIVER, NEW JERSEY

These tasty stuffed burgers are perfect fare for gatherings throughout the year.
They're great with a cool, creamy macaroni salad and an icy cold drink.

1 pound lean ground beef (90% lean)
¼ cup chunky salsa
4 frozen breaded cheddar cheese jalapeno peppers, thawed

¼ cup guacamole
4 hamburger buns, split and toasted
4 lettuce leaves
¼ cup salsa con queso dip
¼ cup sliced plum tomatoes
2 tablespoons sliced ripe olives
4 thin slices sweet onion

1. In a large bowl, combine the beef and salsa. Shape into four patties. Place a jalapeno in the center of each; wrap beef around jalapeno, forming a ball. Reshape into patties, about 3½ to 4 in. in diameter and 1 in. thick.
2. Grill, covered, over medium-hot heat for 7-8 minutes on each side or until meat is no longer pink and a thermometer reads 160°.
3. Spread guacamole over toasted side of bun tops. On each bun bottom, layer with lettuce, a burger, con queso dip, tomatoes, olives and onion; replace tops.
YIELD: 4 servings.

We like grilling because it's a no-fuss way to make a great meal. This tantalizing combo of vegetables and chicken is one we enjoy all summer.

honey-mustard chicken kabobs

MARILYN DICK ⚑ CENTRALIA, MISSOURI

4 boneless skinless chicken breast halves

4 small zucchini

4 small yellow squash

2 medium sweet red peppers

4 ounces small fresh mushrooms

GLAZE:

¾ cup honey

½ cup prepared mustard

¼ cup water

2 tablespoons soy sauce

2 tablespoons cornstarch

1 tablespoon cider vinegar

1. Cut chicken, zucchini, squash and peppers into 1-in. pieces; thread with mushrooms alternately onto metal or soaked wooden skewers. In a saucepan, combine glaze ingredients; bring to a boil. Boil for 1 minute or until thickened.

2. Grill kabobs over hot heat for 10 minutes, turning often. Brush with glaze; grill 5 minutes more or until the chicken is no longer pink and vegetables are tender.

YIELD: 4 servings.

GRILLING SAFETY
Place the grill on a level solid surface away from the main activities so that no one accidentally bumps into it.

Everyone comes running when they hear the sizzle—and smell the wonderful aroma of these burgers on the grill. Nothing else captures the taste of summer quite like these stuffed sandwiches.

stuffed bacon burgers

JOHNNIE MCLEOD ▷ BASTROP, LOUISIANA

1 envelope dry onion soup mix

¼ cup water

1½ pounds ground beef

6 slices (1 ounce *each*) process American cheese

6 bacon strips

6 hamburger buns, toasted

Lettuce leaves

Tomato slices

1. In a bowl, combine soup mix and water. Crumble beef over mixture and blend well. Shape into 12 thin patties. Place a cheese slice on six of the patties. Cover each with another patty. Pinch edges to seal. Wrap a strip of bacon around each; fasten with a wooden toothpick.

2. Grill for 8-10 minutes, turning once, or until meat is no longer pink. Remove the toothpicks. Serve on buns with the lettuce and tomato.

YIELD: 6 servings.

grilled tarragon chicken

JANIE THORPE ⚑ TULLAHOMA, TENNESSEE

Just a few ingredients are all that's needed to make this moist chicken. It's easy to prepare for a party!

2 teaspoons Dijon mustard

4 boneless skinless chicken breast halves

¼ teaspoon pepper

⅓ cup butter, melted

2 teaspoons lemon juice

2 teaspoons minced fresh tarragon *or*
½ teaspoon dried tarragon

½ teaspoon garlic salt

1. Spread mustard on both sides of the chicken; sprinkle with pepper. Cover and refrigerate at least 2 hours. Combine butter, lemon juice, tarragon and garlic salt.
2. Grill the chicken over medium-hot heat until juices run clear, basting with butter mixture during the last 3-5 minutes.

YIELD: 4 servings.

grilled orange chicken strips

MARION LOWERY ⚑ MEDFORD, OREGON

These savory marinated chicken strips are great for a picnic or backyard barbecue. Skewering the chicken makes it easy to handle, but you can put the strips directly on the grill or broil them in the oven if you prefer.

2 tablespoons chopped fresh orange segments

¼ cup orange juice

¼ cup olive oil

2 teaspoons lime juice

3 garlic cloves, minced

1 teaspoon *each* dried thyme, oregano and cumin

½ teaspoon salt

1 pound boneless skinless chicken breasts, cut into ¼-inch strips

1. Combine the first nine ingredients in a resealable plastic bag; add chicken and turn to coat. Seal and refrigerate for 1 hour.
2. Drain and discard marinade. Thread meat onto metal or soaked wooden skewers. Grill, uncovered, over medium-hot heat for 6-8 minutes or until juices run clear, turning often.

YIELD: 4 servings.

spicy bacon-wrapped shrimp

JANE BONE ☞ CAPE CORAL, FLORIDA

This grilling recipe has been in our family for many years and always gets rave reviews. I combine tender marinated shrimp with bacon strips to produce these delightful appetizers. They disappear in a hurry!

¼ cup sugar
¼ cup lemon juice
2 tablespoons olive oil
4 teaspoons paprika
1 teaspoon *each* salt, pepper, curry powder, ground cumin and ground coriander
½ to 1 teaspoon cayenne pepper
18 uncooked jumbo shrimp, peeled and deveined
9 bacon strips, halved lengthwise

1. In a small bowl, combine the sugar, lemon juice, oil and seasonings. Pour ¼ cup marinade into a large resealable plastic bag; add the shrimp. Seal bag and turn to coat; refrigerate for 30-60 minutes. Cover and refrigerate remaining marinade for basting.
2. In a skillet, cook bacon over medium heat until cooked but not crisp. Drain on paper towels. Remove shrimp from marinade; discard marinade. Wrap each shrimp with a piece of bacon and secure with a toothpick.
3. Coat grill rack with nonstick cooking spray before starting the grill. Grill bacon-wrapped shrimp, covered, over medium heat for 5-10 minutes or until shrimp turn pink, turning and basting with reserved marinade.

YIELD: 1½ dozen.

german bratwurst

TASTE OF HOME TEST KITCHEN

What a tasty use for bacon drippings! The tangy mustard and brown sugar make this quick and easy German bratwurst recipe something special.

1 teaspoon cornstarch
¼ cup chicken broth
2 tablespoons Dijon mustard
1 tablespoon brown sugar
1 tablespoon white wine *or* additional chicken broth
1 tablespoon cider vinegar
⅛ teaspoon celery seed
5 uncooked bratwurst

1. In a small saucepan, combine the first seven ingredients. Bring to a boil; cook and stir until thickened. Cool. Cover and refrigerate until serving.
2. Grill bratwurst, covered, over medium heat for 15-20 minutes or until no longer pink, turning frequently. In a small disposable foil pan, heat mustard mixture. Add bratwurst and turn to coat.

YIELD: 5 servings.

Be sure to use your fresh bounty of summer basil for this fantastic corn recipe. Steaming the basil under the husks adds lots of flavor to the ears. Lime makes their sweet taste pop even more.

basil corn on the cob

DIANE EATON ⚑ CAMPBELL, CALIFORNIA

6 **large ears sweet corn in husks**
6 **tablespoons butter, softened**
½ **teaspoon dried basil**
¼ **teaspoon sugar**
Dash salt
Dash garlic salt
1 **cup fresh basil leaves**
Lime wedges

1. Carefully peel back corn husks to within 1 in. of bottoms; remove silk. In a small bowl, combine the butter, dried basil, sugar, salt and garlic salt; spread over corn. Place basil leaves over butter mixture. Rewrap corn in husks and secure with kitchen string. Place in a stockpot; cover with cold water. Soak for 20 minutes; drain.

2. Grill corn, covered, over medium heat for 25-30 minutes or until tender, turning often. Serve with lime wedges.

YIELD: 6 servings.

I've been making this recipe ever since I can remember. It's so simple to fix, doesn't take a lot of ingredients or time, and is always a favorite with my guests. You can change it for different crowds by varying the seasoning for a mild to extra-spicy kick.

grilled jerk chicken wings

CAREN ADAMS ✒ FONTANA, CALIFORNIA

½ cup Caribbean jerk seasoning
18 fresh chicken wingettes (2 to 3 pounds)
2 cups honey barbecue sauce
⅓ cup packed brown sugar
2 teaspoons prepared mustard
1 teaspoon ground ginger

1. Coat grill rack with nonstick cooking spray before starting the grill. Place jerk seasoning in a large resealable plastic bag; add chicken wings, a few at a time, and shake to coat. In a small bowl, combine the barbecue sauce, brown sugar, mustard and ginger; set aside.

2. Grill chicken wings, covered, over medium heat for 12-16 minutes, turning occasionally. Brush with sauce. Grill, covered, 8-10 minutes longer or until juices run clear, basting and turning several times.

YIELD: 3 servings.

EDITOR'S NOTE: Caribbean jerk seasoning may be found in the spice aisle of your grocery store. This recipe was prepared with the first and second sections of the chicken wings.

BRUSH UP ON USING SAUCES
Brush on thick or sweet sauces during the last 10 to 15 minutes of cooking, basting and turning every few minutes to prevent burning.

zippy corn on the cob

BARB SASS ⚑ BURTON, OHIO

Dijon mustard and horseradish perk up this summertime favorite. You can prepare this sweet corn on the grill or in the oven. I can't remember where I found this recipe, but it's a real keeper!

- 6 medium ears sweet corn
- ½ cup butter, melted
- 2 tablespoons Dijon mustard
- 1 tablespoon minced fresh parsley
- 2 teaspoons prepared horseradish
- ½ teaspoon salt
- ¼ teaspoon pepper

1. Place ears of corn on a large sheet of double-layered heavy-duty foil. In a small bowl, combine the remaining ingredients; brush over corn. Fold foil around corn and seal tightly.
2. Grill, covered, over medium heat for 25-30 minutes or until corn is tender, turning once.

YIELD: 6 servings.

---

brats in beer

JILL HAZELTON ⚑ HAMLET, INDIANA

The flavor of the marinade really comes through in the grilled onions that top off these brats.

- 1 can (12 ounces) beer *or* nonalcoholic beer
- 2 tablespoons brown sugar
- 2 tablespoons soy sauce
- 1 tablespoon chili powder
- 1 tablespoon prepared mustard
- ⅛ teaspoon garlic powder
- 8 uncooked bratwurst
- 1 large onion, thinly sliced
- 8 brat *or* hot dog buns, split

1. In a small bowl, combine the first six ingredients. Pour 1¾ cups into a large resealable plastic bag; add bratwurst. Seal bag and turn to coat; refrigerate for 4 hours or overnight. Cover and refrigerate remaining marinade.
2. Add onion to remaining marinade; toss to coat. Place on a double thickness of heavy-duty foil (about 18 in. square). Fold foil around onion mixture and seal tightly. Drain and discard marinade from bratwurst.
3. Grill bratwurst and onion, covered, over medium heat or broil 4 in. from the heat for 15-20 minutes or until meat is no longer pink and onion is tender, turning frequently. Open foil carefully to allow steam to escape. Serve brats in buns with onion mixture.

YIELD: 8 servings.

marinated spiedis

PHYLLIS HOUSE ⚑ AVERILL PARK, NEW YORK

Marinating the tenderloin overnight makes it moist and flavorful. Plus, this recipe is easy on the cook. Just broil or grill when you're ready and serve dinner in a matter of minutes.

1 cup olive oil
⅓ cup fresh lemon juice
4 garlic cloves, minced
2 to 3 bay leaves, crushed
1 teaspoon dried oregano
1 teaspoon ground cumin
½ teaspoon salt
½ teaspoon pepper
3 medium onions, chopped
4 pounds pork tenderloin, trimmed and cut into 1-inch pieces
12 hot dog buns, split and buttered

1. In a large bowl, combine the first 10 ingredients. Cover and refrigerate for at least 8 hours.
2. Drain, discarding marinade. Thread pork onto 12 metal or soaked wooden skewers. Grill over medium heat or broil 6 in. from the heat, turning frequently, for 15-20 minutes or until the meat is no longer pink and pulls away easily from skewers. Wrap a bun around the meat and pull off the skewer.

YIELD: 12 servings.

grilled pork tenderloin

BETSY CARRINGTON ⚑ LAWRENCEBURG, TENNESSEE

This recipe is one my entire family loves. Serve the pork on a bed of rice for a pretty presentation.

⅓ cup honey
⅓ cup *each* soy sauce and teriyaki sauce
3 tablespoons brown sugar
1 tablespoon minced fresh gingerroot
3 garlic cloves, minced

4 teaspoons ketchup
½ teaspoon onion powder
½ teaspoon ground cinnamon
¼ teaspoon cayenne pepper
2 pork tenderloins (about 1 pound *each*)
Hot cooked rice

1. In a bowl, combine the first 10 ingredients; mix well. Pour half of the marinade into a large resealable plastic bag; add tenderloins. Seal bag and turn to coat; refrigerate for 8 hours, turning occasionally. Cover and refrigerate remaining marinade.
2. Drain and discard marinade from meat. Grill, uncovered, over indirect medium-hot heat for 8-10 minutes on each side, basting with reserved marinade, until a thermometer reads 160° and juices run clear. Let stand for 5 minutes. Serve with rice.

YIELD: 8-10 servings.

My husband and I love to grill burgers year-round. This variation with a creamy and flavorful filling is a hit with our family and friends.

horseradish burgers

CHRIS ANDERSON ⚑ MORTON, ILLINOIS

2 pounds ground beef

2 tablespoons steak sauce

¾ teaspoon seasoned salt

1 package (3 ounces) cream cheese, softened

1 to 2 tablespoons prepared horseradish

1 teaspoon prepared mustard

8 hamburger buns, split

1. In a large bowl, combine beef, steak sauce and seasoned salt; mix well. Shape into 16 patties. In a small bowl, combine cream cheese, horseradish and mustard. Spoon about 1 tablespoonful into the center of half of the patties; top with remaining patties. Press edges to seal.

2. Grill, covered, over medium-hot heat for 8-10 minutes on each side or until meat is no longer pink. Serve on buns.

YIELD: 8 servings.

sausage veggie grill

LAURA HILLYER ⚑ BAYFIELD, COLORADO

1 pound Italian sausage links, cut into ½-inch slices
1 medium zucchini, cut into 1-inch slices
1 medium yellow summer squash, cut into 1-inch slices
1 medium sweet red pepper, sliced
1 medium onion, cut into wedges
1 cup quartered fresh mushrooms
¼ cup olive oil
1 tablespoon dried oregano
1 tablespoon dried parsley flakes
1 teaspoon garlic salt
1 teaspoon paprika

1. In a large bowl, combine the first six ingredients. In a small bowl, combine the oil, oregano, parsley, garlic salt and paprika. Pour over sausage mixture; toss to coat. Divide between two pieces of heavy-duty foil (about 14 in. x 12 in.). Fold foil around sausage mixture and seal tightly.
2. Grill, covered, over medium heat for 25-30 minutes or until meat is no longer pink. Open foil carefully to allow steam to escape.

YIELD: 4 servings.

beef stir-fry on a stick

GWENDOLYN LAMBERT ⚑ FRISCO CITY, ALABAMA

*A slightly sweet hoisin glaze coats these tender beef and veggie kabobs.
They're a family favorite and always a hit.*

½ cup hoisin sauce

3 tablespoons water

2 tablespoons canola oil

1 tablespoon reduced-sodium soy sauce

1 garlic clove, minced

¼ to ½ teaspoon crushed red pepper flakes

3 cups large fresh broccoli florets

2 medium yellow summer squash, cut into ¾-inch slices

1 large sweet red pepper, cut into 1-inch pieces

1 pound beef tenderloin, cut into 1-inch cubes

Hot cooked rice

1. For glaze, in a small bowl, combine hoisin sauce, water, oil, soy sauce, garlic and pepper flakes.

2. On four metal or soaked wooden skewers, alternately thread the broccoli, squash, red pepper and beef.

3. Grill, covered, over medium heat or broil 4 in. from the heat for 6-7 minutes on each side or until meat reaches desired doneness and vegetables are tender, basting occasionally with glaze. Serve with rice.

YIELD: 4 servings.

sweet and spicy grilled chicken

MELISSA BALL ⚑ PEARISBURG, VIRGINIA

This simple recipe has become our favorite way to eat chicken. The blend of sweet and spicy is perfect.

2 tablespoons brown sugar

1 tablespoon paprika

2 teaspoons onion powder

1½ teaspoons salt

1 teaspoon chili powder

6 boneless skinless chicken breast halves (6 ounces *each*)

1. Combine the first five ingredients; rub over chicken breasts. Moisten a paper towel with cooking oil; using long-handled tongs, lightly coat the grill rack.

2. Grill chicken, covered, over medium heat or broil 4 in. from the heat for 4-5 minutes on each side or until a thermometer reads 170°.

YIELD: 6 servings.

giant mushroom burger

JANICE DELAGRANGE ⚑ MT. AIRY, MARYLAND

I add mushrooms and onion to lean ground beef before forming it into one giant, family-pleasing patty. After grilling it, all I need to do is slice and serve.

- 1 can (4 ounces) mushroom stems and pieces, drained
- ¼ cup egg substitute
- ½ cup chopped onion
- ¼ cup ketchup
- 1 teaspoon Italian seasoning
- 1 teaspoon fennel seed, crushed
- ¼ teaspoon pepper
- ¼ teaspoon Worcestershire sauce
- 1½ pounds lean ground beef

1. In a bowl, combine first eight ingredients. Crumble beef over mixture and blend well. Pat into a 9-in. circle on a large sheet of waxed paper. Invert onto a greased wire grill basket; peel off waxed paper.

2. Grill, covered, over medium heat for 20-25 minutes or until meat is no longer pink, turning once. Cut into six wedges.

YIELD: 6 servings.

veggie skewers

MONICA MEEK FLATFORD ⚑ KNOXVILLE, TENNESSEE

I discovered this recipe while trying to spruce up plain vegetables for dinner guests. A mild spice blend coats colorful skewers of fresh zucchini, summer squash and mushrooms.

- 2 medium zucchini, cut into 1-inch slices
- 2 medium yellow summer squash, cut into 1-inch slices
- ½ pound whole fresh mushrooms
- ⅓ cup olive oil
- 2 tablespoons lemon juice
- 1½ teaspoons dried basil
- 1½ teaspoons dried parsley flakes
- ¾ teaspoon garlic powder
- ¾ teaspoon dried oregano
- ½ teaspoon salt
- ⅛ teaspoon pepper

1. On metal or soaked wooden skewers, alternately thread zucchini, yellow squash and mushrooms. In a bowl, combine the remaining ingredients. Brush some of the mixture over vegetables.

2. Grill, covered, over medium heat for 10-15 minutes or until vegetables are tender, turning and basting occasionally with herb mixture.

YIELD: 4 servings.

CLEAN THAT PLATE!
Always be sure to place cooked food on a clean plate—never place it on a plate that held uncooked food.

If you're like me, you can never have enough delicious ways to grill chicken. The savory sauce in this recipe gives the chicken a fantastic herb flavor.

barbecued chicken

JOANNE SHEW CHUK ► ST. BENEDICT, SASKATCHEWAN

¼ cup water
¼ cup white vinegar
¼ cup butter, cubed
¼ teaspoon garlic powder
¼ teaspoon dried thyme
¼ teaspoon dried oregano
¼ teaspoon dried rosemary, crushed
⅛ teaspoon salt
⅛ teaspoon pepper
1 broiler/fryer chicken (3½ to 4 pounds), quartered

1. In a small saucepan, combine the first nine ingredients; bring to a gentle boil. Remove from heat; cool to room temperature. Place chicken in a large resealable plastic bag; add marinade. Seal bag and turn to coat; refrigerate for 4 hours, turning once.

2. Drain and discard marinade. Grill chicken, covered, over medium heat for 30-40 minutes or until juices run clear.

YIELD: 4 servings.

A grilling goal of mine has been to cook barbecued ribs to tender perfection. These are the most tender and best-tasting ribs I have ever made. Everyone who tries them agrees!

baby back ribs

JOANNE PARKS ⚑ STEGER, ILLINOIS

2 racks pork baby back ribs (about 4½ pounds)
2 tablespoons olive oil
¼ cup packed brown sugar
¼ cup paprika
1 tablespoon pepper
1 teaspoon onion powder
1 teaspoon garlic powder
½ teaspoon cayenne pepper

SAUCE:
½ cup barbecue sauce
¼ cup beer *or* beef broth

1. Rub ribs with oil. In a small bowl, combine the brown sugar, paprika, pepper, onion powder, garlic powder and cayenne; rub over ribs. Wrap in a large piece of heavy-duty foil (about 28 in. x 18 in.). Seal the edges of foil. In a small bowl, combine barbecue sauce and beer; set aside.

2. Grill ribs, covered, over indirect medium heat for 1 hour. Carefully remove ribs from foil. Place over direct heat; baste with sauce mixture. Grill 20 minutes or until meat is tender, turning and basting occasionally with sauce.

YIELD: 4 servings.

tailgate sausages
TASTE OF HOME TEST KITCHEN

You'll need just a handful of ingredients to fix these tasty sandwiches. Fully cooked sausages are stuffed with cheese and a homemade relish, then wrapped in foil so they're easy to transport and a breeze to grill.

½ cup giardiniera
½ teaspoon sugar
4 cooked Italian sausage links
4 slices provolone cheese, cut into strips
4 brat buns *or* hot dog buns, split

1. In a small food processor, combine giardiniera and sugar; cover and process until blended. Make a lengthwise slit three-fourths of the way through each sausage to within ½ in. of each end. Fill with giardiniera mixture and cheese.

2. Place sausages in buns; wrap individually in a double thickness of heavy-duty foil (about 12 in. x 10 in.). Grill, covered, over medium-hot heat for 8-10 minutes or until heated through and cheese is melted. Open foil carefully to allow steam to escape.

YIELD: 4 servings.

EDITOR'S NOTE: Giardiniera, a pickled vegetable mixture, is available in mild and hot varieties and can be found in the Italian or pickle section of your grocery store.

chipotle cheeseburgers
CRYSTAL BRUNS ⚑ ILIFF, COLORADO

Heat up a casual meal with these spiced-up burgers. You can substitute ground turkey for the beef and your favorite sliced cheese for the mozzarella.

1 small onion, finely chopped
2 tablespoons minced fresh cilantro
1 chipotle pepper in adobo sauce, finely chopped
1 teaspoon onion powder
1 teaspoon garlic powder
1 teaspoon seasoned salt
¼ teaspoon pepper
1 pound ground beef
4 slices part-skim mozzarella cheese
4 hamburger buns, split and toasted
Lettuce leaves and tomato slices, optional

1. In a small bowl, combine first seven ingredients. Crumble beef over mixture and mix well. Shape into four patties.
2. Grill, covered, over medium heat or broil 4 in. from the heat for 5-7 minutes on each side or until a thermometer reads 160° and juices run clear. Top with cheese. Cook 1-2 minutes longer or until cheese is melted. Serve on buns with lettuce and tomato if desired.

YIELD: 4 servings.

15-minute marinated chicken

PAM SHINOGLE ⚑ ARLINGTON, TEXAS

For tailgating, spread the marinade on the chicken and put in resealable plastic bags just before packing up.

¼ cup Dijon mustard
2 tablespoons fresh lemon juice
1½ teaspoons Worcestershire sauce
½ teaspoon dried tarragon
¼ teaspoon pepper
4 boneless skinless chicken breast halves

1. Combine the first five ingredients; spread on both sides of chicken. Place chicken on plate. Marinate at room temperature for 10-15 minutes or for several hours in the refrigerator.
2. Grill, uncovered, over medium heat, for 10-15 minutes or until juices run clear, turning once.
YIELD: 4 servings.

MARINADE DO'S AND DON'TS
Reserve some marinade for basting and add the meat to the remaining marinade. Discard the marinade from the meat—any marinade that comes in contact with uncooked meat, poultry or seafood should be discarded.

brats with sauerkraut

DARLENE DIXON ⚑ HANOVER, MINNESOTA

I've made many variations of this excellent main dish. The bratwurst can be plain, smoked or cheese-flavored, served whole or cut in slices, with a bun or without. It would be popular at a party or potluck.

1 can (14 ounces) sauerkraut, rinsed and well drained
2 medium apples, peeled and finely chopped
3 bacon strips, cooked and crumbled
¼ cup packed brown sugar
¼ cup finely chopped onion
1 teaspoon ground mustard
8 uncooked bratwurst
8 brat buns, split

1. In a 1½-qt. slow cooker, combine the first six ingredients. Cover and cook on low for 4-6 hours or until apples are tender. Keep hot until serving. Grill the bratwurst, covered, over medium heat for 15-20 minutes or until no longer pink, turning frequently. Place bratwurst in buns. Using a slotted spoon, top with sauerkraut mixture.
YIELD: 8 servings.

This is my favorite recipe for grilled shrimp. The mild flavor of the marinade works equally well with cod or haddock.

shrimp on the grill

CHER GRIFFIN MANCHESTER, NEW HAMPSHIRE

1 cup canola oil
2 tablespoons olive oil
2 teaspoons garlic powder
1 teaspoon dried thyme
1 teaspoon lemon juice
1 teaspoon cider vinegar
½ teaspoon pepper
30 large shrimp, peeled and deveined
1 large green pepper, cut into 1-inch pieces
1 medium yellow squash, cut into ¾-inch pieces
6 green onions, cut into 2-inch pieces
⅓ cup butter, melted
2 teaspoons snipped fresh dill
Hot cooked rice

1. In a blender, combine the first seven ingredients; cover and process for 1-2 minutes.

2. On 12 metal or soaked wooden skewers, alternately thread shrimp and vegetables, leaving a small space between pieces. Place in a shallow glass container. Pour oil mixture over kabobs; cover and refrigerate for 2-3 hours.

3. Drain and discard marinade. Grill kabobs, uncovered, over medium heat for 6-8 minutes on each side or until shrimp turn pink and vegetables are tender. Combine butter and dill; baste over skewers. Serve with rice.

YIELD: 6 servings.

all-american hamburgers

DIANE HIXON NICEVILLE, FLORIDA

2 tablespoons diced onion

2 tablespoons chili sauce

2 teaspoons Worcestershire sauce

2 teaspoons prepared mustard

1 pound ground beef

4 slices American *or* cheddar cheese, halved diagonally

2 slices Swiss cheese, halved diagonally

4 hamburger buns, split and toasted

Lettuce leaves, sliced tomato and onion, cooked bacon, ketchup and mustard, optional

1. In a bowl, combine the first four ingredients. Crumble beef over mixture and mix well. Shape into four patties. Grill, covered, over medium heat for 6 minutes on each side or until meat is no longer pink.

2. During the last minute of cooking, top each patty with two triangles of American cheese and one triangle of Swiss cheese. Serve on buns with lettuce, tomato, onion, bacon, ketchup and mustard if desired.

YIELD: 4 servings.

grilled italian sausage sandwiches

MIKE YAEGER ⚑ BROOKINGS, SOUTH DAKOTA

4 large green peppers, thinly sliced
½ cup chopped onion
4 garlic cloves, minced
2 tablespoons olive oil
1 can (15 ounces) tomato sauce
1 can (12 ounces) tomato paste
1 cup water
1 tablespoon sugar
2 teaspoons dried basil
1 teaspoon salt
1 teaspoon dried oregano
20 uncooked Italian sausage links
20 sandwich buns
Shredded part-skim mozzarella cheese, optional

1. In a large saucepan, saute the peppers, onion and garlic in oil until crisp-tender; drain. Stir in the tomato sauce, tomato paste, water, sugar, basil, salt and oregano. Bring to a boil. Reduce heat; cover and simmer for 30 minutes or until heated through.

2. Meanwhile, grill sausages, covered, over medium heat for 10-16 minutes or until no longer pink, turning occasionally. Serve on buns with sauce and cheese if desired.

YIELD: 20 servings.

When my wife and I have friends over, we love to serve these sandwiches. This is a convenient recipe, since the sauce can be prepared the day before and reheated.

eggplant-portobello sandwich loaf

TASTE OF HOME TEST KITCHEN

This grilled sandwich uses fresh eggplant and tasty marinara to make a hearty vegetarian dinner for four. If you can't find smoked mozzarella, regular works just fine.

1 loaf (1 pound) Italian bread
½ cup olive oil
2 teaspoons minced garlic
1 teaspoon Italian seasoning
½ teaspoon salt
¼ teaspoon pepper
1 large eggplant (1 pound), cut into ½-inch slices
1 package (6 ounces) sliced portobello mushrooms
1 cup marinara sauce
2 tablespoons minced fresh basil
4 ounces smoked fresh mozzarella cheese, cut into ¼-inch slices

1. Cut bread lengthwise in half. Carefully hollow out top and bottom, leaving a ½-in. shell; set aside. In a small bowl, combine the oil, garlic, Italian seasoning, salt and pepper. Brush over eggplant and mushrooms.
2. Grill, covered, over medium heat for 3-5 minutes on each side or until vegetables are tender.
3. Spread half of the marinara sauce over bottom of bread. Top with eggplant and mushrooms. Spread with remaining sauce; top with basil and cheese. Replace bread top.
4. Wrap loaf in a large piece of heavy-duty foil (about 28 in. x 18 in.); seal tightly. Grill, covered, over medium heat for 4-5 minutes on each side.

YIELD: 4 servings.

campfire potatoes

JOANN DETTBARN ⌂ BRAINERD, MINNESOTA

Butter, onion and cheddar cheese combine to make a delicious potato side dish for any grilled meat. Cooking in the foil packet makes cleanup a breeze.

5 medium potatoes, peeled and thinly sliced
1 medium onion, sliced
6 tablespoons butter
⅓ cup shredded cheddar cheese
2 tablespoons minced fresh parsley
1 tablespoon Worcestershire sauce
Salt and pepper to taste
⅓ cup chicken broth

1. Place the potatoes and onion on a large piece of heavy-duty foil (about 20 in. x 20 in.); dot with butter. Combine the cheese, parsley, Worcestershire sauce, salt and pepper; sprinkle over potatoes.
2. Fold foil up around potatoes and add broth. Seal the edges of foil well. Grill, covered, over medium heat for 35-40 minutes or until potatoes are tender.

YIELD: 4-6 servings.

Get ready to rock the grill with this spicy and wonderfully fragrant chicken. The zippy marinade includes hints of cinnamon, cayenne and thyme. We like to think of this dish as "chicken with attitude."

caribbean jerk chicken

JUDY KAMALIEH ⚑ NEBRASKA CITY, NEBRASKA

4 **chicken leg quarters, skin removed**
¼ **cup olive oil**
2 **tablespoons brown sugar**
2 **tablespoons reduced-sodium soy sauce**
1 **envelope Italian salad dressing mix**
1 **teaspoon dried thyme**
1 **teaspoon ground cinnamon**
½ **teaspoon cayenne pepper**

1. With a sharp knife, separate leg quarters at the joints if desired. In a large resealable plastic bag, combine the remaining ingredients; add chicken. Seal bag and turn to coat; refrigerate for 2-4 hours.

2. Drain and discard marinade. Moisten a paper towel with cooking oil; using long-handled tongs, lightly coat the grill rack. Grill chicken, covered, over medium heat for 35-45 minutes or until a thermometer reads 180°, turning occasionally.

YIELD: 4 servings.

This is a variation of an old Southern recipe with a Texas twist. I've been making it at least once a month for the last 15 years. The marinade gives the beef a wonderful taste.

flavorful flank steak

JANICE MONTIVERDI ⚑ SUGAR LAND, TEXAS

½ cup soy sauce
½ cup canola oil
3 tablespoons red wine vinegar
3 tablespoons barbecue sauce
3 tablespoons steak sauce
2 tablespoons dried minced onion
1 tablespoon Liquid Smoke, optional
½ teaspoon garlic powder
1 beef flank steak (1½ pounds)

1. In a large resealable plastic bag, combine the first eight ingredients. Add the steak; seal bag and turn to coat. Refrigerate for 8 hours or overnight. Drain and discard the marinade.

2. Grill steak, covered, over medium-hot heat for 6-8 minutes on each side or until the meat reaches desired doneness (for medium-rare, a thermometer should read 145°; medium, 160°; well-done, 170°). Slice steak across the grain.
YIELD: 6 servings.

PUT OUT THE FIRE
If you're using a charcoal grill, bring along extra water to douse the embers and a plastic garbage bag to put the cold coals in.

individual grilled pizzas

MARTHA HASEMAN 〰 HINCKLEY, ILLINOIS

1½ cups all-purpose flour

½ cup whole wheat flour

1 package (¼ ounce) quick-rise yeast

½ teaspoon salt

½ teaspoon sugar

¾ cup warm water (120° to 130°)

1 tablespoon olive oil

PESTO:

1 cup chopped fresh basil

¼ cup plain yogurt

2 tablespoons unsalted sunflower kernels

1 tablespoon olive oil

1 garlic clove, minced

⅛ teaspoon salt

⅛ teaspoon pepper

TOPPINGS:

1 cup (4 ounces) shredded part-skim mozzarella cheese, *divided*

2 medium tomatoes, thinly sliced

2 green onions, finely chopped

Coarsely ground pepper

2 tablespoons grated Parmesan cheese

1. Coat grill rack with nonstick cooking spray before starting grill. Prepare grill for indirect medium heat. In a mixing bowl, combine flours, yeast, salt and sugar. Add water and oil; mix just until a soft dough forms.

2. Turn onto a floured surface; knead until smooth and elastic, about 5-7 minutes. Cover and let stand for 10-15 minutes. Meanwhile, combine the pesto ingredients in a blender or food processor; cover and process until smooth, scraping sides often. Set aside.

3. Divide dough into fourths. Roll each portion into a 6-in. circle; place on grill over directly heated area.

4. Cover and cook for 1 minute or until puffed and golden. Turn; place over indirectly heated area of grill. Spread pesto over crusts; top with ⅔ cup mozzarella cheese, tomatoes, onions, pepper, Parmesan and remaining mozzarella. Grill for 3-5 minutes or until the cheese is melted and the crust is lightly browned.

YIELD: 4 servings.

These are especially popular because each person can add whatever toppings they like. Just set out the fixings and guests can enjoy.

grilled onion

STANLEY PICHON ⚑ SLIDELL, LOUISIANA

This side dish may be simple, but it always gets a terrific reaction, even from folks who don't usually care for onions.

1 large onion, peeled
1 tablespoon butter
1 teaspoon beef bouillon granules

1. Hollow center of onion to a depth of 1 in.; chop the removed onion. Place butter and bouillon in center of onion; top with the chopped onion.
2. Wrap tightly in heavy-duty foil. Cook on a covered grill over medium heat for 25-30 minutes or until tender. Cut onion into wedges.

YIELD: 4 servings.

SWEET ON ONIONS
Grilling brings out the natural sweetness of onions, while adding a rich and smoky flavor. Grilled onions are a great accompaniment to steak, burgers and sausages. For an extra-special treat, try Vidalia or other sweet onions.

chili burgers

SUE ROSS ⚑ CASA GRANDE, ARIZONA

These are hearty, easy-to-assemble sandwiches. The savory chili and french-fried onions are a fun alternative to traditional burger toppings like ketchup and mustard.

1 pound ground beef
1½ teaspoons chili powder
1 can (15 ounces) chili with beans
4 hamburger buns, split and toasted
½ cup shredded cheddar cheese
1 can (2.8 ounces) french-fried onions

1. In a bowl, combine beef and chili powder. Shape into four patties. Pan-fry, grill or broil until meat is no longer pink.
2. Meanwhile, in a saucepan, heat chili. Place burgers on bun bottoms; top with chili, cheese and onions. Replace bun tops.

YIELD: 4 servings.

With these colorful fajitas, it's easy to bring a taste of Mexico to your next gathering! The fresh flavor of the meat and peppers appeals to everyone.

chicken fajitas

MELINDA EWBANK ⚑ FAIRFIELD, OHIO

2 tablespoons white wine vinegar

2 tablespoons fresh lime juice

1 tablespoon canola oil

1 tablespoon Worcestershire sauce

1 tablespoon chopped onion

1 garlic clove, minced

½ teaspoon salt, optional

½ teaspoon dried oregano

¼ teaspoon ground cumin

1 pound boneless skinless chicken breasts

Canola oil

1 medium green pepper, halved and seeded

1 medium sweet red pepper, halved and seeded

1 medium sweet onion, sliced

6 flour tortillas (8 inches)

Salsa, guacamole, sour cream and shredded cheddar cheese, optional

1. In a large resealable plastic bag, combine vinegar, lime juice, oil, Worcestershire sauce, onion, garlic, salt if desired, oregano and cumin. Add chicken. Close bag and refrigerate at least 4 hours. Drain, discarding marinade.

2. Lightly oil vegetables. Grill vegetables and chicken, uncovered, over medium heat for 12-15 minutes or until vegetables begin to soften and chicken juices run clear.

3. Meanwhile, warm tortillas according to package directions. Quickly slice chicken and peppers into strips and separate onion slices into rings. Spoon chicken and vegetables down the center of tortillas; fold in sides. Garnish as desired with salsa, guacamole, sour cream and cheese.

YIELD: 6 servings.

With a slice of bacon inside and a tasty barbecue-mayo sauce on top, these are definitely not ordinary burgers. We think you'll agree.

bbq bacon burgers

JOAN SCHOENHERR ⚐ EASTPOINTE, MICHIGAN

¼ cup mayonnaise
¼ cup barbecue sauce
4 bacon strips, cooked and crumbled
1½ teaspoons dried minced onion
1½ teaspoons steak seasoning
1 pound ground beef
4 slices Swiss cheese
4 hamburger buns, split
Lettuce leaves and tomato slices

1. In a small bowl, combine mayonnaise and barbecue sauce. In another bowl, combine the bacon, 2 tablespoons mayonnaise mixture, onion and steak seasoning; crumble beef over mixture and mix well. Shape into four patties.

2. Grill burgers, covered, over medium heat for 5-7 minutes on each side or until a thermometer reads 160° and juices run clear. Top with cheese. Cover and cook 1-2 minutes longer or until cheese is melted. Spread remaining mayonnaise mixture over buns; top each with a burger, lettuce and tomato.

YIELD: 4 servings.

tangy shrimp kabobs

PAT WAYMIRE  YELLOW SPRINGS, OHIO

*You'd never guess that a pair of these colorful kabobs has only 2 grams of fat total!
An easy tomato-based mixture is used as a marinade and basting sauce
to add just the right amount of sweet-sour taste to the shrimp, pineapple and veggies.*

1 can (20 ounces) unsweetened pineapple chunks
1 can (8 ounces) tomato sauce
½ cup fat-free Italian salad dressing
4½ teaspoons brown sugar
1 teaspoon prepared mustard
1½ pounds uncooked large shrimp, peeled and deveined
12 pearl onions
1 large sweet red pepper, cut into 1-inch pieces
1 large green pepper, cut into 1-inch pieces
Hot cooked rice, optional

1. Drain pineapple, reserving ¼ cup juice; set aside. In a small bowl, combine the tomato sauce, Italian dressing, brown sugar, mustard and reserved pineapple juice. Pour ¾ cup marinade into a large resealable plastic bag; add shrimp. Seal bag and turn to coat; refrigerate for 3 hours, turning occasionally. Cover and refrigerate remaining mixture for sauce.

2. In a Dutch oven, bring 6 cups water to a boil. Add onions; boil for 2 minutes. Add peppers and boil 2 minutes longer. Drain and rinse in cold water; peel onions. Refrigerate vegetables until ready to grill.

3. In a small saucepan, bring ¾ cup of reserved tomato sauce mixture to a boil. Reduce heat; simmer, uncovered, for 5 minutes or until slightly thickened. Keep warm.

4. Drain and discard marinade. On 12 metal or soaked wooden skewers, alternately thread shrimp and vegetables. Moisten a paper towel with cooking oil; using long-handled tongs, lightly coat the grill rack.

5. Grill kabobs, covered, over medium heat or broil 4 in. from the heat for 3-5 minutes on each side or until shrimp turn pink, basting occasionally with remaining tomato sauce mixture. Drizzle kabobs with warm sauce. Serve the kabobs over rice if desired.

YIELD: 6 servings.

KABOBS FOR THE ROAD
For fuss-free tailgating, thread kabobs onto soaked disposable wooden skewers, then transport them in resealable plastic bags. Make a variety of kabobs, including vegetable, and pack them into separate bags.

smoked linkburgers

JUNE BURKERT ⚑ EVANS CITY, PENNSYLVANIA

We enjoy these sandwiches as a change from plain hamburgers or hot dogs.

1 tablespoon brown sugar
1 tablespoon lemon juice
1 tablespoon finely chopped onion
½ teaspoon salt
Dash pepper
1½ pounds ground beef
1 package (14 ounces) smoked sausage links
8 hot dog *or* hoagie buns, split

1. In a large bowl, combine the first five ingredients. Crumble beef over mixture and mix well. Divide into eight portions and shape each portion around a sausage link.
2. Grill or broil until beef is no longer pink, turning frequently. Serve on buns.
YIELD: 8 servings.

grill bread

TASTE OF HOME TEST KITCHEN

Get creative for your next cookout and try your hand at this tasty vegetable sandwich. Prepare the bread in advance and grill it when it's time to eat. It's worth the extra few minutes of prep time.

4 frozen Texas rolls (2 ounces *each*), thawed
2 garlic cloves, minced
2 tablespoons olive oil
½ pound fresh mushrooms, sliced
1 small onion, cut into thin wedges
1 medium green pepper, sliced
1 medium sweet yellow pepper, sliced
1 medium sweet red pepper, sliced
½ cup fresh snow peas
¾ teaspoon salt
⅛ teaspoon pepper
½ teaspoon dried oregano

1. On a lightly floured surface, roll out each roll into an 8-in. to 10-in. circle, turning dough frequently; set aside.
2. In a large skillet, saute garlic in oil until tender. Add mushrooms; saute for 2-3 minutes. Add onion, peppers, peas, salt, pepper and oregano; stir-fry until vegetables are crisp-tender, about 3 minutes.
3. Meanwhile, grill bread, uncovered, over medium-high heat for 30-45 seconds on each side or until lightly browned. Fill with vegetable mixture and serve immediately. The bread can be reheated in the microwave.
YIELD: 4 servings.

Unlike traditional kabobs, these call for turkey breast slices, potatoes and apple chunks. The honey-mustard salad dressing shines through in each delicious bite.

tangy turkey kabobs
TASTE OF HOME TEST KITCHEN

½ cup honey-mustard salad dressing

2 teaspoons dried rosemary, crushed

12 small red potatoes, cut in half

1 pound turkey breast slices, cut into 1-inch strips

2 unpeeled green apples, cut into 1-inch pieces

1. In a small bowl, combine salad dressing and rosemary; set aside. Place potatoes in a saucepan and cover with water; bring to a boil. Cook for 5 minutes; drain. Fold turkey strips in thirds; thread onto metal or soaked wooden skewers alternately with potatoes and apples. Spoon half of the dressing over kabobs.

2. Grill, uncovered, over medium-hot heat for 6-8 minutes. Turn; brush with remaining dressing. Continue grilling until meat juices run clear.

YIELD: 4 servings.

These grilled portobello mushroom burgers taste like the classic with a meatless twist.

portobello burgers

THERESA SABBAGH ⌇ WINSTON-SALEM, NORTH CAROLINA

2 tablespoons balsamic vinegar

1 tablespoon olive oil

3 garlic cloves, minced

1½ teaspoons minced fresh basil *or* ½ teaspoon dried basil

1½ teaspoons minced fresh oregano *or* ½ teaspoon dried oregano

Dash salt

Dash pepper

2 large portobello mushrooms, stems removed

2 slices reduced-fat provolone cheese

2 hamburger buns, split

2 lettuce leaves

2 slices tomato

1. In a small bowl, whisk the first seven ingredients. Add mushroom caps; let stand for 15 minutes, turning twice. Drain and reserve marinade.

2. Moisten a paper towel with cooking oil; using long-handled tongs, lightly coat the grill rack. Grill mushrooms, covered, over medium heat or broil 4 in. from the heat for 6-8 minutes on each side or until tender, basting with reserved marinade. Top with cheese during the last 2 minutes.

3. Serve on buns with lettuce and tomato.

YIELD: 2 servings.

pacific rim salmon

AMY SAUSER ⚑ OMAHA, NEBRASKA

½ cup unsweetened pineapple juice

¼ cup reduced-sodium soy sauce

2 tablespoons prepared horseradish

2 tablespoons minced fresh parsley

5 teaspoons sesame oil, *divided*

2 teaspoons honey

½ teaspoon coarsely ground pepper

8 salmon fillets (6 ounces *each*)

5 green onions, coarsely chopped

1. In a small bowl, combine the pineapple juice, soy sauce, horseradish, parsley, 3 teaspoons sesame oil, honey and pepper. Pour ⅔ cup marinade into a large resealable plastic bag; add salmon and green onions. Seal bag and turn to coat; refrigerate for 1 to 1½ hours, turning occasionally. Add remaining sesame oil to remaining marinade. Cover and refrigerate for basting.

2. Drain and discard marinade. Moisten a paper towel with cooking oil; using long-handled tongs, lightly coat the grill rack. Grill salmon, skin side down, covered, over medium heat or broil 4 in. from the heat for 8-12 minutes or until fish flakes easily with a fork, basting frequently with reserved marinade.

YIELD: 8 servings.

I came across this recipe in a local fund-raiser cookbook. We've made some slight adjustments to it since then, but it is a great recipe to use when grilling. It's a favorite summer meal.

bacon-stuffed burgers

SANDRA MCKENZIE ⚑ BRAHAM, MINNESOTA

 4 slices bacon
¼ cup chopped onion
 1 can (4 ounces) mushroom stems and pieces, finely chopped
¼ cup grated Parmesan cheese
½ teaspoon pepper
¼ teaspoon garlic powder
 2 tablespoons steak sauce
 1 pound lean ground beef
 1 pound bulk pork sausage
 8 hamburger buns, split and toasted
Leaf lettuce, optional

1. Cook bacon until crisp. Remove bacon and discard all but 2 tablespoons drippings. Saute onions in drippings until tender. Crumble bacon; add with mushrooms to skillet and set aside.

2. In a bowl, combine cheese, pepper, garlic powder and steak sauce; crumble meat over mixture and blend well. Shape into 16 patties. Divide bacon mixture and place over eight of the patties. Place remaining patties on top and press edges tightly to seal.

3. Grill over medium heat until well-done (the pork sausage in burgers requires thorough cooking). Serve on buns with lettuce if desired.

YIELD: 8 servings.

SUPER SANDWICHES

This giant sandwich is perfect for backyard parties and large gatherings. It's a terrific way to feed your hungry bunch.

sandwich for 12

MELISSA COLLIER ✒ WICHITA FALLS, TEXAS

½ cup old-fashioned oats
½ cup boiling water
2 tablespoons butter
1 package (16 ounces) hot roll mix
¾ cup warm water (110° to 115°)
2 eggs, beaten
1 tablespoon dried minced onion

TOPPING:
1 egg
1 teaspoon garlic salt
1 tablespoon dried minced onion
1 tablespoon sesame seeds

FILLING:
½ cup mayonnaise
4 teaspoons prepared mustard
½ teaspoon prepared horseradish
8 lettuce leaves
8 ounces thinly sliced fully cooked ham
8 ounces thinly sliced cooked turkey
6 ounces thinly sliced Swiss cheese
1 medium onion, thinly sliced
2 large tomatoes, thinly sliced
1 medium green pepper, thinly sliced

1. In a large bowl, combine oats, boiling water and butter; let stand for 5 minutes. Meanwhile, dissolve yeast from hot roll mix in warm water. Add to the oat mixture. Add eggs and onion. Add flour mixture from hot roll mix; stir well (do not knead).

2. Spread dough into a 10-in. circle on a well-greased pizza pan. Cover with plastic wrap coated with nonstick cooking spray; let rise in a warm place until doubled, about 45 minutes.

3. Beat egg and garlic salt; brush gently over dough. Sprinkle with onion and sesame seeds. Bake at 350° for 25-30 minutes or until golden brown. Remove from pan; cool on a wire rack. Split lengthwise. Combine mayonnaise, mustard and horseradish; spread over cut sides of loaf. Layer with remaining filling ingredients. Cut into wedges.

YIELD: 12 servings.

bbq chicken sandwiches

LETICIA LEWIS  KENNEWICK, WASHINGTON

½ cup chopped onion
½ cup diced celery
1 garlic clove, minced
1 tablespoon butter
½ cup salsa
½ cup ketchup
2 tablespoons brown sugar
2 tablespoons cider vinegar
1 tablespoon Worcestershire sauce
½ teaspoon chili powder
¼ teaspoon salt
⅛ teaspoon pepper
2 cups shredded cooked chicken
6 hamburger buns, split and toasted

1. In a saucepan, saute the onion, celery and garlic in butter until tender. Stir in salsa, ketchup, brown sugar, vinegar, Worcestershire sauce, chili powder, salt and pepper. Add the chicken; stir to coat. Bring to a boil. Reduce heat; cover and simmer for 15 minutes. Serve about ⅓ cup of the chicken mixture on each bun.

YIELD: 6 servings.

INSTEAD OF MAYO
Are you out of mayonnaise? Try spreading your bread or roll with ranch or a creamy Caesar salad dressing instead. You just might discover a new favorite combination!

These yummy BBQs are a cinch to make. For a spicier taste, omit the ketchup and increase the salsa to 1 cup.

layered deli loaf

SARAH KRAEMER ROCKFORD, ILLINOIS

A tangy sauce, flavored with horseradish and Dijon mustard, complements a hearty assortment of meats and cheeses. This feeds a crowd, so it's perfect for a party.

¼ cup mayonnaise
2 tablespoons prepared horseradish, drained
1 tablespoon Dijon mustard
1 round loaf (1 pound) unsliced bread
2 tablespoons butter, softened
⅓ pound thinly sliced deli ham
⅓ pound sliced Monterey Jack *or* Muenster cheese
⅓ pound thinly sliced deli turkey
⅓ pound sliced cheddar *or* Colby cheese
⅓ pound thinly sliced deli roast beef
1 medium tomato, sliced
1 large dill pickle, sliced lengthwise
1 small red onion, thinly sliced
Lettuce leaves

1. In a small bowl, combine the mayonnaise, horseradish and mustard. Cut bread in half. Carefully hollow out bottom and top of loaf, leaving ¾-in. shell (discard removed bread or save for another use). Spread butter on cut sides of bread.

2. In the shell, layer ham, a third of the mayonnaise mixture, Monterey Jack cheese, turkey, a third of the mayonnaise mixture, cheddar cheese, roast beef, remaining mayonnaise mixture, tomato, pickle, onion and lettuce. Replace top. Wrap tightly in plastic wrap; cover and refrigerate for at least 1 hour.

YIELD: 8 servings.

fresh veggie pockets

LINDA REEVES CLOVERDALE, INDIANA

One summer I worked at a health food store that sold sandwiches. We were close to a college campus, so I made lots of these fresh filled pitas for the students. Crunchy with crisp vegetables and nutty sunflower kernels, they make a fast-to-fix lunch when you're in a hurry.

1 carton (8 ounces) spreadable cream cheese
¼ cup sunflower kernels
1 teaspoon seasoned salt *or* salt-free seasoning blend
4 wheat pita breads, halved
1 medium tomato, thinly sliced
1 medium cucumber, thinly sliced
1 cup sliced fresh mushrooms
1 ripe avocado, peeled and sliced

1. In a bowl, combine the cream cheese, sunflower kernels and seasoned salt; spread about 2 tablespoons on the inside of each pita half. Layer with the tomato, cucumber, mushrooms and avocado.

YIELD: 4 servings.

I created this recipe mainly to help get more veggies into my diet. I'm busy and on the go like many other mothers. These wraps give me energy and taste delicious.

veggie hummus wraps

AMBER INDRA THOUSAND OAKS, CALIFORNIA

6 tablespoons hummus
2 flour tortillas (8 inches), room temperature
½ cup shredded carrots
1 cup fresh baby spinach
6 slices tomato
2 tablespoons green goddess salad dressing

1. Spread hummus over each tortilla. Layer with carrots, spinach and tomato; drizzle with dressing. Roll up tightly.
YIELD: 2 servings.

A mustard-flavored dressing coats the colorful combination of chicken, broccoli, tomatoes and bacon in this tasty filling. It's great for an outdoor get-together because you can prepare the filling ahead and assemble the pitas at the party site. Your guests will love it!

picnic chicken pitas

MARLA BRENNEMAN ⚑ GOSHEN, INDIANA

1 package (10 ounces) frozen broccoli florets, cooked and drained

2 cups shredded cooked chicken

1 cup (4 ounces) shredded cheddar cheese

1 medium tomato, chopped

¼ cup mayonnaise

2 tablespoons prepared mustard

½ teaspoon salt, optional

⅛ teaspoon pepper

4 pita breads (6 inches), halved

4 bacon strips, cooked and crumbled, optional

1. In a large bowl, combine the broccoli, chicken, cheese and tomato. In a small bowl, combine the mayonnaise, mustard, salt if desired and pepper; pour over the broccoli mixture and toss to coat. Spoon about ¾ cup into each pita half; top with bacon if desired.

YIELD: 4 servings.

barbecued pork sandwiches

THELMA WAGGONER ⚑ HOPKINSVILLE, KENTUCKY

*These taste even better if the pork is prepared a day ahead so the flavors can blend.
We welcomed Mother's pork sandwiches for any occasion, but especially
for our birthday celebrations. We never wanted to change that menu!*

1 pork shoulder roast (about 5 pounds),
  trimmed and cut into 1-inch cubes
2 medium onions, coarsely chopped
2 tablespoons chili powder
½ teaspoon salt, optional
1½ cups water
1 cup ketchup
¼ cup white vinegar
Hamburger rolls, split

1. In a Dutch oven, combine meat, onions, chili powder, salt if desired, water, ketchup and vinegar. Cover and simmer for 4 hours or until the meat falls apart easily. Skim off excess fat.
2. With a slotted spoon, remove meat, reserving cooking liquid. Shred the meat with two forks or a pastry blender. Return to the cooking liquid and heat through. Serve on rolls.

YIELD: 16 servings.

champion roast beef sandwiches

ANN EASTMAN ⚑ GREENVILLE, CALIFORNIA

*When I have time, I like to prepare a roast with this much-requested recipe in mind.
But when I need a quick meal in a hurry, I use deli roast beef with delicious results.*

½ cup sour cream
1 tablespoon dry onion soup mix
1 tablespoon prepared horseradish, drained
⅛ teaspoon pepper
8 slices rye *or* pumpernickel bread
½ pound sliced roast beef
Lettuce leaves

1. In a small bowl, combine the first four ingredients. Spread 1 tablespoon on each slice of bread. Top four slices of bread with roast beef and lettuce; cover with remaining bread.

YIELD: 4 servings.

orange turkey croissants

JENNIFER MOORE ⚑ CENTERVILLE, IOWA

6 tablespoons spreadable cream cheese
6 tablespoons orange marmalade
6 croissants, split
½ cup chopped pecans
1 pound thinly sliced deli turkey

1. Spread cream cheese and marmalade onto bottom half of croissants. Sprinkle with pecans. Top with turkey; replace tops.

YIELD: 6 servings.

Here's an easy, amazing sandwich that feels special. Sweet and tangy orange and crunchy pecans make it truly delicious. And only five ingredients!

There's a funny story involving this recipe. Years ago, our older daughter dipped her sandwich into the broth, took a bite and piped up, "Mom, I like these coffee sandwiches." We've kept that nickname for them ever since.

philly steak sandwiches

SHERYL CHRISTIAN ⚑ WATERTOWN, WISCONSIN

½ pound fresh mushrooms, sliced
2 medium onions, thinly sliced
1 medium green pepper, sliced
2 tablespoons butter
1 pound thinly sliced cooked roast beef
6 hoagie rolls, split
6 slices (8 ounces) part-skim mozzarella cheese
4 beef bouillon cubes
2 cups water

1. In a skillet, saute mushrooms, onions and green pepper in butter until tender. Divide beef among rolls. Top with vegetables and cheese; replace roll tops. Place on an ungreased baking sheet; cover with foil.
2. Bake at 350° for 15 minutes or until heated through. In a small saucepan, heat bouillon and water until cubes are dissolved; serve as a dipping sauce.

YIELD: 6 servings.

barbecue sandwiches

TINA WUNKER ☞ WINSTON-SALEM, NORTH CAROLINA

1 boneless beef chuck roast (2½ pounds), trimmed

1 boneless pork shoulder roast (2½ pounds), trimmed

8 cups water

2 celery ribs, cut into 3-inch pieces

2 bay leaves

8 whole cloves

1 teaspoon salt

¼ teaspoon pepper

BARBECUE SAUCE:

1 cup chopped onion

2 tablespoons butter

1 cup ketchup

½ cup cider vinegar

⅓ cup sugar

4 teaspoons Worcestershire sauce

1 tablespoon brown sugar

1 tablespoon celery salt

2 teaspoons paprika

½ teaspoon *each* salt, pepper, chili powder and ground cumin

16 to 20 hamburger buns, split

1. Place the first eight ingredients in a large roasting pan; cover and bake at 325° for 3-4 hours or until pork is tender. Remove pork roast; set aside.

2. Bake chuck roast, covered, 40 minutes longer or until beef is tender. Cut pork and beef into bite size pieces. Strain pan drippings and set aside ½ cup sauce.

3. In a large Dutch oven, saute onion in butter until tender. Add ketchup, vinegar, sugar, Worcestershire sauce, brown sugar and seasonings. Stir in reserved pan drippings. Add meat; bring to a boil. Reduce heat; cover and simmer for 15 minutes, stirring occasionally. Serve on buns.

YIELD: 16-20 servings.

california clubs

DIANE CIGEL ⚑ STEVENS POINT, WISCONSIN

Ranch dressing and Dijon mustard create a tasty sauce, and pairing tomato and avocado with the chicken and bacon is just the right combination on sourdough bread. These will liven up any casual lunch.

½ cup ranch salad dressing
¼ cup Dijon mustard
8 slices sourdough bread, toasted
4 boneless skinless chicken breast halves, cooked and sliced
1 large tomato, sliced
1 medium ripe avocado, peeled and sliced
12 bacon strips, cooked and drained

1. In a small bowl, combine salad dressing and mustard; spread on each slice of bread. On four slices of bread, layer the chicken, tomato, avocado and bacon. Top with remaining bread

YIELD: 4 servings.

italian steak sandwiches

MARIA REGAKIS ⚑ SOMERVILLE, MASSACHUSETTS

My sister came up with these quick sandwiches that use minced garlic and other seasonings to bring pizzazz to deli roast beef. Add some carrot sticks or a tomato salad for a fantastic lunch in minutes.

2 garlic cloves, minced
⅛ teaspoon crushed red pepper flakes
2 tablespoons olive oil
16 slices deli roast beef
½ cup beef broth
2 tablespoons red wine *or* additional beef broth
2 teaspoons dried parsley flakes
2 teaspoons dried basil
¼ teaspoon salt
¼ teaspoon dried oregano
⅛ teaspoon pepper
4 sandwich rolls, split
4 slices provolone cheese

1. In a large skillet, saute garlic and pepper flakes in oil. Add the roast beef, broth, wine or additional broth and seasonings; heat through. Place beef slices on rolls; drizzle with the broth mixture. Top with cheese.

YIELD: 4 servings.

greek hero

MARGARET WILSON ⚑ HEMET, CALIFORNIA

This Greek-style hero is made by spreading a loaf of bread with hummus, then adding veggies, seasonings and feta cheese. With plenty of garden-fresh flavors and a hearty bean spread that packs protein, this stacked submarine makes a satisfying, nutritious meal.

2 tablespoons lemon juice
1 tablespoon olive oil
1 can (15 ounces) garbanzo beans *or* chickpeas, rinsed and drained
2 garlic cloves, minced
1 teaspoon dried oregano
¼ teaspoon salt
⅛ teaspoon pepper

SANDWICH:

1 unsliced loaf (8 ounces) French bread
2 medium sweet red peppers, cut into thin strips
½ medium cucumber, sliced
2 small tomatoes, sliced
¼ cup thinly sliced red onion

¼ cup chopped ripe olives
¼ cup chopped stuffed olives
½ cup crumbled feta cheese
4 lettuce leaves

1. For hummus, place the lemon juice, oil and beans in a food processor; cover and process until smooth. Add garlic, oregano, salt and pepper; mix well.
2. Slice bread in half horizontally. Carefully hollow out bottom half, leaving a ½-in. shell. Spread hummus into shell. Layer with red peppers, cucumber, tomatoes, onion, olives, cheese and lettuce. Replace bread top. Cut into four portions.

YIELD: 4 servings.

corned beef & cabbage sandwiches

TASTE OF HOME TEST KITCHEN

You don't have to wait for St. Patrick's Day to serve these. Your family is sure to enjoy creamy cabbage and tender corned beef on hard rolls any time of year—and feel lucky as leprecauns.

⅓ cup mayonnaise
1 tablespoon white vinegar
¼ teaspoon ground mustard
¼ teaspoon celery seed
¼ teaspoon pepper
1½ cups thinly shredded raw cabbage
4 kaiser *or* hard rolls, split
¾ to 1 pound fully cooked corned beef, sliced

1. In a bowl, combine the mayonnaise, vinegar, mustard, celery seed and pepper until smooth. Stir in the cabbage and mix well. Spoon onto the bottom halves of rolls. Cover with the corned beef; replace tops of the rolls. Serve immediately.

YIELD: 4 servings.

Olive lovers will rejoice over this stacked sub! Stuffed and ripe olives are marinated in white wine vinegar and garlic before being spooned onto these speedy salami, ham and provolone subs.

italian subs

DELORES CHRISTNER ☞ SPOONER, WISCONSIN

⅓ cup olive oil

4½ teaspoons white wine vinegar

1 tablespoon dried parsley flakes

2 to 3 garlic cloves, minced

1 can (2¼ ounces) sliced ripe olives, drained

½ cup chopped stuffed olives

6 submarine sandwich buns (10 inches), split

24 thin slices hard salami

24 slices provolone *or* part-skim mozzarella cheese

24 slices fully cooked ham

Lettuce leaves, optional

1. In a bowl, combine the oil, vinegar, parsley and garlic. Stir in olives. Cover and refrigerate for 8 hours or overnight.
2. Place about 2 tablespoons olive mixture on the bottom of each bun. Top each with four slices of salami, cheese and ham; add lettuce if desired. Replace tops.

YIELD: 6 servings.

antipasto-stuffed baguettes

DIANNE HOLMGREN PRESCOTT, ARIZONA

1 can (2¼ ounces) sliced ripe olives, drained
2 tablespoons olive oil
1 teaspoon lemon juice
1 garlic clove, minced
⅛ teaspoon *each* dried basil, thyme, marjoram and rosemary, crushed
2 French bread baguettes (8 ounces *each*)
1 package (4 ounces) crumbled feta cheese
¼ pound thinly sliced Genoa salami
1 cup fresh baby spinach
1 jar (7¼ ounces) roasted red peppers, drained and chopped
1 can (14 ounces) water-packed artichoke hearts, rinsed and drained

1. In a blender, combine the olives, oil, lemon juice, garlic and herbs; cover and process until the olives are chopped. Set aside ⅓ cup olive mixture (refrigerate remaining mixture for another use).

2. Cut the top third off each baguette; carefully hollow out bottoms, leaving a ¼-in. shell (discard removed bread or save for another use).

3. Spread olive mixture in the bottom of each loaf. Sprinkle with feta cheese. Fold salami slices in half and place over cheese. Top with the spinach, red peppers and artichokes, pressing down as necessary. Replace the bread tops. Wrap loaves tightly in foil. Refrigerate for at least 3 hours or overnight.

4. Serve cold, or place foil-wrapped loaves on a baking sheet and bake at 350° for 20-25 minutes or until heated through. Cut into slices; secure with a toothpick.

YIELD: 3 dozen.

EDITOR'S NOTE: ⅓ cup purchased tapenade (olive paste) may be substituted for the olive mixture.

peppy meatball subs

CRISTINE COSTELLO  SONORA, CALIFORNIA

1 jar (28 ounces) spaghetti sauce, *divided*

1 egg

1 cup seasoned bread crumbs

1 medium onion, chopped

½ cup chopped sweet red pepper

1 garlic clove, minced

½ teaspoon Italian seasoning

¼ teaspoon salt

¼ teaspoon pepper

1 pound ground beef

6 submarine *or* hoagie buns, split

1 jar (11½ ounces) pepperoncinis, drained and sliced

1 can (2¼ ounces) sliced ripe olives, drained, optional

Shredded Parmesan cheese and thinly sliced red onion, optional

1. In a large bowl, combine ½ cup of spaghetti sauce, egg, bread crumbs, onion, red pepper, garlic, Italian seasoning, salt and pepper. Crumble beef over mixture and mix well. Shape into 1-in. balls.

2. Place meatballs on a greased rack in a shallow baking pan. Bake at 350° for 15-20 minutes or until meat is no longer pink, turning once; drain.

3. Transfer to a large saucepan; add the remaining spaghetti sauce. Bring to a boil. Reduce heat; cover and simmer for 15 minutes. Spoon meatballs and sauce onto bun bottoms. Top with pepperoncinis, olives, Parmesan cheese and red onion if desired. Replace bun tops.

YIELD: 6 servings.

A store in town used to sell the most amazing meatball subs. When I discovered they no longer offered them, I decided to get creative and make my own. My husband and young children love my version.

vegetarian sloppy joes

LINDA WINTER ⚑ OAK HARBOR, WASHINGTON

The meat won't be missed in my version of sloppy joes. It tastes like the classic recipe, but is lower in fat and a great option for vegetarians.

- 1 small onion, finely chopped
- 2 teaspoons butter
- 1 package (12 ounces) frozen vegetarian meat crumbles
- ½ teaspoon pepper
- 2 tablespoons all-purpose flour
- 1 can (8 ounces) no-salt-added tomato sauce
- ⅔ cup ketchup
- 6 hamburger buns, split and toasted

1. In a large nonstick skillet coated with cooking spray, saute onion in butter until tender. Stir in meat crumbles and pepper; heat through.
2. Sprinkle flour over mixture and stir until blended. Stir in tomato sauce and ketchup. Bring to a boil; cook and stir for 1-2 minutes or until thickened. Spoon ½ cup onto each bun.

YIELD: 6 servings.

EDITOR'S NOTE: Vegetarian meat crumbles are a nutritious protein source made from soy. Look for them in the natural foods freezer section.

hawaiian deli sandwiches

TAMMY BLOMQUIST ⚑ TAYLORVILLE, ILLINOIS

When our kids were in sports, we were often on the road for meals. These easy sandwiches can be made ahead of time, and they travel well. They're great for potlucks and entertaining, too.

- 1 package (4.4 ounces) Hawaiian sweet rolls
- 1 tablespoon ranch salad dressing
- 1 tablespoon prepared mustard
- 2 slices deli ham
- 4 slices hard salami
- 2 slices deli turkey

1. Leaving the rolls attached, cut in half horizontally; remove top. Spread ranch dressing over cut side of top; spread mustard over cut side of bottom. Layer with ham, salami and turkey; replace top. Cut into four sandwiches.

YIELD: 2 servings.

SANDWICH SATURDAY
Get your family together to create sandwiches in assembly-line fashion. Use freezer-friendly fillings, wrap the sandwiches in heavy-duty foil, label them, and store them in the freezer for fast lunch packing later in the week.

Rustic ciabatta is the perfect match for tender roast beef with bold blue cheese and chipotle in this easy, tasty recipe.

chipotle roast beef sandwiches

ANDRE HOUSEKNECHT ⚑ FEASTERVILLE, PENNSYLVANIA

1 loaf (14 ounces) ciabatta bread, halved lengthwise

⅔ cup mayonnaise

1 tablespoon chopped chipotle pepper in adobo sauce

1 small garlic clove, minced

1 teaspoon lime juice

¼ teaspoon pepper

⅛ teaspoon salt

½ cup crumbled blue cheese

¾ pound sliced deli roast beef

1 small onion, thinly sliced

1 medium tomato, sliced

4 lettuce leaves

1. Place bread, cut side up, on a baking sheet. Broil 3-4 in. from heat for 2-3 minutes or until toasted.

2. Meanwhile, in a small bowl, combine mayonnaise, chipotle pepper, garlic, lime juice, pepper and salt; spread over cut sides of bread.

3. Sprinkle bottom half with blue cheese. Layer with roast beef, onion, tomato and lettuce; replace top. Cut into four sandwiches.

YIELD: 4 servings.

Before leaving for work, I often put these ingredients in the slow cooker. Supper is ready when I get home. This recipe is good to take to tailgate parties.

italian beef sandwiches

CAROL ALLEN ⚑ MCLEANSBORO, ILLINOIS

1 boneless beef chuck roast (3 to 4 pounds), trimmed
3 tablespoons dried basil
3 tablespoons dried oregano
1 cup water
1 envelope onion soup mix
10 to 12 Italian rolls *or* sandwich buns

1. Place roast in a slow cooker. Combine basil, oregano and water; pour over roast. Sprinkle with soup mix. Cover and cook on low for 7-8 hours or until meat is tender. Remove meat; shred with a fork and keep warm. Strain broth; skim off fat. Serve meat on rolls; use broth for dipping if desired.

YIELD: 10-12 servings.

SHREDDING MEAT FOR SANDWICHES
Cook meat until very tender, then place in a shallow pan to catch drips. Cool slightly. With two forks, pull the meat into thin shreds. Return to the slow cooker to keep warm.

salami pork sub

SHIRLEY NORDBLUM 🏴 YOUNGSVILLE, PENNSYLVANIA

Our family used to drive 22 miles to enjoy these sandwiches at a restaurant. After the place was torn down to make room for a highway, I was able to get the recipe. Now I fix them at home all the time.

- 1 loaf (1 pound) unsliced French bread
- 12 slices salami
- 16 slices cooked pork (⅛ inch thick)
- 8 slices provolone cheese
- 24 thin dill pickle slices
- Lettuce leaves
- ¼ cup mayonnaise
- 2 tablespoons prepared mustard

1. Cut bread in half lengthwise. On the bottom half, layer the salami, pork, cheese, pickles and lettuce. Combine mayonnaise and mustard; spread over cut side of top half of loaf. Replace bread top. Cut into fourths.

YIELD: 4 servings.

favorite sloppy joes

ELEANOR MIELKE 🏴 SNOHOMISH, WASHINGTON

I've prepared sloppy joes for years. I've tried many recipes, but this one is the best by far. It also travels well for picnics or potlucks. My family loves it!

- 2 pounds ground beef
- ½ cup chopped onion
- ¾ cup chili sauce
- ½ cup water
- ¼ cup prepared mustard
- 2 teaspoons chili powder
- 12 hamburger buns, split
- 12 slices cheddar cheese

1. In a skillet, cook beef and onion over medium heat until meat is no longer pink; drain. Add chili sauce, water, mustard and chili powder. Simmer, uncovered, for 20 minutes, stirring occasionally. Spoon ½ cup of meat mixture onto each bun; top with a cheese slice.

YIELD: 12 servings.

turkey hero

TASTE OF HOME TEST KITCHEN

1 package (3 ounces) cream cheese, softened
2 tablespoons ranch salad dressing
1 teaspoon poppy seeds
Pinch garlic powder
1 loaf (1 pound) French bread, split lengthwise
Shredded lettuce
¾ pound thinly sliced cooked turkey
¼ pound thinly sliced Swiss cheese
2 medium tomatoes, sliced

1. In a small bowl, beat the first four ingredients until smooth. Spread on both cut surfaces of bread. Layer lettuce, turkey, cheese and tomatoes on bottom half of bread. Top with the other half. Cut into serving-size pieces.

YIELD: 6 servings.

A special cream cheese and ranch dressing spread adds zest to the hearty turkey, cheese and vegetables. Get set to slice up second helpings!

A traditional club gets a fun change of pace when the bread is replaced with soft flour tortillas.

club quesadillas

VICTORIA HAHN ⚑ NORTHAMPTON, PENNSYLVANIA

½ cup mayonnaise
8 flour tortillas (8 inches)
4 lettuce leaves
2 medium tomatoes, sliced
8 slices deli turkey
8 slices deli ham
8 slices provolone cheese
8 bacon strips, cooked
Salsa

1. Spread mayonnaise on each tortilla. On tortillas, layer the lettuce, tomatoes, turkey, ham, cheese and bacon; top with the remaining tortillas. Cut into quarters. Serve with salsa.

YIELD: 4 servings.

My Italian husband grew up eating this flavorful sandwich his mother used to make on Saturdays. It can easily be made a few hours ahead and refrigerated, then served with chips, veggies and dip for a delicious meal.

italian submarine

CHRISTINE LUPELLA ⚑ FIFTY LAKES, MINNESOTA

1 loaf (1 pound) unsliced Italian bread
2 to 3 tablespoons olive oil
2 to 4 tablespoons shredded Parmesan cheese
1 to 1½ teaspoons dried oregano
1 medium tomato, thinly sliced
½ pound thinly sliced deli ham
¼ pound sliced provolone cheese
¼ pound thinly sliced hard salami

1. Cut bread in half lengthwise. Hollow out bottom half, leaving a ¼-in. shell (discard removed bread or save for another use). Brush oil over cut sides of bread.

2. Combine the Parmesan cheese and oregano; sprinkle over bread. On the bottom half, layer the tomato, ham, provolone and salami. Replace bread top. Cut into four slices.

YIELD: 4 servings.

pita pocket chicken salad

NATASHA RANDALL ⚑ AUSTIN, TEXAS

We wanted something cool for lunch one summer day, so I tossed together whatever I had in the refrigerator. This wonderful salad was the result. People enjoy the sweet grapes, tender chicken and crunchy almonds—and they always ask for the recipe.

2 cups cubed cooked chicken

1½ cups seedless red grapes, halved

1 cup chopped cucumber

¾ cup sliced almonds

¾ cup shredded part-skim mozzarella cheese

½ cup poppy seed salad dressing

6 pita pocket halves

Leaf lettuce, optional

1. In a large bowl, combine the chicken, grapes, cucumber, almonds and mozzarella cheese. Drizzle with salad dressing and toss to coat. Line pita breads with lettuce if desired; fill with chicken salad.

YIELD: 6 servings.

spinach pastrami wraps

RHONDA WILKINSON ⚑ LEVITTOWN, PENNSYLVANIA

Instead of using tortillas for this recipe, you can simply wrap the meat around the other ingredients and fasten with a toothpick. Either way, the wraps can be sliced and served for appetizers or kept whole.

4 flour tortillas (10 inches), room temperature

4 ounces cream cheese, softened

¾ cup shredded cheddar cheese

¼ cup chopped red onion

¼ cup sliced Greek olives

½ pound thinly sliced deli pastrami

1½ cups fresh baby spinach

1. Spread the tortillas with cream cheese; sprinkle with cheddar cheese, onion and olives. Top with pastrami and spinach. Roll up tightly; secure wraps with toothpicks.

YIELD: 4 servings.

fancy ham 'n' cheese

JAMES GAUTHIER ⚑ OAK CREEK, WISCONSIN

Garden-fresh ingredients such as spinach, cucumber and onion add appeal to this zippy ham stacker.

- ¼ cup butter, softened
- 8 slices rye bread
- 12 fresh spinach leaves
- 16 cucumber slices
- 4 thin slices red onion
- 12 slices fully cooked ham
- 2 tablespoons Dijon mustard
- 8 slices cheddar cheese

1. Spread butter on one side of each slice of bread. On half of the slices, layer the spinach, cucumber, onion, ham, mustard and cheese. Top with the remaining bread.

YIELD: 4 servings.

giant focaccia sandwich

MARINA GELLING ⚑ ROWLETT, TEXAS

A flavorful Italian flatbread made with oats and molasses turns this sandwich into something special.

- 5½ cups all-purpose flour
- 1 cup quick-cooking oats
- 2 packages (¼ ounce *each*) active dry yeast
- 2 teaspoons salt
- 2¼ cups water
- ½ cup molasses
- 1 tablespoon butter
- 1 egg, lightly beaten
- 1 tablespoon *each* dried minced onion, sesame seeds and garlic salt

SANDWICH FILLING:
- 6 tablespoons mayonnaise
- 2 tablespoons prepared mustard
- 6 to 8 lettuce leaves
- ¾ to 1 pound thinly sliced fully cooked ham
- 6 to 8 thin slices Swiss *or* cheddar cheese
- 4 slices red onion, separated into rings
- 1 medium green pepper, sliced
- 2 medium tomatoes, thinly sliced

1. In a large mixing bowl, combine flour, oats, yeast and salt. In a saucepan, heat water, molasses and butter to 120°-130°. Add to dry ingredients; beat just until moistened.

2. Place in a greased bowl; turn once to grease top. Cover and let rise in a warm place until doubled, about 45 minutes.

3. Press the dough onto a greased 14-in. pizza pan. Cover and let rise until doubled, about 30 minutes. Brush with egg. Sprinkle with onion, sesame seeds and garlic salt. Bake at 350° for 30-35 minutes or until golden brown.

4. Remove to wire rack to cool. Split the focaccia in half horizontally; spread mayonnaise and mustard on cut sides. On bottom half, layer lettuce, ham, cheese, onion, green pepper and tomatoes. Replace top half. Chill until serving. Cut into wedges.

YIELD: 12 servings

Flour tortillas are available in a variety of flavors, including sun-dried tomato, spinach and whole wheat. Serve chips with the leftover guacamole to accompany the sandwiches.

guacamole chicken roll-ups
TASTE OF HOME TEST KITCHEN

¼ cup guacamole

4 flavored flour tortillas of your choice (10 inches)

4 large lettuce leaves

1⅓ cups chopped fresh tomatoes

2 packages (6 ounces *each*) thinly sliced deli smoked chicken breast

2 cups (8 ounces) shredded Mexican cheese blend

1. Spread 1 tablespoon of guacamole over each tortilla. Layer with lettuce, tomatoes, chicken and cheese. Roll up tightly.

YIELD: 4 servings.

TASTY SANDWICH TOPPERS
Enhance a sandwich with toppings such as guacamole, salsa, cheese spreads, mayonnaise, Swiss cheese, blue cheese, sauteed mushrooms or bacon strips.

mile-high shredded beef

BETTY SITZMAN ☞ WRAY, COLORADO

1 boneless beef chuck roast (3 pounds)
1 can (14½ ounces) beef broth
1 medium onion, chopped
1 celery rib, chopped
¾ cup ketchup
¼ cup packed brown sugar
2 tablespoons white vinegar
1 teaspoon salt
1 teaspoon ground mustard
1 teaspoon Worcestershire sauce
1 garlic clove, minced
1 bay leaf
¼ teaspoon garlic powder
¼ teaspoon paprika
3 drops hot pepper sauce
12 to 15 hoagie buns

1. Place the roast in a Dutch oven; add broth, onion and celery. Bring to a boil. Reduce heat; cover and simmer for 2½ to 3 hours or until the meat is tender.
2. Remove roast and cool slightly; shred meat with two forks. Strain vegetables and set aside. Skim fat from cooking liquid and reserve 1½ cups. Return meat, vegetables and reserved cooking liquid to pan.
3. Stir in ketchup, brown sugar, vinegar, salt, mustard, Worcestershire sauce, garlic, bay leaf, garlic powder, paprika and hot pepper sauce. Bring to a boil. Reduce heat; cover and simmer for 30 minutes. Discard bay leaf. Serve beef on buns.

YIELD: 12-15 servings.

sandwich for a crowd

HELEN HOUGLAND ⚐ SPRING HILL, KANSAS

2 unsliced loaves (1 pound *each*)
  Italian bread
1 package (8 ounces) cream cheese, softened
1 cup (4 ounces) shredded cheddar cheese
¾ cup sliced green onions
¼ cup mayonnaise
1 tablespoon Worcestershire sauce
1 pound thinly sliced fully cooked ham
1 pound thinly sliced roast beef
12 to 14 thin slices dill pickle

1. Cut the bread in half lengthwise. Hollow out top and bottom of loaves, leaving a ½-in. shell (discard removed bread or save for another use). Combine cheeses, onions, mayonnaise and Worcestershire sauce; spread over cut sides of bread.
2. Layer ham and roast beef on bottom and top halves; place pickles on bottom halves. Gently press halves together. Wrap in plastic wrap and refrigerate for at least 2 hours. Cut sandwich into 1½-in. slices.

YIELD: 12-14 servings.

My husband and I live on a 21-acre horse ranch and are pleased to invite friends to enjoy it with us. When entertaining, I rely on no-fuss make-ahead entrees.

reunion barbecues

MARGERY BRYAN ⚑ ROYAL CITY, WASHINGTON

*I found this recipe in our local CattleWomen's cookbook. It's a favorite when
I need to make lots of sandwiches for a crowd, and I never have to worry about leftovers!*

5 pounds ground beef
2 cups chopped onion
3 cups water
2 tablespoons ketchup
2 to 3 tablespoons chili powder
2 tablespoons salt
1 tablespoon pepper
1 teaspoon ground mustard
1 cup quick-cooking oats
24 hamburger buns, split

1. In a large saucepan or Dutch oven, cook beef and onion over medium heat until meat is no longer pink; drain.

2. Add water, ketchup, chili powder, salt, pepper and mustard; bring to a boil. Add oats; mix well. Reduce heat; cover and simmer for 30 minutes. Serve on buns, ½ cup on each.

YIELD: 24 servings.

pumpernickel turkey hero

MILDRED SHERRER ⚑ ROANOKE, TEXAS

*Thousand Island dressing lends flavor to each bite of this hearty turkey and Swiss sandwich. A friend brought
this loaf to a sandwich luncheon. I asked for the recipe so I could serve it to my family. They liked it, too.*

1 loaf (1 pound) unsliced pumpernickel bread
⅓ cup Thousand Island salad dressing
6 lettuce leaves
2 medium tomatoes, sliced
3 slices red onion, separated into rings
6 slices Swiss cheese
1 package (12 ounces) thinly sliced deli turkey

1. Cut bread in half horizontally; spread salad dressing over cut sides. On the bottom half, layer the lettuce, tomatoes, onion, half of the cheese and half of the turkey. Top with remaining cheese and turkey. Replace bread top. Slice before serving.

YIELD: 6 servings.

These tortilla wraps make a convenient portable lunch. We simply love them!

beef 'n' cheese wraps

SUE SIBSON HOWARD, SOUTH CAROLINA

4 flour tortillas (10 inches)
1 carton (8 ounces) spreadable chive and onion cream cheese
1 cup shredded carrots
1 cup (4 ounces) shredded Monterey Jack cheese
1 pound thinly sliced cooked roast beef
Leaf lettuce

1. Spread one side of each tortilla with cream cheese; top with carrots and Monterey Jack cheese. Layer with beef and lettuce. Roll up tightly and wrap in plastic wrap. Refrigerate for at least 30 minutes. Cut in half or into 1-in. slices using a serrated knife.

YIELD: 4 servings.

pigskin barbecue

BOBBIE LOVE ⚑ KAPAA, HAWAII

1 bone-in pork blade roast (about 5 pounds), cut in half
1 tablespoon canola oil
1 cup water
1 can (8 ounces) tomato sauce
¼ cup packed brown sugar
¼ cup cider vinegar
¼ cup Worcestershire sauce
2 to 3 tablespoons hot pepper sauce
1 tablespoon chili powder
1½ teaspoons celery seed
1 to 2 teaspoons salt
1 medium onion, halved and thinly sliced
1 cup chopped sweet red *or* green pepper
1 to 2 tablespoons cornstarch
3 tablespoons cold water
14 to 16 kaiser rolls, split

1. In a large kettle, brown pork in oil on all sides; drain. Combine the water, tomato sauce, brown sugar, vinegar, Worcestershire sauce, hot pepper sauce, chili powder, celery seed and salt; pour over roast. Bring to a boil. Reduce heat; cover and simmer for 1¾ hours.

2. Stir in onion and sweet pepper. Cover and simmer 30-45 minutes longer or until the meat is tender. Remove roast. When cool enough to handle, shred meat with two forks; set aside.

3. Skim fat from pan juices. Combine cornstarch and cold water until smooth; gradually add to pan juices. Bring to a boil; cook and stir for 2 minutes or until slightly thickened. Return pork to pan and heat through. Serve on rolls.

YIELD: 14-16 servings.

I've taken these saucy sandwiches to potlucks and tailgate parties with our polo club and served them at our own backyard picnics. They're simple to make and always draw rave reviews.

SAUCES, RELISHES & MORE

This colorful combination of broiled peppers and eggplant is nicely seasoned with garlic and oregano. Serve it warm or cold, as a side dish, sandwich topper or on toasted bread rounds as an appetizer. My family loves it!

eggplant pepper relish

JEANNE VITALE ☞ LEOLA, PENNSYLVANIA

3 medium sweet red peppers, cut in half lengthwise

3 medium sweet yellow peppers, cut in half lengthwise

1 medium eggplant, cut in half lengthwise

2 tablespoons olive oil

1 garlic clove, minced

¼ cup minced fresh parsley

1 tablespoon minced fresh oregano *or* 1 teaspoon dried oregano

¾ teaspoon salt

¼ teaspoon pepper

1. Place peppers skin side up on a broiler pan. Broil for 10-15 minutes or until tender and skin is blistered. Place in a bowl; cover and let stand for 15-20 minutes. Peel off and discard charred skin.

2. Broil eggplant skin side up for 5-7 minutes or until tender and skin is blistered. Place in a bowl; cover and let stand for 15-20 minutes. Peel off and discard charred skin. Cut peppers into strips and eggplant into cubes.

3. In a large bowl, combine oil and garlic. Add peppers, eggplant, parsley, oregano, salt and pepper. Toss to coat. Serve at room temperature.

YIELD: 12 servings.

ginger honey mustard

LYNNE ELLIS  LAWRENCE, KANSAS

This mustard makes a tangy addition to burgers, brats or subs.
We've found it tastes great with pretzels, too!

½ cup Dijon mustard
¼ cup honey
¾ teaspoon ground ginger
1 teaspoon lemon juice
1 teaspoon vegetable oi

1. In a blender, combine all the ingredients; cover and process until smooth. Transfer to a jar or container. Refrigerate for 2 hours before serving. Store in the refrigerator.

YIELD: about ¾ cup.

ALL IN ONE
Going to grill hot dogs and hamburgers at your tailgate? Mix the ketchup, mustard, pickle relish and chopped onion together in one container. It's a breeze to use this instead of dragging out all the separate condiments.

dijon tartar sauce

KRISTEN FLAHERTY  SOUTH PORTLAND, MAINE

Fat-free mayonnaise mixed only with pickle relish seemed so flavor-free,
so I began experimenting and came up with my own version of tartar sauce.
It adds lots of flavor to fish, but fewer calories than regular tartar sauce.

½ cup fat-free mayonnaise
3 tablespoons sweet pickle relish
3 tablespoons chopped onion
4 teaspoons Dijon mustard
2 teaspoons lemon juice
¼ teaspoon sugar
¼ teaspoon salt
⅛ teaspoon pepper

1. In a bowl, combine all the ingredients. Store in the refrigerator for up to 1 week.

YIELD: ¾ cup.

steak sauce

This savory recipe is just the thing for folks who don't think a steak is ready until each morsel is dripping with sauce.

2 cups ketchup
2 garlic cloves, minced
⅔ cup chopped onion
½ cup *each* lemon juice, water, Worcestershire sauce and white vinegar
¼ cup soy sauce
¼ cup packed dark brown sugar
2 tablespoons prepared mustard

1. Combine all ingredients in a 3-qt. saucepan; bring to a boil over medium heat. Reduce heat and simmer, uncovered, for 30 minutes. Strain if desired. Cover and refrigerate.

YIELD: about 3 cups.

RETURNING HOME
When you arrive back home, promptly refrigerate all perishable items. Drain the cooler and wash it with hot, soapy water; allow it to air-dry overnight before storing.

bread and butter pickles

KAREN OWEN ☞ RISING SUN, INDIANA

My mom always made these crisp pickles when we were kids, and she gave me the recipe. They are pleasantly tart and so good.

4 pounds cucumbers, sliced
8 small onions, sliced
½ cup canning salt
5 cups sugar
4 cups white vinegar
2 tablespoons mustard seed
2 teaspoons celery seed
1½ teaspoons ground turmeric
½ teaspoon ground cloves

1. In a large container, combine cucumbers, onions and salt. Cover with crushed ice; mix well. Let stand for 3 hours. Drain; rinse and drain again.
2. In a large kettle, combine the sugar, vinegar and seasonings; bring to a boil. Add cucumber mixture; return to a boil. Ladle hot mixture into hot jars, leaving ¼-in. headspace. Adjust caps. Process for 15 minutes in a boiling-water bath. Remove jars to a wire rack to cool completely.

YIELD: 4 pints.

sweet brown mustard

RHONDA HOLLOWAY ⚑ PORT RICHEY, FLORIDA

This versatile, sweet and slightly spicy mustard goes well with a variety of meats.

- 1 can (14 ounces) sweetened condensed milk
- 1 cup spicy brown mustard
- 2 tablespoons prepared horseradish
- 2 tablespoons Worcestershire sauce

1. In a small bowl, combine all of the ingredients until smooth. Cover and store in the refrigerator for up to 2 weeks.

YIELD: 2⅓ cups.

riverboat barbecue sauce

BARB LOFTIN ⚑ FLORENCE, KENTUCKY

Maple and orange are the flavors that accent this sweet and tangy sauce. I gave it this name because we live near the Ohio River and love to watch the riverboats go by. The sauce is especially good on ribs or pork chops.

- ½ cup maple syrup
- ½ cup ketchup
- ¼ cup orange juice
- 1 tablespoon dried minced onion
- 1 tablespoon white vinegar
- 1 tablespoon steak sauce
- 1 teaspoon grated orange peel
- 1 teaspoon prepared mustard
- ½ teaspoon Worcestershire sauce
- ¼ teaspoon salt
- ¼ teaspoon pepper
- ¼ teaspoon hot pepper sauce
- 3 whole cloves

1. In a small saucepan, combine all ingredients. Bring to a boil. Reduce heat; simmer, uncovered, for 15 minutes or until the flavors are blended. Remove from heat. Discard cloves. Cool. Store in refrigerator.

YIELD: 1⅓ cups.

Here's a sweet and spicy combination that also looks attractive on a buffet spread. Plus, it can be used as a condiment or an appetizer!

pineapple chutney

SHIRLEY WATANABE KULA, HAWAII

2 cans (20 ounces *each*) pineapple tidbits, drained
4 cups diced onions
3 cups packed brown sugar
2 cups golden raisins
2 cups white vinegar
4 teaspoons grated orange peel
2 teaspoons salt
2 teaspoons mustard seed
2 teaspoons ground turmeric
2 teaspoons grated lemon peel
2 medium yellow banana peppers, seeded and chopped, optional

1. In a large saucepan over medium heat, combine the first 10 ingredients; add peppers if desired. Bring to a boil. Reduce heat; simmer, uncovered, for 1 to 1½ hours or until chutney reaches desired thickness.
2. Refrigerate. Serve with meat or with cream cheese as an appetizer spread.
YIELD: 6 cups.

pickled asparagus

MARIE HATTRUP ⚑ THE DALLES, OREGON

These tangy spears make a great addition to a relish tray. They liven up the beginning of any meal.

9 quarts water, *divided*
16 pounds fresh asparagus, trimmed
2 quarts white vinegar
1 cup canning salt
1 tablespoon mixed pickling spices
1 garlic clove, minced

1. In a large kettle, bring 6 qts. of water to a boil. Cook the asparagus in batches, uncovered, for 2½ minutes. Remove the asparagus and rinse in cold water.
2. In a Dutch oven, combine the vinegar, salt, pickling spices, garlic and remaining water; bring to a boil. Pack asparagus in quart jars to within ½ in. of top. Ladle boiling liquid over asparagus, leaving ¼-in. headspace. Adjust caps. Process for 20 minutes in a boiling-water bath. Remove jars to wire racks to cool completely.

YIELD: 8 quarts.

spicy mustard

JOYCE LONSDALE ⚑ UNIONVILLE, PENNSYLVANIA

I like to make this using fresh horseradish from my garden and vinegar seasoned with homegrown tarragon. It's a delightful dipper for pretzel rods or as a sandwich spread.

½ cup tarragon vinegar
½ cup water
¼ cup olive oil
2 tablespoons prepared horseradish
½ teaspoon lemon juice
1 cup ground mustard
½ cup sugar
½ teaspoon salt

1. In blender or food processor, combine all ingredients; cover and process for 1 minute. Scrape down sides of the container and process for 30 seconds.
2. Transfer to a small saucepan and let stand for 10 minutes. Cook over low heat until bubbly, stirring constantly. Cool completely. If a thinner mustard is desired, stir in an additional 1-2 tablespoons water. Pour into small containers with tight-fitting lids. Store in the refrigerator.

YIELD: 1½ cups.

barbecue sauce with mustard

CHARLIE AND RUTHIE KNOTE ⚑ CAPE GIRARDEAU, MISSOURI

This is a simple yet delightful way to add flavor to grilled fare. Try it for your next cookout.

½ cup sugar
¼ teaspoon ground oregano
½ teaspoon ground thyme
1 teaspoon salt
½ teaspoon pepper
⅛ teaspoon cayenne pepper
½ teaspoon cornstarch
½ cup white vinegar, *divided*
1 cup molasses
1 cup ketchup
1 cup prepared mustard
2 tablespoons canola oil

1. Combine the first seven ingredients in a small saucepan. Stir in enough vinegar to make a paste. Combine the molasses, ketchup, mustard, oil and remaining vinegar; add to herb paste. Bring to a boil, stirring constantly. Reduce heat and simmer 10 minutes. Remove from the heat; cool completely.

2. Pour into a glass jar; cover tightly. Store refrigerated for up to 3 months. Baste over smoked chicken, turkey, ham or hot dogs.

YIELD: 4 cups.

sweet 'n' tasty sauce

TASTE OF HOME TEST KITCHEN

Try this sauce as an alternative topping on hot dogs, brats or burgers. It also makes for great basting.

½ cup ketchup
⅓ cup orange juice
2 tablespoons brown sugar

1. In a small saucepan, combine all ingredients. Cook and stir over medium heat until the sugar is dissolved. Cool slightly.

YIELD: 1 cup.

Well coated with a tangy sour cream and celery seed dressing, these sweet-sour onions can sure dress up a juicy burger. My sister likes to serve them as a side salad when our family gets together in summer up at the lake.

creamy sweet onions

ETHEL LOWEY FORT FRANCES, ONTARIO

5 **large white onions, thinly sliced**
2¼ **cups sugar**
1½ **cups cider vinegar**
1½ **cups water**
4 **teaspoons salt**
1 **cup (8 ounces) sour cream**
3 **tablespoons mayonnaise**
¼ **teaspoon celery seed**
Salt and pepper to taste

1. Place the onions in a large bowl; set aside. In a small saucepan, combine the sugar, vinegar, water and salt. Bring to a boil; pour over onions. Cover and refrigerate overnight.

2. Drain onions, discarding liquid. In a large bowl, combine the sour cream, mayonnaise, celery seed, salt and pepper. Add onions and toss to coat.

YIELD: 4 cups.

easy freezer pickles

LUCILE JOHNSON ⌖ RED OAK, IOWA

These crispy no-cook pickles are so simple to fix. They can be frozen for up to 6 weeks.

8 pounds cucumbers, thinly sliced
1 cup thinly sliced onion
3 tablespoons salt
4 cups sugar
2 cups white vinegar
1 teaspoon celery seed
1 teaspoon ground turmeric
1 teaspoon mustard seed
½ teaspoon alum

1. In a large container, combine cucumbers, onion and salt; mix well. Let stand for 3 hours, stirring occasionally. Drain and rinse. In a bowl, combine remaining ingredients; let stand for 2-3 hours, stirring often.
2. Pour over the cucumber mixture and stir well. Pack into 1-pt. freezer containers, leaving 1-in. headspace. Cover and freeze up to 6 weeks. Thaw before serving.

YIELD: 6 pints.

rhubarb ketchup

FAITH MCLILLIAN ⌖ RAWDON, QUEBEC

I received this recipe from a friend about 15 years ago. It's a nice surprise for ketchup lovers, and so easy to prepare. The spicy flavor makes this one of the tastiest ketchups I've ever had!

4 cups diced fresh *or* frozen rhubarb
3 medium onions, chopped
1 cup white vinegar
1 cup packed brown sugar
1 cup sugar
1 can (28 ounces) diced tomatoes, undrained
2 teaspoons salt
1 teaspoon ground cinnamon
1 tablespoon pickling spice

1. In a large saucepan, combine all ingredients. Cook for 1 hour or until thickened. Cool. Refrigerate in covered containers.

YIELD: 6-7 cups.

EDITOR'S NOTE: If using frozen rhubarb, measure rhubarb while still frozen, then thaw completely. Drain in a colander, but do not press liquid out.

maple barbecue sauce

LORNA CROWE ⚑ EAST MAPLETON, NOVA SCOTIA

Guests at your outdoor party will love this sweet sauce on just about any meat you choose.

¾ cup maple syrup
¾ cup ketchup
½ cup cold water
½ teaspoon onion salt
¼ teaspoon celery seed
Salt and pepper to taste

1. In a small bowl or jar with a tight-fitting lid, combine all ingredients; mix or shake well. Serve over ribs, chicken, pork or ham or use as a marinade. Store in the refrigerator.

YIELD: 1¾ cups.

USE A GENTLE TOUCH
Homemade barbecue sauces are simple but delicious. If you're using any spices on your meat, make sure you dab the sauce on gently in the last few minutes of cooking. If you brush too hard, you might lose some of the spices.

pickled beets

EDNA HOFFMAN ⚑ HEBRON, INDIANA

With sweet, tangy and spiced flavors, these pickled beets are so good, they'll convert any naysayers!

3 pounds small fresh beets
2 cups sugar
2 cups water
2 cups cider vinegar
2 cinnamon sticks (3 inches)
1 teaspoon whole cloves
1 teaspoon whole allspice

1. Scrub beets and trim tops to 1 in. Place in a Dutch oven and cover with water. Bring to a boil. Reduce heat; cover and simmer for 25-35 minutes or until tender. Remove from the water; cool. Peel beets and cut into fourths.

2. Place the beets in a Dutch oven. Add the sugar, water and vinegar. Place the spices on a double thickness of cheesecloth; bring up the corners of the cloth and tie them with string to form a bag. Add to the beet mixture. Bring to a boil. Reduce heat; cover and simmer for 10 minutes. Discard spice bag.

3. Carefully pack beets into hot 1-pint jars to within ½ in. of the top. Carefully ladle hot liquid over beets, leaving ½-in. headspace. Remove air bubbles; wipe rims and adjust lids. Process for 35 minutes in a boiling-water canner.

YIELD: 4 pints.

EDITOR'S NOTE: The processing time listed is for altitudes of 1,000 feet or less. For altitudes up to 3,000 feet, add 5 minutes; 6,000 feet, add 10 minutes; 8,000 feet, add 15 minutes; 10,000 feet, add 20 minutes.

pecan barbecue sauce

VICKIE PATTERSON ▷ GRAND PRAIRIE, TEXAS

After 18 years, I haven't found anything that this sauce doesn't taste great on. Pecans are the deliciously different ingredient.

1 can (12 ounces) tomato paste
1 cup ground pecans
¾ cup water
⅓ cup packed brown sugar
¼ cup cider vinegar
¼ cup chopped onion
¼ cup honey
2 tablespoons lemon juice
1 tablespoon prepared mustard
1 teaspoon seasoned salt
2 garlic cloves, minced

1. In a large saucepan, combine all ingredients. Bring to a boil. Reduce heat; simmer, uncovered, for 20 minutes or until thickened, stirring occasionally. **YIELD:** 3 cups.

MAKING VEGETABLE RELISHES
If you plan to prepare a lot of relish, make the chopping easier by using a food processor or a food grinder with a coarse grinding blade.

german-style pickled eggs

MARJORIE HENNIG ▷ GREEN VALLEY, ARIZONA

I make these eggs and refrigerate them in a glass gallon jar for my husband to sell at his tavern. The customers love them! I found the recipe in an old cookbook years ago.

2 cups cider vinegar
1 cup sugar
½ cup water
2 tablespoons prepared mustard
1 tablespoon salt
1 tablespoon celery seed
1 tablespoon mustard seed
6 whole cloves
2 medium onions, thinly sliced
12 hard-cooked eggs, peeled

1. In a large saucepan, combine the first eight ingredients. Bring to a boil. Reduce heat; cover and simmer for 10 minutes. Cool completely. Place onions and eggs in a large jar; add enough vinegar mixture to completely cover.

2. Cover and refrigerate for at least 8 hours or over night. Use a clean spoon each time you remove eggs for serving. May be refrigerated for up to 1 week. **YIELD:** 12 servings.

My two grown sons actually eat this as a salad, but that's a bit too hot for me! The recipe's from my late husband's mother, and I haven't varied it over the years. I usually make a batch as soon as the first tomatoes of the season are ready. It also keeps for months in the freezer.

fresh tomato relish

LELA BASKINS WINDSOR, MISSOURI

2 cups white vinegar
½ cup sugar
8 cups chopped tomatoes (about 11 large)
½ cup chopped onion
1 medium green pepper, diced
1 celery rib, diced
¼ cup prepared horseradish
2 tablespoons salt
1 tablespoon mustard seed
1½ teaspoons pepper
½ teaspoon ground cinnamon
½ teaspoon ground cloves

1. In a large saucepan, bring vinegar and sugar to a boil. Remove from the heat; cool completely.

2. In a large bowl, combine remaining ingredients; add vinegar mixture and mix well. Spoon into storage containers, allowing ½-in. headspace. Refrigerate up to 2 weeks or freeze up to 12 months. Serve with a slotted spoon.

YIELD: about 6 pints.

You can use fresh or frozen cherries to make this flavorful barbecue sauce. It tastes great on ribs and chicken!

cherry barbecue sauce

ILENE HARRINGTON ⚑ NIPOMO, CALIFORNIA

1 medium onion, chopped
2 garlic cloves, minced
2 tablespoons butter
2 cups fresh *or* frozen dark sweet cherries, pitted and coarsely chopped
1 cup ketchup
⅔ cup packed brown sugar
¼ cup cider vinegar
1 tablespoon Worcestershire sauce
2 teaspoons ground mustard
½ teaspoon pepper
⅛ teaspoon liquid smoke, optional

1. In a large saucepan, saute onion and garlic in butter until tender. Stir in the remaining ingredients. Cook, uncovered, over medium-low heat for 20 minutes or until cherries are tender and sauce is thickened, stirring occasionally.

YIELD: about 3½ cups.

microwave pickles

MARIE WLADYKA ⚑ LAND O'LAKES, FLORIDA

You can enjoy a small batch of these sweet, crunchy pickles anytime without the work of traditional canning methods. They're loaded with flavor and so easy to make. We just love them!

1 medium cucumber, thinly sliced
2 small onions, thinly sliced
¾ cup sugar
½ cup white vinegar
1 teaspoon salt
½ teaspoon celery seed
½ teaspoon mustard seed

1. In a large microwave-safe bowl, combine all ingredients. Microwave, uncovered, on high for 3 minutes; stir. Cook 2-3 minutes longer or until mixture is bubbly and cucumbers and onions are crisp-tender.

2. Cover and refrigerate for at least 4 hours. Serve with a slotted spoon.

YIELD: 4-6 servings.

EDITOR'S NOTE: This recipe was tested in a 1,100-watt microwave.

bruce's hot barbecue sauce

PATTY KILE ⚑ GREENTOWN, PENNSYLVANIA

The heat is on when you brush meat with this tongue-tingling sauce! You'll also detect a hint of fruity sweetness, thanks to the apricots. I've been making this barbecue sauce for 20 years and get requests for the recipe every summer. I'm always happy to share it.

2 cans (15 ounces *each*) apricot halves, drained
4 cups packed brown sugar
4 cups cider vinegar
1 can (29 ounces) tomato sauce
2 cups ketchup
1 cup maple syrup
1 cup prepared mustard
½ cup orange juice
½ cup honey
3 tablespoons salt
½ cup molasses
3 tablespoons chicken bouillon granules
2 to 4 tablespoons crushed red pepper flakes
2 tablespoons garlic powder
2 tablespoons onion powder
2 tablespoons Worcestershire sauce
2 tablespoons soy sauce
1 tablespoon pepper
2 tablespoons liquid smoke, optional

1. In a blender or food processor, puree apricots until smooth. Pour into a large soup kettle or Dutch oven; add the next 17 ingredients. Bring to a boil.

2. Reduce heat; simmer, uncovered, for 1 hour or until flavors are blended, stirring occasionally. Stir in liquid smoke if desired. Cool. Store in the refrigerator.

YIELD: 4 quarts.

happy hot dog relish

ELIZABETH CARLSON ⚑ CORVALLIS, OREGON

*This sweet-tart relish combining cranberry sauce and sauerkraut is so good!
It's also a nice complement to hamburgers, baked ham and roast pork.*

1 medium onion, chopped
1 tablespoon olive oil
1 cup whole-berry cranberry sauce
1 tablespoon Dijon mustard
1 teaspoon sugar
½ teaspoon garlic powder
¼ teaspoon hot pepper sauce
½ cup sauerkraut, rinsed and drained

1. In a small saucepan, saute the onion in oil until tender. Add the cranberry sauce, mustard, sugar, garlic powder and pepper sauce. Cook and stir for 5-10 minutes or until cranberry sauce is melted. Add sauerkraut; heat through.

YIELD: 1½ cups.

MEAL PLANNING POINTERS
Plan well-balanced meals that contain foods from all of the basic food groups. Begin your menu planning with the main dish, then add a vegetable, side dish and/or salad and starch. Lastly, choose any relishes and a dessert.

spicy mustard spread

AUDREY THIBODEAU ⚑ GILBERT, ARIZONA

*This zippy spread makes taste buds sit up and take notice. It's super on
vegetables, hot dogs and hamburgers, in potato salad and more.*

¼ cup butter, softened
2 tablespoons ground mustard
2 tablespoons white vinegar
¼ teaspoon garlic salt
4 drops hot pepper sauce

1. In a small bowl, combine all the ingredients until smooth. Serve mustard spread with hot dogs, vegetables, hamburgers, chicken or steak. Store in the refrigerator.

YIELD: about ⅓ cup.

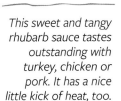

This sweet and tangy rhubarb sauce tastes outstanding with turkey, chicken or pork. It has a nice little kick of heat, too.

rhubarb barbecue sauce

CAROL ANDERSON ⚑ COALDALE, ALBERTA

1 cup chopped fresh *or* frozen rhubarb

⅔ cup water

1 medium onion, finely chopped

1 teaspoon canola oil

1 garlic clove, minced

1 cup ketchup

⅔ cup packed brown sugar

½ cup dark corn syrup

2 tablespoons cider vinegar

2 tablespoons Worcestershire sauce

1 tablespoon Dijon mustard

1½ teaspoons hot pepper sauce

¼ teaspoon salt

1. In a small saucepan, bring rhubarb and water to a boil. Reduce heat; simmer, uncovered, for 5-6 minutes or until tender. Remove from the heat; cool slightly.

2. Place rhubarb in a blender or food processor; cover and process until smooth. Set aside.

3. In the same saucepan, saute onion in oil until tender. Add garlic; saute 1 minute longer. Add the remaining ingredients.

4. Whisk in the rhubarb puree until blended. Bring to a boil. Reduce heat; simmer, uncovered, for 5 minutes. Use as a basting sauce for grilled meats. Store in the refrigerator.

YIELD: 2⅓ cups.

refrigerator dill pickles

JAKE HAEN ☞ OCALA, FLORIDA

Easy and economical, these pickles are tangy, zesty and crispy. No one will believe you made them yourself!

6 to 8 pounds pickling cucumbers
40 fresh dill sprigs
2 large onions, thinly sliced
5 garlic cloves, sliced
1 quart water
1 quart white vinegar
¾ cup sugar
½ cup canning salt

1. Cut each cucumber lengthwise into four spears. In a large bowl, combine the cucumbers, dill, onions and garlic; set aside. In a Dutch oven, combine the remaining ingredients. Bring to a boil; cook and stir just until salt is dissolved. Pour over cucumber mixture; cool.
2. Cover tightly and refrigerate for at least 24 hours. Store in the refrigerator for up to 2 months.
YIELD: 100 pickle spears.

raspberry barbecue sauce

GARNET PIRRE ☞ HELENA, MONTANA

Raspberries replace the traditional tomatoes in this thick, ruby-red sauce, while red pepper flakes add a little heat. This is great over chicken breasts or pork tenderloin. Just brush on the sauce near the end of the grilling time.

3 garlic cloves, peeled
¼ teaspoon olive oil
1¼ cups unsweetened raspberries
3 tablespoons brown sugar
1 tablespoon balsamic vinegar
1 tablespoon light corn syrup
1 teaspoon molasses
½ teaspoon lemon juice
¼ to ½ teaspoon crushed red pepper flakes
⅛ teaspoon salt
⅛ teaspoon pepper
Dash onion powder

1. Place garlic on a double thickness of heavy-duty foil; drizzle with oil. Wrap foil around garlic. Bake at 425° for 15-20 minutes. Cool for 10-15 minutes.
2. Place softened garlic in a small saucepan. Add the remaining ingredients. Cook over medium-low heat for 15-20 minutes until sauce is thickened and bubbly. Remove from the heat; cool slightly.
3. Transfer to a food processor; cover and process until smooth. Strain seeds. Store in the refrigerator.
YIELD: 4 servings.

homemade horseradish sauce

PATRICIA WOLF ⚑ LEWES, DELAWARE

A little of this fresh, zippy relish goes a long way to liven up beef, sausage, chops and deli sandwiches. It's also a fantastic dip for fresh vegetables.

- 6 tablespoons white wine vinegar
- 8 teaspoons water
- 2 tablespoons sugar
- 1 small jalapeno pepper, seeded and chopped
- ⅛ teaspoon white pepper
- 1 cup finely shredded horseradish root

1. In a bowl, combine the first five ingredients and mix well. Stir in the horseradish. Cover and refrigerate overnight before serving.

YIELD: 1 cup.

EDITOR'S NOTE: When cutting or seeding hot peppers, use rubber or plastic gloves to protect your hands. Avoid touching your face.

spicy plum sauce

SUZANNE VEVERKA ⚑ WHITE CLOUD, MICHIGAN

This flavorful fruit sauce is delicious over pork or poultry. The pepper imparts the perfect level of heat.

- 4 pounds fresh plums, pitted and quartered
- 1 small onion, quartered
- 1 garlic clove, peeled
- 3½ cups sugar
- 2 cups cider vinegar
- 1 tablespoon ground ginger
- 1 tablespoon ground mustard
- 1 teaspoon ground cinnamon
- 1 teaspoon crushed red pepper flakes
- ½ teaspoon ground cloves

1. In a blender or food processor, process the plums, onion and garlic in batches until smooth. Transfer to a large saucepan or Dutch oven. Stir in the remaining ingredients. Bring to a boil. Reduce heat; simmer for 60-90 minutes or until reduced by a third.

2. Ladle hot mixture into hot jars, leaving ¼-in. headspace. Adjust caps. Process for 15 minutes in a boiling-water bath. Remove jars to wire racks to cool completely.

YIELD: 9 half-pints.

creamy mustard sauce

ESTELLE HARP ⚑ SHAWNEE, OKLAHOMA

The delectable combination of mustard, mayonnaise and other handy pantry ingredients nicely enhances the smoky flavor of ham but would be great on any sandwich meat. Try it next time you crave more than an ordinary sandwich. Friends and family are sure to ask for the recipe.

1 tablespoon butter
1 tablespoon all-purpose flour
1 tablespoon ground mustard
⅓ cup water
⅓ cup white vinegar
¼ cup sugar
⅓ cup mayonnaise

1. In a saucepan, melt butter. Stir in flour and mustard until smooth. Add water, vinegar and sugar; mix well. Bring to a boil; cook and stir for 2 minutes or until slightly thickened. Remove from the heat; add mayonnaise and mix well.

YIELD: 1 cup.

ADD APPLES TO SAUCE
To thicken and sweeten bottled barbecue sauce, blend in apples that have been mashed in a food processor. It's wonderful when brushed on ribs, chicken or pork chops.

molasses barbecue sauce

SANDRA PICHON ⚑ SLIDELL, LOUISIANA

The secret to this favorite sauce is in the very first ingredient...a can of soup! It's a no-fuss recipe that comes in handy for chicken, ribs and burgers.

1 can (10¾ ounces) condensed tomato soup, undiluted
1 can (8 ounces) tomato sauce
1 cup molasses
½ cup cider vinegar
¼ cup canola oil
1 tablespoon dried minced onion
1 tablespoon grated orange peel
1 tablespoon Worcestershire sauce
2 teaspoons ground mustard
1½ teaspoons paprika
1 teaspoon seasoned salt
½ teaspoon pepper
¼ teaspoon garlic powder

1. In a large saucepan, combine all ingredients. Bring to a boil. Reduce heat; simmer, uncovered, for 20 minutes. Store in the refrigerator.

YIELD: 3½ cups.

As a salad or appetizer, these mushrooms are a welcome addition to any meal or party buffet table. It doesn't take long for a whole bowl to be devoured. I love to cook with fresh mushrooms—a crop our state is well-known for.

pickled mushrooms

SANDRA JOHNSON ⚑ TIOGA, PENNSYLVANIA

⅔ cup tarragon vinegar
½ cup canola oil
2 tablespoons water
1 tablespoon sugar
1½ teaspoons salt
1 garlic clove, minced
Dash hot pepper sauce
1 pound fresh mushrooms
1 medium onion, thinly sliced into rings
Finely diced sweet red pepper

1. In a glass bowl, combine the first seven ingredients. Add mushrooms and onion; toss to coat. Cover and refrigerate 8 hours or overnight. Sprinkle with red pepper before serving.
YIELD: 4 cups.

tangy barbecue sauce

MARY KAYE RACKOWITZ ⚑ MARYSVILLE, WASHINGTON

My mother-in-law created this recipe, and we just can't get enough of her delectable sauce! I always take a little out of the basting dish prior to using it on the grill so we have some to serve at the table. It tastes terrific on grilled poultry, beef or pork.

1 cup ketchup
2 tablespoons lemon juice
2 tablespoons cider vinegar
¼ cup packed brown sugar
2 teaspoons prepared mustard
1 teaspoon salt
½ to 1 teaspoon hot pepper sauce
1 bay leaf
1 garlic clove, minced
½ cup water
2 teaspoons Worcestershire sauce

1. Combine all of the ingredients in a small saucepan; bring to a boil, stirring occasionally. Reduce the heat; cover and simmer 30 minutes. Discard the bay leaf. Use as a basting sauce when grilling chicken, pork or beef.

YIELD: 1½ cups.

gingered cranberry chutney

MARION LOWERY ⚑ MEDFORD, OREGON

This colorful chutney is a super side dish or condiment served with pork, ham or poultry. My family enjoys the pears, cranberries and tongue-tingling spices.

1 cup packed brown sugar
⅓ cup red wine vinegar
½ teaspoon ground ginger
⅛ teaspoon cayenne pepper
⅛ teaspoon salt
2 pounds fresh pears, peeled and diced
1 package (12 ounces) fresh *or* frozen cranberries, thawed
½ teaspoon ground cinnamon

1. In a large saucepan, combine the brown sugar, vinegar, ginger, cayenne and salt. Bring to a boil. Add pears. Reduce heat; cover and simmer for 10 minutes or until pears are tender.
2. Strain, reserving liquid. Return liquid to pan; set pears aside. Stir cranberries into pan. Cook over medium heat until berries pop, about 3 minutes, stirring occasionally.
3. Strain berries, reserving liquid. Return liquid to pan; set berries aside. Bring liquid to a boil; cook, uncovered, until liquid is reduced to ½ cup. Stir in pears, cranberries and cinnamon. Serve warm or cold. Store in the refrigerator.

YIELD: 3 cups.

CHILI, SOUPS & STEWS

cider beef stew

CAROL HENDRICKSON 🏳 LAGUNA BEACH, CALIFORNIA

3 tablespoons all-purpose flour

1 teaspoon salt

½ teaspoon pepper

1 pound beef stew meat, cut into 1-inch pieces

2 tablespoons canola oil

1 cup apple cider

½ cup water

1 tablespoon white vinegar

½ teaspoon dried thyme

2 large carrots, cut into 1-inch pieces

1 celery rib, cut into 1-inch pieces

1 large potato, peeled and cubed

1 medium onion, sliced

1. In a bowl or bag, combine flour, salt and pepper; add beef and toss to coat. In a large saucepan, brown beef in oil. Add cider, water, vinegar and thyme; bring to a boil.

2. Reduce heat; cover and simmer for 1 hour and 45 minutes or until the meat is tender. Add the carrots, celery, potato and onion; return to a boil. Reduce the heat; cover and simmer for 45 minutes or until the vegetables are tender.

YIELD: 4 servings.

spinach garlic soup

MARILYN PARADIS ⚑ WOODBURN, OREGON

During the years I owned and operated a deli, this was one of the most popular soups I had on the menu.

- 1 package (10 ounces) fresh spinach, trimmed and coarsely chopped
- 4 cups chicken broth
- ½ cup shredded carrots
- ½ cup chopped onion
- 8 garlic cloves, minced
- ⅓ cup butter
- ¼ cup all-purpose flour
- ¾ cup heavy whipping cream
- ¼ cup milk
- ½ teaspoon pepper
- ⅛ teaspoon ground nutmeg

1. In a 5-qt. Dutch oven, bring the spinach, broth and carrots to a boil. Reduce heat; simmer 5 minutes, stirring occasionally. Remove from heat; cool to lukewarm.
2. Meanwhile, in a skillet, saute onion and garlic in butter until onion is soft, about 5-10 minutes. Add flour; cook and stir over low heat for 3-5 minutes. Add to spinach mixture.
3. Puree in small batches in a blender or food processor until finely chopped. Place in a large saucepan. Add the cream, milk, pepper and nutmeg; heat through but do not boil.

YIELD: 4-6 servings.

gazpacho

ROBYNN SHANNON ⚑ ALEXANDRIA, VIRGINIA

Nothing equals the taste of an ice-cold serving of gazpacho on a hot day.
This is a wonderful way to use up an abundance of tomatoes from your garden.

- 3 cups chopped, seeded, peeled fresh tomatoes
- 2 celery ribs, finely chopped
- 1 medium green pepper, finely chopped
- 1 medium cucumber, peeled, seeded and finely chopped
- ¼ cup minced fresh parsley
- 1 tablespoon minced chives
- 1 green onion, thinly sliced
- 1 garlic clove, minced
- 1 can (46 ounces) tomato juice
- ⅓ cup red wine vinegar
- ¼ cup olive oil
- 1 teaspoon salt
- ½ teaspoon Worcestershire sauce
- ½ teaspoon pepper
Seasoned croutons

1. In a large bowl, combine the first 14 ingredients. Cover and refrigerate for several hours or overnight. Garnish each serving with croutons.

YIELD: 10 servings (2½ quarts).

sausage onion chili

DENISE VONSTEIN ⚑ SHILOH, OHIO

When people see this recipe, they're surprised to see onion soup as an ingredient. It's great!

1 pound bulk pork sausage
1 pound ground beef
1 can (10½ ounces) condensed French onion soup, undiluted
2 tablespoons chili powder
1 teaspoon ground cumin
½ teaspoon salt
½ teaspoon pepper
1 can (15½ ounces) kidney beans, rinsed and drained
1 can (8 ounces) tomato sauce
1 can (6 ounces) tomato paste
½ cup water

1. In a large saucepan, cook sausage and beef until no longer pink; drain. Add remaining ingredients and mix well; bring to boil. Reduce the heat; cook and stir for 10-15 minutes or until thickened.

YIELD: 6 servings (about 1½ quarts).

SERVE SOUP
A hearty soup can really satisfy on a cool day. For outdoor events, consider serving it with prepared sandwiches, crackers or wholesome crusty bread. Disposable bowls are available at most grocery stores to make cleanup a breeze.

super-duper chili

ELIZABETH MAYS ⚑ NUNNELLY, TENNESSEE

No one ever guesses the secret ingredient in this recipe that I created. A can of mushroom soup is what makes the chili so thick and creamy.

1 pound bulk pork sausage
1 pound ground beef
2 cans (15½ ounces *each*) hot chili beans
1 jar (16 ounces) salsa
1 can (16 ounces) kidney beans, rinsed and drained
1 can (15 ounces) pinto beans, rinsed and drained
1 can (14½ ounces) diced tomatoes, undrained
1 can (10¾ ounces) condensed cream of mushroom soup, undiluted
1 can (8 ounces) tomato sauce
8 ounces process cheese (Velveeta), cubed
1½ teaspoons chili powder
½ teaspoon cayenne pepper

1. In a soup kettle or Dutch oven, cook the sausage and beef over medium heat until no longer pink; drain. Stir in the remaining ingredients. Bring to a boil. Reduce heat; cover and simmer for 30 minutes or until heated through.

YIELD: 14 servings (3½ quarts).

> When the weather gets chilly, we enjoy comfort foods like this hearty chowder. It's easy to prepare, and the aroma of it as it simmers makes my mouth water.

autumn chowder

SHEENA HOFFMAN ⚑ NORTH VANCOUVER, BRITISH COLUMBIA

2 bacon strips, diced
¼ cup chopped onion
1 medium red potato, diced
1 small carrot, halved lengthwise and thinly sliced
½ cup water
¾ teaspoon chicken bouillon granules
1 cup milk
⅔ cup frozen corn
⅛ teaspoon pepper
2½ teaspoons all-purpose flour
2 tablespoons cold water
¾ cup shredded cheddar cheese

1. In a saucepan, cook bacon over medium heat until crisp; remove to paper towels and reserve. Drain, reserving 1 teaspoon drippings. In the drippings, saute onion until tender. Add the potato, carrot, water and bouillon. Bring to a boil. Reduce heat; cover and simmer for 15-20 minutes or until the vegetables are almost tender.

2. Stir in the milk, corn and pepper. Cook 5 minutes longer. Combine the flour and cold water until smooth; gradually whisk into soup. Bring to a boil; cook and stir for 1-2 minutes or until thickened. Remove from the heat; stir in the cheese until melted. Sprinkle with the bacon.

YIELD: 2 servings.

This veggie-packed beef stew is great with homemade bread and a green salad served alongside.

autumn vegetable beef stew

MARTHA TONNIES ⚑ FT. MICHELL, KENTUCKY

1 teaspoon salt
¼ teaspoon pepper
¼ teaspoon paprika
1 pound round steak, cut into 1-inch cubes
1 tablespoon canola oil
1 tablespoon all-purpose flour
1½ cups water
1 medium onion, chopped
½ cup tomato sauce
2 beef bouillon cubes
½ teaspoon caraway seeds
1 bay leaf
2 medium potatoes, peeled and cut into 1-inch cubes
2 medium turnips, peeled and cut into 1-inch cubes
2 medium carrots, cut into 1-inch slices

1. Combine salt, pepper and paprika; toss with beef. In a large saucepan over medium heat, brown beef in oil. Sprinkle with flour; stir well. Add water, onion, tomato sauce, bouillon, caraway seeds and bay leaf.
2. Cover and simmer for 1 hour. Add potatoes, turnips and carrots; cover and simmer 45 minutes or until meat and vegetables are tender. Discard bay leaf.

YIELD: 4 servings.

chili verde

JO OLIVERIUS ⚑ ALPINE, CALIFORNIA

2 cups cubed cooked pork (about 1 pound)

1 can (16 ounces) kidney beans, rinsed and drained

1 can (15 ounces) pinto beans, rinsed and drained

1 can (15 ounces) chili with beans, undrained

1 can (14½ ounces) stewed tomatoes

1½ to 2 cups green salsa

1 large onion, chopped

2 cans (4 ounces *each*) chopped green chilies

2 garlic cloves, minced

1 tablespoon minced fresh cilantro

2 teaspoons ground cumin

1. In a large saucepan, combine all ingredients. Bring to a boil. Reduce heat; simmer, uncovered, for 10 minutes.

YIELD: 8 servings (2 quarts).

This chili is great on a cool night with a stack of tortillas. I've taken it to many gatherings and it's sure to be gone when the party's over.

turkey chili

CELESTA ZANGER ⚑ BLOOMFIELD HILLS, MICHIGAN

I've taken my mother's milder recipe for chili and made it more robust. It's a favorite with all who try it.

1 pound lean ground turkey
¾ cup chopped onion
¾ cup chopped celery
¾ cup chopped green pepper
1 can (28 ounces) diced tomatoes, undrained
1 jar (26 ounces) meatless spaghetti sauce
1 can (15½ ounces) hot chili beans
1½ cups water
½ cup frozen corn
2 tablespoons chili powder
1 teaspoon ground cumin
¼ teaspoon pepper
⅛ to ¼ teaspoon cayenne pepper

1 can (16 ounces) kidney beans, rinsed and drained
1 can (15 ounces) pinto beans, rinsed and drained

1. In a large nonstick skillet, cook the turkey, onion, celery and green pepper over medium heat until meat is no longer pink and vegetables are tender. Drain; transfer to a slow cooker. Add tomatoes, spaghetti sauce, chili beans, water, corn and seasonings. Cover and cook on high for 1 hour.
2. Reduce heat to low; cook for 5-6 hours. Add kidney and pinto beans; cook 30 minutes longer.

YIELD: 12 servings (3 quarts).

chalupa (mexican stew)

ANNE FATOUT ⚑ PHOENIX, ARIZONA

We've lived in Arizona for more than 36 years, so Mexican cooking has become the same as "Arizona cooking" for us. Nothing tastes better than this stew!

1 pork roast (3 pounds), trimmed
1 package (16 ounces) pinto beans, soaked overnight
4 to 5 garlic cloves, minced
2 tablespoons chili powder
1 to 1½ teaspoons ground cumin
1 teaspoon dried oregano
2 cans (4 ounces *each*) chopped green chilies
Pepper to taste
5 carrots, peeled and sliced
4 celery ribs, sliced
1 can (14½ ounces) diced tomatoes, undrained
3 small zucchini, sliced
Flour tortillas, warmed

1. Put first eight ingredients into a large Dutch oven or kettle. Cover with water and cook, covered, over low heat 3-4 hours or until meat and beans are tender. Cool slightly; remove meat from bones. Cut or shred meat into bite-size pieces; return meat to kettle.

2. Add carrots, celery, tomatoes and tomato liquid; cover and cook until vegetables are tender. In last 10 minutes of cooking, add zucchini. Serve with warmed flour tortillas.

YIELD: 16 servings (4 quarts).

Several people told me this is the best soup that they've ever had. The biggest compliment I ever received, though, came from my 93-year-old grandfather. He usually ate as few vegetables as possible—but he asked for a second bowl!

cream of vegetable soup

MARY PARKER ⚑ COPPERAS COVE, TEXAS

1 medium onion, chopped

¾ cup butter

½ cup all-purpose flour

3 cans (10½ ounces *each*) condensed chicken broth *or* 4 cups chicken broth

2 cups milk

2 cups half-and-half cream

1 teaspoon dried basil

½ teaspoon salt

½ teaspoon pepper

¼ teaspoon garlic powder

5 cups chopped leftover cooked mixed vegetables (such as broccoli, carrots and cauliflower)

1. In a large kettle or Dutch oven, saute onion in butter until tender. Add flour; cook and stir until bubbly. Gradually add chicken broth; cook and stir until thickened, about 5 minutes.

2. Stir in the milk, cream, basil, salt, pepper and garlic powder. Add the vegetables; cook gently until heated through.

YIELD: 8-10 servings (about 3 quarts).

wild west chili

FRANCES HANSON ☞ MILLS, WYOMING

2 bacon strips, diced

1 pound ground beef *or* venison

2 teaspoons chili powder

1½ teaspoons salt

¼ teaspoon garlic salt

¼ teaspoon dried oregano

⅛ teaspoon cayenne pepper

3 to 5 drops hot pepper sauce

1 can (14½ ounces) diced tomatoes, undrained

1 cup *each* finely chopped celery, onion and carrots

½ cup finely chopped green pepper

1 can (16 ounces) chili beans, undrained

1. In a large saucepan over medium heat, cook bacon and the beef or venison until no longer pink; drain. Add the seasonings; cook and stir for 5 minutes. Stir in the tomatoes, celery, onion, carrots and green pepper; bring to a boil. Reduce the heat; cover and simmer for 40 minutes. Stir in the beans; cook 30 minutes longer.

YIELD: 6 servings.

clam chowder

ROSEMARY PETERSON ⚑ ARCHIE, MISSOURI

This chowder is quick and easy to prepare. Bowlfuls are so satisfying on colder days.

2 cans (6½ ounces *each*) minced clams
6 potatoes, peeled and diced
6 carrots, diced
½ cup chopped onion
½ cup butter
1½ cups water
2 cans (10¾ ounces *each*) condensed cream of mushroom soup, undiluted
2 cans (12 ounces *each*) evaporated milk
1 teaspoon salt
½ teaspoon pepper

1. Drain clams, reserving liquid. Set the clams aside. In a large kettle, combine clam juice, potatoes, carrots, onion, butter and water. Cook over medium heat for 15 minutes or until the vegetables are tender. Stir in soup, milk, salt and pepper; simmer until heated through. Stir in clams.

YIELD: 10-12 servings (3 quarts).

white chili

KAREN GARDINER ⚑ EUTAW, ALABAMA

The recipe for this chili was given to me by a friend. The day after I served it, someone called for the recipe, too!

2 pounds dried great northern beans
1½ cups diced onion
1 tablespoon canola oil
1 tablespoon ground oregano
2 teaspoons ground cumin
1½ teaspoons seasoned salt
½ teaspoon cayenne pepper
4½ quarts chicken broth
2 garlic cloves, minced
8 boneless skinless chicken breast halves, cubed
2 cans (4 ounces *each*) chopped green chilies

1. Place beans in a saucepan; cover with water and bring to a boil. Boil 2 minutes. Remove from heat. Soak 1 hour; drain and rinse. In an 8-qt. Dutch oven, saute onion in oil until tender. Combine seasonings; add half to Dutch oven. Saute 1 minute.

2. Add beans, broth and garlic; bring to a boil. Reduce heat; simmer 2 hours. Coat chicken with remaining seasoning mixture; place in 15-in. x 10-in. x 1-in. baking pan. Bake at 350° for 15 minutes or until juices run clear; add to beans. Stir in chilies. Simmer 1½ to 2 hours.

YIELD: 20 servings (5 quarts).

bratwurst stew

DEBORAH ELLIOTT ⚑ RIDGE SPRING, SOUTH CAROLINA

Using leftover brats hurries along the preparation of this satisfying stew. When time is short, this flavorful combination is so good and so easy. I usually have all the ingredients handy.

2 cans (14½ ounces *each*) chicken broth
4 medium carrots, cut into ¾-inch chunks
2 celery ribs, cut into ¾-inch chunks
1 medium onion, chopped
½ to 1 teaspoon dried thyme
½ teaspoon dried basil
½ teaspoon salt
¼ to ½ teaspoon garlic powder
3 cups chopped cabbage
2 cans (15½ ounces *each*) great northern beans, rinsed and drained
5 fully cooked bratwurst links, cut into ¾-inch slices

1. In a large saucepan, combine the broth, carrots, celery, onion and seasonings. Bring to a boil. Reduce heat; cover and simmer for 15 minutes. Add the cabbage; cover and cook for 10 minutes. Stir in beans and bratwurst; heat through.

YIELD: 10 servings (2½ quarts).

GENERATING POWER
Serious tailgaters bring a small generator for powering a TV, stereo system or electric space heater during cold-weather games.

zucchini soup

SUE FRIEND ⚑ LYNDEN, WASHINGTON

When there's an abundance of zucchini in our garden, I know it's time for this fresh-tasting vegetable medley.

1 cup chopped onion
1 cup thinly sliced celery
1 garlic clove, minced
¼ cup chopped green pepper
1 tablespoon canola oil
2 pounds zucchini, chopped
2 medium tomatoes, chopped
3 cups chicken broth
½ teaspoon dried basil
¼ teaspoon dried thyme
1 cup half-and-half cream *or* milk

1. In a large saucepan, saute onion, celery, garlic and green pepper in oil until tender. Add zucchini, tomatoes, broth, basil and thyme; bring to a boil. Reduce heat; simmer, uncovered, for 20-30 minutes or until the vegetables are tender. Stir in cream; heat through. Serve hot or cold.

YIELD: 8 servings (2 quarts).

This tempting chili is big on flavor and simple to prepare. Sometimes on a Sunday, I'll get a good start on it—up to where it's time to add the beans. Then the next day, I'll take it out of the fridge and finish it off in just a few minutes. Voila!

bold bean and pork chili

NATERCIA YAILAIAN SOMERVILLE, MASSACHUSETTS

1 pork shoulder *or* butt roast (4 to 5 pounds), trimmed and cut into ¾-inch cubes

3 tablespoons olive oil

2 large onions, chopped

8 garlic cloves, minced

4 cans (14½ ounces *each*) chicken broth

1 can (28 ounces) crushed tomatoes

½ to ⅔ cup chili powder

3 tablespoons dried oregano

2 to 3 tablespoons ground cumin

4½ teaspoons salt

2 teaspoons cayenne pepper

4 cans (15 ounces *each*) black beans, rinsed and drained

Minced fresh cilantro, optional

1. In a Dutch oven, saute pork in oil until no longer pink; drain. Add onions; cook and stir for 3 minutes. Add garlic; cook 2 minutes longer. Stir in the broth, tomatoes and seasonings. Bring to a boil. Reduce heat; simmer, uncovered, for 1 hour, stirring several times.

2. Skim fat; stir in beans. Simmer 15-30 minutes longer or until chili reaches desired thickness. Garnish with cilantro if desired.

YIELD: 14 servings (3½ quarts).

spinach bisque

PATRICIA TUCKWILLER ⚑ LEWISBURG, WEST VIRGINIA

½ cup chopped onion

2 tablespoons butter

⅓ cup all-purpose flour

½ to 1 teaspoon salt

⅛ teaspoon ground nutmeg

2½ cups milk

1 cup water

¾ cup cubed process cheese (Velveeta)

1 package (10 ounces) frozen chopped spinach, thawed and drained

Oyster crackers, optional

1. In a large saucepan, saute onion in butter until tender. Stir in the flour, salt and nutmeg until blended. Gradually whisk in milk and water. Bring to a boil.

2. Cook and stir for 2 minutes or until thickened. Reduce heat to medium; add the cheese and stir until melted. Stir in the spinach; heat through. Serve with oyster crackers if desired.

YIELD: 5-6 servings.

brunswick stew

JUDI BRINEGAR ⚑ LIBERTY, NORTH CAROLINA

Festivals in North Carolina wouldn't be the same without this classic stew. It's a special main dish for any crowd.

4 large onions, halved and thinly sliced

¼ cup butter

1 broiler/fryer chicken (3 to 4 pounds), cut up

2 quarts water

2 cans (28 ounces *each*) crushed tomatoes

1¾ cups ketchup

1 can (6 ounces) tomato paste

1 can (10¾ ounces) condensed tomato soup, undiluted

2 medium jalapeno peppers, seeded and chopped

1 tablespoon salt

1 teaspoon Worcestershire sauce

1 teaspoon hot pepper sauce

1 teaspoon pepper

2 pounds ground beef, cooked and drained

1 pound cubed fully cooked ham

1 package (16 ounces) frozen cut green beans

1 package (16 ounces) frozen butter beans

1 package (16 ounces) frozen corn

6 cups hot mashed potatoes (without added milk and butter)

1. In a large soup kettle, saute onions in butter until tender. Add chicken and water. Bring to a boil. Reduce heat; cover and simmer for 1 hour.

2. Remove chicken; when cool enough to handle, remove meat from bones. Discard bones and dice meat. Skim fat from broth; return chicken to broth. Add the next 14 ingredients; bring to a boil. Reduce heat; cover and simmer for 1 hour or until vegetables are tender. Stir in potatoes; heat through.

YIELD: 25-30 servings (about 8 quarts).

EDITOR'S NOTE: When cutting or seeding hot peppers, use rubber or plastic gloves to protect your hands. Avoid touching your face.

shrimp gazpacho

TASTE OF HOME TEST KITCHEN

This refreshing tomato-based soup features shrimp, cucumber and avocados.

6 cups spicy hot V8 juice

2 cups cold water

1 pound cooked medium shrimp, peeled and deveined

2 medium tomatoes, seeded and diced

1 medium cucumber, seeded and diced

2 medium ripe avocados, diced

½ cup lime juice

½ cup minced fresh cilantro

½ teaspoon salt

¼ to ½ teaspoon hot pepper sauce

1. In a large bowl, combine all ingredients. Cover and refrigerate for 1 hour. Serve cold.

YIELD: 12 servings (about 3 quarts).

EDITOR'S NOTE: This recipe is best served the same day it's made.

easy sausage chowder

SUZANNE VERVERKA ▷ WHITE CLOUD, MICHIGAN

This super soup, flavored with fresh basil, makes a hearty summer lunch.

1 pound fully cooked smoked sausage, halved and thinly sliced

1 medium onion, quartered and thinly sliced

4 cups diced potatoes

3 cups water

2 tablespoons minced fresh parsley *or* 2 teaspoons dried parsley flakes

1 tablespoon minced fresh basil *or* 1 teaspoon dried basil

1 teaspoon salt

⅛ teaspoon pepper

1 can (15¼ ounces) whole kernel corn, drained

1 can (14¾ ounces) cream-style corn

1 can (12 ounces) evaporated milk

1. In a soup kettle or Dutch oven over medium heat, brown the sausage and onion. Slowly add the potatoes, water, parsley, basil, salt and pepper; bring to a boil.

2. Reduce heat; cover and simmer for 15-20 minutes or until potatoes are tender. Add remaining ingredients; cook 5-10 minutes longer or until heated through.

YIELD: 12 servings (about 3 quarts).

heartwarming chili

CHRISTINE PANZARELLA ▷ BUENA PARK, CALIFORNIA

Loaded with both beef and pork, this chili is extra meaty. I like to keep it mild for the kids to enjoy, too.

1 pound ground beef

1 pound ground pork

1 medium onion, chopped

½ cup chopped green pepper

1½ to 2 cups water

1 can (15 ounces) tomato sauce

1 can (15 ounces) pinto beans, rinsed and drained

1 can (14½ ounces) diced tomatoes, undrained

1 envelope chili seasoning

¼ teaspoon garlic salt

Shredded cheddar cheese, sour cream, chopped green onions *and/or* hot pepper slices, optional

1. In a large saucepan or Dutch oven, cook beef, pork, onion and green pepper over medium heat until meat is no longer pink and vegetables are tender; drain.

2. Add the water, tomato sauce, beans, tomatoes, chili seasoning and garlic salt. Bring to a boil.

Reduce heat and simmer, uncovered, until heated through. Garnish with cheese, sour cream, green onions and/or hot peppers if desired.

YIELD: 10 servings (2½ quarts).

Served with a hot loaf of bread and a side salad, this slow cooker sensation makes a hearty meal.

barbecued beef chili

PHYLLIS SHYAN ⚑ ELGIN, ILLINOIS

7 teaspoons chili powder
1 tablespoon garlic powder
2 teaspoons celery seed
1 teaspoon coarsely ground pepper
¼ to ½ teaspoon cayenne pepper
1 fresh beef brisket (3 to 4 pounds)
1 medium green pepper, chopped
1 small onion, chopped
1 bottle (12 ounces) chili sauce
1 cup ketchup
½ cup barbecue sauce
⅓ cup packed brown sugar
¼ cup cider vinegar
¼ cup Worcestershire sauce
1 teaspoon ground mustard
1 can (15½ ounces) hot chili beans
1 can (15½ ounces) great northern beans,
   rinsed and drained

1. Combine the first five ingredients; rub over brisket. Cut into eight pieces; place in a slow cooker. Combine the green pepper, onion, chili sauce, ketchup, barbecue sauce, brown sugar, vinegar, Worcestershire sauce and mustard; pour over meat. Cover and cook on high for 5-6 hours or until meat is tender.

2. Remove meat; cool slightly. Meanwhile, skim fat from cooking juices. Shred meat with two forks; return to slow cooker. Reduce heat to low. Stir in the beans. Cover and cook for 1 hour or until heated through.

YIELD: 12 servings (3 quarts).

EDITOR'S NOTE: This is a fresh beef brisket, not corned beef.

Any time you're looking for a way to use up your zucchini and squash, this is an out-of-the-ordinary option.

garden harvest chili

DEBBIE COSFORD ⚑ BAYFIELD, ONTARIO

1 medium sweet red pepper, chopped
1 medium onion, chopped
4 garlic cloves, minced
2 tablespoons canola oil
1 tablespoon chili powder
1 teaspoon ground cumin
1 teaspoon dried oregano
2 cups cubed peeled butternut squash
1 can (28 ounces) diced tomatoes, undrained
2 cups diced zucchini
1 can (15 ounces) black beans, rinsed and drained
1 can (8¾ ounces) whole kernel corn, drained
¼ cup minced fresh parsley

1. In a 3-qt. saucepan, saute red pepper, onion and garlic in oil until tender. Stir in chili powder, cumin, oregano, butternut squash and tomatoes; bring to a boil.

2. Reduce heat; cover and simmer for 10-15 minutes or until squash is almost tender. Stir in remaining ingredients; cover and simmer 10 minutes more.

YIELD: 7 servings (1¾ quarts).

tomato dill bisque

SUSAN BRECKBILL  LINCOLN UNIVERSITY, PENNSYLVANIA

2 medium onions, chopped
1 garlic clove, minced
2 tablespoons butter
2 pounds tomatoes, peeled and chopped
½ cup water
1 chicken bouillon cube
1 teaspoon sugar
1 teaspoon dill weed
½ teaspoon salt
¼ teaspoon pepper
½ cup mayonnaise, optional

1. In a large saucepan, saute onions and garlic in butter until tender. Add tomatoes, water, bouillon, sugar and seasonings. Cover and simmer 10 minutes or until tomatoes are tender. Remove from heat; cool slightly.

2. Place the tomato mixture in a blender, cover and process until pureed. Return to saucepan. If creamy soup is desired, stir in mayonnaise. Cook and stir over low heat until heated through. Serve warm.

YIELD: 5 servings (5 cups).

My family really enjoys this soup made from our garden tomatoes. I prepare a big batch (without mayonnaise) and freeze it to enjoy it after the garden is gone for the season.

Living in Wisconsin, I like to make dishes featuring cheese, and this chowder is one of my favorites. It's a great meal served with salad greens and rye rolls.

ham cheddar chowder

RUTH PROTZ ⚑ OSHKOSH, WISCONSIN

3 cups water
3 cups diced, peeled potatoes
1 cup diced carrots
1 cup diced celery
1 medium onion, chopped
2 teaspoons salt
½ teaspoon pepper
6 tablespoons butter
6 tablespoons all-purpose flour
4 cups milk
3 cups (12 ounces) shredded cheddar cheese
1 cup cubed fully cooked ham

1. In a large saucepan or Dutch oven, bring water to a boil. Add the potatoes, carrots, celery, onion, salt and pepper. Reduce heat. Cover and simmer for 20 minutes or until vegetables are tender; drain and set vegetables aside.

2. In same pan, melt butter. Stir in the flour until smooth. Gradually add milk. Bring to a boil; cook and stir for 2 minutes or until thickened. Remove from the heat; stir in cheese until melted. Add ham and reserved vegetables. Cook on low until heated through. Do not boil.

YIELD: 8 servings (about 2 quarts).

campfire stew

LAURIE SCHAFER ⚑ AURORA, COLORADO

My dad concocted this recipe by using all the leftovers from a Labor Day camping trip. It's delicious!

- 2 pounds ground beef
- 6 medium potatoes, peeled and cubed
- 1½ pounds carrots, sliced
- 4 cups water
- 1 can (15¼ ounces) whole kernel corn, drained
- 1 can (15 ounces) peas, drained
- 1 can (14½ ounces) cut green beans, drained
- 2 medium onions, chopped
- 1 cup ketchup
- ¾ cup medium pearl barley
- 1 tablespoon Worcestershire sauce

Dash white vinegar

Salt and pepper to taste

1. In a soup kettle or Dutch oven, cook beef over medium heat until no longer pink; drain. Add the potatoes, carrots and water. Bring to a boil. Reduce heat; cover and simmer for 20 minutes or until vegetables are tender. Add remaining ingredients. Cover and simmer for 1 hour.

YIELD: 20 servings (5 quarts).

garbanzo gazpacho

MARY ANN GOMEZ ⚑ LOMBARD, ILLINOIS

*This chunky chilled soup is terrific in warm weather, but our family loves it so much
I often prepare it in winter, too. I made some slight changes to suit our tastes,
and the fresh flavorful combination has been a favorite ever since.*

- 1 can (15 ounces) garbanzo beans *or* chickpeas, rinsed and drained
- 1 can (14½ ounces) Italian diced tomatoes, undrained
- 1¼ cups V8 juice
- 1 cup beef broth
- 1 cup quartered cherry tomatoes
- ½ cup chopped seeded cucumber
- ¼ cup chopped red onion
- ¼ cup minced fresh cilantro
- 3 tablespoons lime juice
- 1 garlic clove, minced
- ½ teaspoon salt
- ¼ teaspoon hot pepper sauce

1. In a large bowl, combine all the ingredients; cover and refrigerate until serving.

YIELD: 6 servings.

cheesy floret soup

JANICE RUSSELL ⚑ KINGFISHER, OKLAHOMA

Talk about comfort food! I received this recipe from my mom, and my family requests it often. It's especially good with crusty French bread.

- 3 cups fresh broccoli florets
- 3 cups fresh cauliflowerets
- 3 celery ribs, sliced
- 1 small onion, chopped
- 2 cups water
- ½ teaspoon celery salt
- 3 tablespoons butter
- 3 tablespoons all-purpose flour
- 2⅓ cups milk
- 1 pound process cheese (Velveeta), cubed

1. In a large saucepan, combine first six ingredients. Bring to a boil. Reduce heat; cover and simmer for 12-15 minutes or until vegetables are tender.
2. Meanwhile, in a small saucepan, melt butter; stir in flour until smooth. Gradually stir in milk. Bring to a boil; cook and stir for 2 minutes or until thickened. Reduce heat; add cheese. Cook and stir until cheese is melted. Drain vegetables; add cheese sauce and heat through.

YIELD: 6 servings.

spicy tomato soup

JAIME HAMPTON ⚑ RICHMOND, VIRGINIA

When you'd rather be playing than cooking, you might want to give this tomato soup a try. Using canned corn and black beans, it goes together fast and is a great accompaniment to sandwiches.

- 8 ounces uncooked elbow macaroni
- 1 can (46 ounces) tomato juice
- 1 can (15¼ ounces) whole kernel corn, drained
- 1 can (15 ounces) black beans, rinsed and drained
- ¼ cup salsa
- 3 teaspoons dried oregano
- 1½ teaspoons garlic powder
- 1 teaspoon dried basil
- 1 teaspoon ground cumin
- ½ to 1 teaspoon crushed red pepper flakes, optional

Shredded cheddar *or* Monterey Jack cheese, optional

1. Cook macaroni according to package directions. Meanwhile, in a large saucepan, combine tomato juice, corn, beans, salsa, oregano, garlic powder, basil, cumin and pepper flakes if desired; bring to a boil. Reduce heat; cover and simmer for 8-10 minutes.
2. Drain macaroni; stir into the soup. Garnish with cheese if desired.

YIELD: 10 servings (2½ quarts).

Here is one yummy dish. My husband loves the kick that Italian sausage gives this quick gumbo, and it's such a cinch to assemble.

gumbo in a jiffy

AMY FLACK HOMER CITY, PENNSYLVANIA

3 Italian sausage links, sliced
1 can (14½ ounces) diced tomatoes with green peppers and onions, undrained
1 can (14½ ounces) chicken broth
½ cup water
1 cup uncooked instant rice
1 can (7 ounces) whole kernel corn, drained

1. In a large saucepan, cook sausage until no longer pink; drain. Stir in the tomatoes, broth and water; bring to a boil. Stir in rice and corn; cover and remove from the heat. Let stand for 5 minutes.

YIELD: 6 servings.

My family loves stew, and this recipe is perfect for the last few vegetables left in the garden. The best part of this recipe is that you can substitute whatever is available.

summer's end stew

LAURA GARTON LENOX, MASSACHUSETTS

1½ pounds beef stew meat, trimmed

1 tablespoon canola oil

8 to 12 medium fresh tomatoes, peeled and cut up

2 cups tomato juice *or* water

2 medium onions, chopped

1 garlic clove, minced

½ teaspoon pepper

2 teaspoons salt, optional

4 to 6 medium potatoes, peeled and quartered

3 to 5 carrots, sliced

2 cups frozen corn

2 cups fresh cut green beans

2 cups frozen peas

2 to 3 celery ribs, sliced

1 cup sliced zucchini

¼ cup snipped fresh parsley

1 teaspoon sugar

1. In a Dutch oven, brown the meat in oil over medium-high heat. Add the tomatoes, tomato juice or water, onions, garlic, pepper and salt if desired. Bring to a boil; reduce the heat and simmer for 1 hour.

2. Add potatoes, carrots, corn, green beans, peas and celery. Cover and simmer 30 minutes. Add zucchini; simmer 10-15 minutes or until meat and vegetables are tender. Stir in parsley and sugar.

YIELD: 16 servings (4 quarts).

santa fe chicken chili

SONIA GALLANT ⚑ ST. THOMAS, ONTARIO

2 pounds boneless skinless chicken breasts, cut into ½-inch cubes

4 medium sweet red peppers, diced

4 garlic cloves, minced

2 large onions, chopped

¼ cup olive oil

3 tablespoons chili powder

2 teaspoons ground cumin

¼ teaspoon cayenne pepper

1 can (28 ounces) diced tomatoes, undrained

2 cans (14½ ounces *each*) chicken broth

2 cans (15½ ounces *each*) kidney beans, rinsed and drained

1 jar (12 ounces) salsa

1 package (10 ounces) frozen corn

½ teaspoon salt

½ teaspoon pepper

1. In a 5-qt. kettle or Dutch oven over medium heat, saute chicken, peppers, garlic and onions in oil until the chicken is no longer pink and vegetables are tender, about 5-7 minutes. Add chili powder, cumin and cayenne pepper; cook and stir for 1 minute. Add the tomatoes and broth; bring to a boil.

2. Reduce heat; simmer, uncovered, for 15 minutes. Stir in remaining ingredients; bring to a boil. Reduce heat; cover and simmer for 10-15 minutes or until the chicken is tender.

YIELD: 16 servings (4 quarts).

Stir up this chili on Sunday, and you'll be set for a couple weekday meals. Or serve a large group of friends at a fall party.

One day when I was making Italian sausages, I decided to do something different. After browning them, I put the sausages in a pot and added other things, ending up with this stew that my husband and I like very much.

italian sausage stew

ANN ERNEY ☞ MIDDLEBURY CENTER, PENNSYLVANIA

1½ pounds Italian sausage links, cut into 1-inch pieces

3 cups water

4 medium potatoes, peeled and cut into chunks

2 medium carrots, cut into chunks

2 celery ribs, cut into chunks

2 small onions, cut into wedges

¼ cup Worcestershire sauce

1 teaspoon dried oregano

½ teaspoon *each* dried basil, thyme and rosemary, crushed

1 bay leaf

Salt and pepper to taste

¾ cup ketchup

½ large green *or* sweet red pepper, cut into chunks

1 tablespoon minced fresh parsley

1 tablespoon cornstarch

1 tablespoon cold water

1. In a soup kettle or Dutch oven over medium heat, brown sausage; drain. Add water, potatoes, carrots, celery, onions, Worcestershire sauce and seasonings. Bring to a boil. Reduce heat; cover and cook over low heat for 1 hour or until sausage is no longer pink and vegetables are tender.

2. Add the ketchup, green pepper and parsley; cook 12-15 minutes longer or until pepper is tender. Discard bay leaf. Combine cornstarch and cold water until smooth; stir into stew. Bring to a boil; cook and stir for 2 minutes or until thickened.

YIELD: 6 servings.

SIDES
& SALADS

This colorful combination of strawberries, pear, peach, pineapple and banana is tossed with yogurt and rice for a delightful side dish that really says summer.

fruit 'n' rice salad

VIOLET BEARD ▷ MARSHALL, ILLINOIS

1 can (8 ounces) unsweetened
    pineapple chunks
2 cups cooked rice
½ cup quartered fresh strawberries
½ cup sliced peeled fresh pear
½ cup sliced peeled peach
½ cup sliced firm banana
2 tablespoons fat-free plain yogurt
1 tablespoon honey
4 cups fresh baby spinach

1. Drain pineapple, reserving ¼ cup juice. In a large bowl, combine the pineapple, rice, strawberries, pear, peach and banana. In a small bowl, whisk the yogurt, honey and reserved pineapple juice. Pour over fruit mixture; toss to coat. Line salad plates with spinach; top with fruit mixture.
YIELD: 8 servings.

corn cobbler

VIVIAN HIPPERT ⚐ RICHLAND, PENNSYLVANIA

While thinking of a shortcut for what we Pennsylvania Dutch call "corn pie,"
I thought of using biscuit mix instead of pie dough. I tried my version on
some friends who were visiting, and they scraped the dish clean!

2 cups diced peeled potatoes
½ cup chopped onion
1½ teaspoons salt
½ teaspoon pepper
2 cups water
4 cups fresh corn
2¾ cups milk, *divided*
¼ cup sliced green onions
2 tablespoons minced fresh parsley
6 hard-cooked eggs, sliced
3 cups biscuit/baking mix

1. Place potatoes, onion, salt, pepper and water in a large saucepan. Bring to a boil and boil, uncovered, for 5 minutes. Add corn; return to boiling and boil for 2 minutes. Drain. Add 1¾ cups milk, green onions and parsley.
2. Pour into a greased 13-in. x 9-in. x 2-in. baking dish. Top with eggs. Mix the biscuit mix and the remaining milk until smooth and drop by teaspoonfuls onto corn mixture. Bake at 450° for 13-15 minutes or until done.

YIELD: 6-8 servings.

ambrosia waldorf salad

JANET SMITH ⚐ SMITHTON, MISSOURI

A lovely light pink salad, this puts a different spin on traditional Waldorf salad. It is super
served with roast turkey or baked ham. People always go back for seconds.
My family didn't think they liked cranberries until they tried this.

2 cups fresh *or* frozen cranberry halves
½ cup sugar
3 cups miniature marshmallows
2 cups diced unpeeled apples
1 cup seedless green grape halves
¾ cup chopped pecans
1 can (20 ounces) pineapple tidbits, drained
1 cup heavy whipping cream, whipped
Shredded *or* flaked coconut

1. Combine cranberries and sugar. In a large bowl, combine the marshmallows, apples, grapes, pecans and pineapple. Add cranberries and mix well. Fold in whipped cream. Cover and chill. Sprinkle with coconut before serving.

YIELD: 12-14 servings.

mediterranean potato salad

JENNY HAEN ⌘ RED WING, MINNESOTA

- 2 pounds small red potatoes, cut into ¼-inch slices
- 3 cups water
- 1 small red onion, thinly sliced and separated into rings
- ½ cup pitted Greek olives
- ½ cup oil-packed sun-dried tomatoes, undrained, chopped
- ½ cup minced fresh parsley
- ⅓ cup pine nuts, toasted
- ⅛ teaspoon salt
- ⅛ teaspoon pepper
- ½ cup sun-dried tomato salad dressing
- 1 package (4 ounces) crumbled tomato and basil feta cheese

1. Place potatoes in a 3-qt. microwave-safe dish; add water. Cover and microwave on high for 10-15 minutes or until tender, stirring once. Drain; rinse in cold water.
2. In a large bowl, combine the potatoes, onion, olives, tomatoes, parsley, pine nuts, salt and pepper. Drizzle with dressing; toss to coat.
3. Let stand at room temperature for 1 hour before serving. Sprinkle with the feta cheese. Refrigerate leftovers.

YIELD: 10 servings.

EDITOR'S NOTE: Recipe was tested in a 1,100-watt microwave.

I use red onions, Greek olives and feta cheese to bring Mediterranean flavors to an all-American classic. With a few minutes of prep and time to chill, it makes an ideal side dish on busy summer days.

You cannot beat this light and refreshing salad on hot summer days! The combination of watermelon, cilantro, lime and two colors of tomatoes is just unusual enough to keep folks commenting on the great flavor— and coming back for more!

watermelon and tomato salad

BEV JONES ⚑ BRUNSWICK, MISSOURI

3 tablespoons lime juice

2 tablespoons white balsamic vinegar

2 tablespoons olive oil

2 tablespoons honey

1 medium mango, peeled and chopped

1 teaspoon grated lime peel

1 teaspoon kosher salt

¼ teaspoon white pepper

8 cups cubed seedless watermelon

1½ pounds yellow tomatoes, coarsely chopped (about 5 medium)

1½ pounds red tomatoes, coarsely chopped (about 5 medium)

2 sweet onions, thinly sliced and separated into rings

⅔ cup minced fresh cilantro

1. For dressing, place the first eight ingredients in a blender; cover and process until pureed.
2. In a large bowl, combine the watermelon, tomatoes, onions and cilantro. Just before serving, add dressing and toss to coat. Serve with a slotted spoon.

YIELD: 12 servings.

If you've been searching for the perfect coleslaw, give this one a try! It has a terrific crunch, and the simple dressing is sweet and tangy all in one.

tangy coleslaw

PATRICIA STAUDT ⚐ MARBLE ROCK, IOWA

½ large head cabbage, shredded
2 large carrots, shredded
½ cup finely chopped green pepper
2 tablespoons finely chopped onion

DRESSING:

¼ cup sugar
3 tablespoons white vinegar
2 tablespoons canola oil
1 teaspoon celery seed
½ teaspoon salt

1. In a large bowl, combine cabbage, carrots, green pepper and onion. In a jar with a tight-fitting lid, combine the dressing ingredients; shake well. Pour over the cabbage mixture and toss. Cover and chill 4 hours before serving.

YIELD: 10 servings.

radish potato salad

LYDIA GARCIA 🏳 HANOVER, PENNSYLVANIA

This summery fare is not only pretty, it is easy to prepare, too.

- 5 medium red potatoes (about 1½ pounds)
- 1 cup sliced radishes
- 2 hard-cooked eggs, chopped
- ¾ cup mayonnaise
- 3 tablespoons minced fresh dill *or* 2 teaspoons dill weed
- 2 tablespoons cider vinegar
- 1 tablespoon sugar
- ¼ teaspoon salt

Dash pepper

1. Place potatoes in a saucepan and cover with water. Bring to a boil. Reduce heat; cover and cook for 15-20 minutes or until tender. Drain and cool. Peel and cube potatoes; place in a large bowl.
2. Add radishes and eggs. In a small bowl, combine mayonnaise, dill, vinegar, sugar, salt and pepper. Gently fold into the potato mixture. Cover and refrigerate for at least 1 hour.

YIELD: 4 servings.

big-batch baked beans

KATHY HERRON 🏳 JAMESTOWN, NEW YORK

My mom got the recipe from my aunt, then shared it with me when she saw how much my husband enjoyed the dish. It's great to take to potlucks and picnics.

- ½ pound ground beef
- ½ cup chopped onion
- 1 can (55 ounces) pork and beans
- 1 can (16 ounces) kidney beans, rinsed and drained
- 1 can (15½ ounces) black-eyed peas, rinsed and drained
- ½ cup ketchup
- 5 bacon strips, cooked and crumbled
- ⅓ cup sugar
- ⅓ cup packed brown sugar
- ⅓ cup barbecue sauce
- 2 tablespoons molasses
- 2 tablespoons prepared mustard
- ½ teaspoon chili powder
- ½ teaspoon salt
- ¼ teaspoon pepper

1. In a Dutch oven, cook beef and onion over medium heat until the meat is no longer pink; drain. Stir in the remaining ingredients. Transfer to a greased 3-qt. baking dish. Cover and bake at 350° for 1 hour or until beans reach desired thickness.

YIELD: 14 servings.

west coast potato salad

PHYLLIS LEE CIARDO ALBANY, CALIFORNIA

1½ pounds medium red potatoes, cooked and cubed

 4 tablespoons lemon juice, *divided*

 2 tablespoons canola oil

 2 tablespoons minced fresh parsley

 ½ teaspoon salt, optional

 ¼ teaspoon pepper

 ¾ cup thinly sliced celery

 ¼ cup chopped green onions

 1 pound fresh asparagus, cut into ¾-inch pieces

 ½ cup sour cream

 2 tablespoons Dijon mustard

 1 teaspoon dried thyme

 1 teaspoon dried tarragon

1. Place potatoes in a large bowl and set aside. In a jar with tight-fitting lid, combine 3 tablespoons lemon juice, oil, parsley, salt if desired and pepper; shake well. Pour over potatoes and toss gently. Add celery and onions; set aside.

2. In a large saucepan, bring ½ in. of water to a boil. Add asparagus; cover and cook for 3 minutes. Drain and immediately place asparagus in ice water. Drain and pat dry. Add to potato mixture.

3. In a small bowl, combine the sour cream, mustard, thyme, tarragon and remaining lemon juice; gently fold into salad. Chill until serving.

YIELD: 12 servings.

four-fruit salad

DEBBIE FITE ⚑ FORT MYERS, FLORIDA

2 cups fresh strawberries, sliced

2 cups green grapes, halved

1 small cantaloupe, cut into chunks

1 to 2 medium firm bananas, sliced

⅓ cup orange juice

1. In a large bowl, combine the fruit. Pour the juice over fruit and toss to coat. Cover and refrigerate for 4 hours. Stir just before serving.

YIELD: 10 servings.

Almost any type of fruit will work in this recipe. The first time I made it, I just used the fruits I had on hand.

stuffed celery sticks

OPAL SCHMIDT ☞ BATTLE CREEK, IOWA

1 package (3 ounces) cream cheese, softened
¼ cup creamy peanut butter
1 tablespoon milk
2 teaspoons soy sauce
4 celery ribs, cut into serving-size pieces

1. In a small mixing bowl, beat the cream cheese, peanut butter, milk and soy sauce until smooth. Transfer to a small resealable plastic bag. Cut a small hole in the corner of the bag; pipe mixture into celery pieces.

YIELD: 4 servings.

I mix cream cheese and soy sauce into peanut butter to give my stuffed celery a rich, unique flavor. The filling is easy to blend together, and kids will have a ball squeezing it into the celery sticks before they start crunching away.

sweet potato slaw

BRENDA SHARON 🏴 CHANNING, MICHIGAN

I grew up in Louisiana, and we ate lots of sweet potatoes.
They look like carrots in this distinctive, crunchy salad.

½ cup mayonnaise

½ cup sour cream

2 tablespoons honey

2 tablespoons lemon juice

1 teaspoon grated lemon peel

½ teaspoon salt

¼ teaspoon pepper

3 cups shredded peeled uncooked
  sweet potatoes

1 medium apple, peeled and chopped

¾ cup pineapple tidbits, drained

½ cup chopped pecans

1. In a large bowl, whisk the first seven ingredients until smooth. In a large bowl, combine the potatoes, apple, pineapple and pecans. Add dressing; toss to coat. Cover and refrigerate for at least 1 hour.

YIELD: 6-8 servings.

---

five-bean salad

JEANETTE SIMEC 🏴 OTTAWA, ILLINOIS

This salad combines five kinds of beans with an oil-and-vinegar dressing in a colorful classic
that's great to take to picnics or tailgate parties. Everyone loves the variety of beans.

1 can (19 ounces) garbanzo beans *or*
  chickpeas, rinsed and drained

1 can (16 ounces) kidney beans, rinsed
  and drained

1 can (15½ ounces) great northern beans,
  rinsed and drained

1 can (14½ ounces) cut wax beans, rinsed
  and drained

1 package (10 ounces) frozen cut
  green beans, thawed

2 small onions, chopped

1 cup white vinegar

¾ cup sugar

¼ cup canola oil

1 teaspoon salt

½ teaspoon pepper

1. In a large bowl, combine the first six ingredients. In another bowl, whisk the vinegar, sugar, oil, salt and pepper. Pour over bean mixture and toss to coat. Cover and refrigerate for several hours or overnight. Serve with a slotted spoon.

YIELD: 15 servings.

spicy ravioli salad

PAULA MARCHESI ⮞ LENHARTSVILLE, PENNSYLVANIA

1 package (25 ounces) frozen beef, sausage *or* cheese ravioli

1 can (10 ounces) diced tomatoes and green chilies, undrained

1 can (8¾ ounces) whole kernel corn, drained

1 bottle (8 ounces) taco sauce

1 can (2¼ ounces) sliced ripe olives, drained

1 small cucumber, peeled, seeded and chopped

1 small red onion, sliced

2 garlic cloves, minced

¼ teaspoon ground cumin

¼ teaspoon salt

¼ teaspoon pepper

1. Cook ravioli according to package directions. Meanwhile, combine remaining ingredients in a large bowl. Drain ravioli and stir into tomato mixture. Cover and refrigerate at least 2 hours.

YIELD: 8-10 servings.

watermelon grape salad

SUE GRONHOLZ ⚑ BEAVER DAM, WISCONSIN

Try this salad that tastes great and is easy to make. It's perfect on a hot summer day when watermelon is at its best. You can even serve it with a scoop of lemon sherbet for a refreshing dessert.

10 cups cubed seedless watermelon

10 cups seedless red grapes

1¼ cups white grape juice

5 teaspoons minced fresh tarragon

5 teaspoons honey

1. In a small bowl, combine the watermelon and grapes. In another bowl, whisk the grape juice, tarragon and honey. Pour over fruit and toss to coat. Serve immediately in a watermelon boat or large bowl.

YIELD: 20 servings.

black 'n' white bean salad

KAY OGDEN ⚑ GRANTS PASS, OREGON

This is a hearty medley I created after tasting a similar one in a restaurant. It goes together in no time and complements most entrees.

1 can (15 ounces) black beans, rinsed and drained

1 can (15 ounces) white kidney beans, rinsed and drained

½ cup chopped cucumber

½ cup chopped sweet red peppers

¼ cup chopped onion

¼ cup minced fresh cilantro

⅓ cup red wine vinegar

¼ cup olive oil

½ teaspoon salt, optional

¼ teaspoon garlic powder

⅛ teaspoon pepper

Lettuce leaves, optional

1. In a large bowl, combine the beans, cucumber, red peppers, onion and cilantro. In a small bowl, whisk the vinegar, oil and seasonings. Pour over bean mixture and toss to coat. Cover and refrigerate until serving. Using a slotted spoon, serve over lettuce if desired.

YIELD: 6 servings.

corn slaw

SUE BURTON ⚑ FRANKFORT, KANSAS

*My mother gave this recipe to me. It's one my husband and two children
ask for in the summer, especially when we're grilling.*

2 cups fresh corn, cooked
1 cup diced carrots
1 cup diced green pepper
½ cup chopped onion
¼ cup mayonnaise
¼ cup sour cream
2 teaspoons white vinegar
1 teaspoon sugar
1 teaspoon prepared yellow mustard
¼ teaspoon salt

1. In a salad bowl, toss corn, carrots, green pepper and onion. In a small bowl, combine remaining ingredients; pour over vegetables and mix well. Refrigerate for several hours before serving.
YIELD: 8 servings.

DON'T HEAD OUT WITHOUT IT
For outdoor parties and events, be sure to have plenty of sunblock, bug repellent and insect bite lotion on hand. Keeping a first-aid kit in the car is also a smart idea.

rainbow fruit bowl

DOROTHY PRITCHETT ⚑ WILLS POINT, TEXAS

*I've found mint gives fruit a delicious zip. Mixed with fruit juices and served over
melon, it's a pleasant blend that's both sweet and refreshing.*

2 cups watermelon balls
2 cups honeydew balls
2 cups cantaloupe balls
½ cup orange juice
¼ cup lime juice
2 tablespoons sugar
1 tablespoon snipped fresh mint
1 tablespoon grated orange peel
1 cup lemon-lime soda

1. Combine melon balls in a glass bowl. In a small bowl, whisk together the juices, sugar, mint and orange peel; pour over the melon and toss gently. Cover and refrigerate for 2 hours. Just before serving, add the soda and toss gently.
YIELD: 6-8 servings.

I created this salad myself and love to serve it when strawberries are at their peak.

apple-strawberry spinach salad

CAROLYN POPWELL ⚑ LACEY, WASHINGTON

1 pound fresh spinach, torn

2 cups chopped unpeeled Granny Smith apples

¾ cup fresh bean sprouts

½ cup sliced fresh strawberries

¼ cup crumbled cooked bacon

DRESSING:

¾ cup canola oil

⅓ cup white wine vinegar

1 small onion, grated

½ cup sugar

2 teaspoons Worcestershire sauce

2 teaspoons salt

1. In a large salad bowl, combine the first five ingredients. In a small bowl, whisk together all dressing ingredients. Just before serving, pour over salad and toss.

YIELD: 4-6 servings.

Luscious fruit, cream cheese and gelatin come together to create an easy side dish for any occasion. The chopped pecans dotting the bottom layer provide a pleasing crunch.

peaches 'n' cream salad

SUE BRAUNSCHWEIG ⚑ DELAFIELD, WISCONSIN

1 package (3 ounces) lemon gelatin
¾ cup boiling water
1 cup orange juice
1 envelope whipped topping mix
1 package (3 ounces) cream cheese, softened
¼ cup chopped pecans, optional
PEACH LAYER:
1 package (3 ounces) lemon gelatin
1 cup boiling water
1 can (21 ounces) peach pie filling

1. In a bowl, dissolve gelatin in water; add orange juice. Refrigerate until partially set. Prepare topping mix according to package directions. In a mixing bowl, beat cream cheese until smooth; fold in whipped topping and pecans if desired. Fold into gelatin mixture. Pour into an ungreased 8-in. square dish. Refrigerate until firm.

2. For peach layer, dissolve gelatin in water; stir in pie filling. Chill until partially set. Carefully pour over creamy gelatin layer (pan will be full). Chill until firm.

YIELD: 9 servings.

pepperoncini pasta salad

ROSEMARY MORGAN ⚑ PACIFICA, CALIFORNIA

My family comes from a very hot part of Italy, so chilled pasta salads are always a big hit. Pepperoncini gives this dish zip, and olive oil dressing adds Mediterranean flavor.

- 3 cups cooked small shell pasta
- 1 cup halved cherry tomatoes
- 1 cup whole pitted ripe olives
- 1 cup pepperoncini, thinly sliced
- 3 tablespoons olive oil
- 3 tablespoons lemon juice
- 1 garlic clove, minced
- 1 teaspoon minced fresh oregano
  or ¼ teaspoon dried oregano
- 1 teaspoon salt
- ¼ teaspoon pepper

1. In a bowl, combine the pasta, tomatoes, olives and pepperoncini. In a small bowl, combine oil, lemon juice, garlic, oregano, salt and pepper. Pour over pasta mixture and toss to coat evenly. Cover and refrigerate for at least 3 hours.

YIELD: 6 servings.

SHREDDING CABBAGE
To shred cabbage without a food processor or grater, cut the cabbage into wedges. Place cut side down on a cutting board. With a large sharp knife, cut wedges into thin slices.

---

fruit slaw in a cabbage bowl

DARLENE BRENDEN ⚑ SALEM, OREGON

This fresh recipe turns ho-hum coleslaw on its head—in more ways than one! I take the traditional blend of vegetables for that dish and mix in juicy fruit pieces. Then I serve the salad inside a hollowed-out cabbage. Both the flavor and "bowl" never fail to draw compliments.

- 1 medium head cabbage
- 1 can (11 ounces) mandarin oranges, drained
- 1 can (8 ounces) pineapple chunks, drained
- 2 medium carrots, shredded
- 1 medium tart apple, chopped
- ½ cup halved green grapes
- 2 tablespoons canola oil
- 2 tablespoons lemon juice
- 2 tablespoons honey
- ⅛ teaspoon ground ginger

1. To prepare the cabbage serving bowl, gently peel back outer leaves of the cabbage. Hollow out cabbage, leaving a ¼-in. shell and the core intact; set aside. Chop removed cabbage leaves. Place 2 cups chopped cabbage in a large bowl (refrigerate remaining cabbage for another use). Add oranges, pineapple, carrots, apple and grapes.

2. In a jar with a tight-fitting lid, combine oil, lemon juice, honey and ginger; shake well. Pour over slaw and toss to coat. Spoon into cabbage bowl. Serve immediately.

YIELD: 6-8 servings.

basil bean salad

MARIAN PLATT ⌖ SEQUIM, WASHINGTON

A light herb vinaigrette makes this zippy delight so refreshing, especially on a hot summer afternoon.

2 pounds fresh green *or* wax beans, trimmed
3 green onions, sliced
⅔ cup minced fresh basil
2 to 4 tablespoons olive oil
2 tablespoons red wine vinegar
½ teaspoon salt
Pepper to taste
⅔ cup grated Romano cheese

1. Cut beans into 1¼-in. pieces. Place in a saucepan; cover with water and bring to a boil. Cook, uncovered, for 10 minutes or until crisp-tender. Rinse with cold water; drain well. In a bowl, combine the beans, onions, basil, oil, vinegar, salt and pepper. Sprinkle with Romano cheese and toss to coat.
YIELD: 10 servings.

steak and potato salad

LINDA EMILY DOW ⌖ PRINCETON JUNCTION, NEW JERSEY

I like to spend a lot of time with our family and friends on weekends. That's when this recipe comes in handy. We marinate the meat in the fridge overnight, then grill it quickly for a fast, filling salad.

2 pounds boneless sirloin steak (1 inch thick)
½ cup red wine vinegar
¼ cup olive oil
¼ cup soy sauce
6 cups cubed cooked potatoes
1 cup diced green pepper
⅓ cup chopped green onions
¼ cup minced fresh parsley
½ cup Caesar salad dressing
Lettuce leaves, optional

1. Place the steak in a large resealable plastic bag or shallow glass container. Combine vinegar, oil and soy sauce; pour over the steak. Cover and refrigerate for 1 hour or overnight. Drain, discarding marinade.
2. Grill or broil steak for 8-10 minutes on each side or until meat reaches desired doneness (for medium-rare, a thermometer should read 145°; medium, 160°; well-done, 170°). Slice into thin strips across the grain and place in bowl. Add potatoes, green pepper, onions, parsley and dressing; toss to coat. Serve on lettuce leaves if desired.
YIELD: 8-10 servings.

confetti bean salad

BONNIE MCKINSEY ⚑ GREENVILLE, SOUTH CAROLINA

1 can (16 ounces) kidney beans, rinsed and drained

1 can (15 ounces) garbanzo beans *or* chickpeas, rinsed and drained

1 can (14½ ounces) Italian diced tomatoes, drained

1½ cups frozen peas

1½ cups frozen corn

½ cup chopped onion

½ cup chopped green pepper

3 tablespoons red wine vinegar

2 tablespoons olive oil

1 garlic clove, minced

½ teaspoon salt

¼ teaspoon pepper

1. In a large bowl, combine first seven ingredients. In a small bowl, combine the vinegar, oil, garlic, salt and pepper until blended. Pour over bean mixture; toss gently to coat. Cover and refrigerate for at least 4 hours.

YIELD: 10 servings.

My kids really enjoy this green salad, made with romaine lettuce, broccoli, corn and crumbled bacon. It uses bottled dressing, so it's quick to fix, too.

baby corn romaine salad

KATHYRN MAXSON ⌐ MOUNTLAKE TERRACE, WASHINGTON

6 cups torn romaine

2 cups broccoli florets

1 can (15 ounces) whole baby corn, rinsed, drained and cut into ½-inch pieces *or* 1½ cups frozen corn, thawed

3 tablespoons crumbled cooked bacon

½ cup Caesar *or* Italian salad dressing

1. In a large bowl, combine the romaine, broccoli, corn and bacon. Drizzle with the dressing and toss to coat.

YIELD: 6 servings.

GREAT GREENS
Just before serving, tear greens into bite-size pieces or use a plastic lettuce knife. Cutting greens with a metal knife will turn the edges brown. Allow greens to stand at room temperature no longer than 15 minutes before serving.

warm dijon potato salad

LAVERNE KAEPPEL 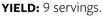 VERO BEACH, FLORIDA

*This satisfying potato salad has so much wonderful flavor, no one will ever guess
it's light. The tang of the Dijon mustard really comes through.*

- 5 medium red potatoes (about 2 pounds)
- ¼ cup reduced-fat mayonnaise
- 1 tablespoon grated Parmesan cheese
- 1 green onion, sliced
- 2 teaspoons cider vinegar
- 1 teaspoon Dijon mustard
- ½ teaspoon salt
- ¼ teaspoon pepper

1. Place potatoes in a large saucepan and cover with water. Bring to a boil. Reduce heat; cover and simmer for 20 minutes or until tender.

2. In a large bowl, combine remaining ingredients. Drain potatoes and cut into cubes; add to the mayonnaise mixture and gently toss to coat. Serve immediately.

YIELD: 8 servings.

---

roasted potato salad

TERRI ADAMS KANSAS CITY, KANSAS

*I pack this delicious potato salad in a cooler to spoon up cold at picnics
or transfer it to a slow cooker to serve it warm.*

- ½ pound fresh green beans, cut into 1½-inch pieces
- 1 large whole garlic bulb
- 2 pounds small red potatoes, quartered
- 2 medium sweet red peppers, cut into large chunks
- 2 green onions, sliced
- ¼ cup chicken broth
- ¼ cup balsamic vinegar
- 2 tablespoons olive oil
- 2 teaspoons sugar
- 1 teaspoon minced fresh rosemary *or* ¼ teaspoon dried rosemary, crushed
- ½ teaspoon salt

1. In a large saucepan, bring 6 cups water to a boil. Add beans; bring to a boil. Cover and cook for 3 minutes. Drain and immediately place beans in ice water; drain and pat dry.

2. Remove papery outer skin from garlic (do not peel or separate cloves). Cut top off garlic bulb. Place cut side up in a greased 15-in. x 10-in. x 1-in. baking pan. Add the potatoes, red peppers, onions and beans; drizzle with broth. Bake, uncovered, at 400° for 30-40 minutes or until garlic is softened.

3. Remove the garlic; set aside. Bake vegetables 30-35 minutes longer or until tender. Cool for 10-15 minutes. Squeeze softened garlic into a large bowl. Stir in the vinegar, oil, sugar, rosemary and salt. Add vegetables; toss to coat. Serve warm or cold.

YIELD: 9 servings.

vegetable pasta salad

HELEN PHILLIPS ⚑ HORSEHEADS, NEW YORK

2 cups broccoli florets

4 cups cooked spiral pasta

2 medium carrots, julienned

½ cup frozen peas, thawed

½ cup cubed fully cooked ham

½ cup cubed cheddar cheese

⅓ cup sliced green onions

DRESSING:

¾ cup mayonnaise

2 tablespoons cider vinegar

1 tablespoon Dijon mustard

1 garlic clove, minced

1 teaspoon dill weed

¼ teaspoon pepper

1. Place 1 in. of water in a small saucepan; add the broccoli. Bring to a boil. Reduce the heat; cover and simmer for 2-3 minutes. Rinse in cold water and drain.

2. In a large bowl, combine the broccoli, pasta, carrots, peas, ham, cheese and onions.

3. In another bowl, combine dressing ingredients. Pour over salad and toss to coat. Cover and refrigerate for at least 1 hour.

YIELD: 10 servings.

creamy coleslaw

DIANNE ESPOSITE  NEW MIDDLETOWN, OHIO

3 to 4 cups shredded cabbage
1 cup shredded carrots
1 cup thinly sliced green pepper
½ cup mayonnaise
¼ cup lemon juice
1 to 2 tablespoons sugar
1 tablespoon prepared mustard
1 teaspoon celery seed
1 teaspoon salt

1. In a large salad bowl, toss cabbage, carrots and green pepper. In a small bowl, combine the remaining ingredients. Pour over the cabbage mixture and toss to coat. Chill for at least 2-3 hours.

YIELD: 6-8 servings.

Cabbage, carrots and green pepper are blended with a tasty dressing that gets its zest from a hint of mustard. When Mom set this slaw on the table, it disappeared fast.

Being from Vermont, the nation's leading maple syrup-producing state, I use pure maple syrup for a special sweet taste. By adding chicken, this salad can be a light main course.

fruity tortellini salad

VICKY MCCLAIN ST. ALBANS, VERMONT

1 package (9 ounces) refrigerated cheese tortellini

1 can (11 ounces) mandarin oranges, drained

1 medium grapefruit, peeled and sectioned

1 medium lemon, peeled and sectioned

2 kiwifruit, peeled and sliced

1 cup halved seedless red grapes

2 cups cubed cooked chicken, optional

½ cup maple syrup

½ cup orange juice

½ cup cashews

1. Cook tortellini according to package directions. Drain and rinse with cold water. In a large bowl, combine the tortellini, fruit and chicken if desired.

2. In a small bowl, whisk the syrup and orange juice; pour over salad and toss to coat. Cover and refrigerate for at least 1 hour. Sprinkle with cashews just before serving.

YIELD: 6-8 servings.

show-off salad

C. NEOMI DRUMMOND ⚑ DES MOINES, IOWA

People tell me they can't stay away from this, with its layers of lettuce, green pepper, cucumber, macaroni, hard-cooked eggs, ham and more.

- 2 cups uncooked elbow macaroni
- 1 tablespoon canola oil
- 3 cups shredded lettuce
- 1 medium green pepper, chopped
- 1 medium cucumber, peeled, seeded and diced
- 3 hard-cooked eggs, sliced
- 1 cup shredded red cabbage
- 1 small red onion, chopped
- 2 medium carrots, shredded
- 1 cup diced fully cooked ham, optional
- 1 package (10 ounces) frozen peas, thawed
- 1 cup (4 ounces) shredded Colby-Monterey Jack *or* Monterey Jack cheese
- 1 cup mayonnaise
- ½ cup sour cream
- ½ cup chopped green onions, *divided*
- 1 tablespoon spicy brown mustard
- 1 teaspoon sugar

Salt and pepper to taste

1. Cook macaroni according to package directions; drain and rinse in cold water. Drizzle with oil; toss to coat. Place lettuce in a shallow 3-qt. dish; top with the green pepper, cucumber, macaroni, eggs, cabbage, red onion, carrots, ham if desired, peas and cheese.
2. In a small bowl, combine the mayonnaise, sour cream, ¼ cup of green onions, mustard, sugar, salt and pepper; spread over the top. Cover and refrigerate overnight. Just before serving, sprinkle with the remaining green onions.

YIELD: 16-18 servings.

rainbow pasta salad

BARBARA CARLUCCI ⚑ ORANGE PARK, FLORIDA

This colorful salad is my mother's recipe. It features an uncommon but tempting mixture of vegetables. Mother always cooks with wonderful flair, and everything she makes is delicious.

- 1 package (16 ounces) tricolor spiral pasta
- 2 cups fresh broccoli florets
- 1 cup chopped carrots
- ½ cup chopped tomato
- ½ cup chopped cucumber
- ¼ cup chopped onion
- 1 can (15¼ ounces) whole kernel corn, drained
- 1 jar (6½ ounces) marinated artichoke hearts, drained and halved
- 1 bottle (8 ounces) Italian salad dressing

1. Cook pasta according to package directions; drain and rinse in cold water. Place in a large bowl; add remaining ingredients and toss to coat. Cover and refrigerate for 2 hours or overnight.

YIELD: 12-14 servings.

fresh mozzarella & tomato salad

LYNN SCULLY ⌖ RANCHO SANTA FE, CALIFORNIA

A splash of lemon brightens up the medley of red tomatoes, creamy mozzarella and rich, buttery avocados in this sensational salad.

6	plum tomatoes, chopped
2	cartons (8 ounces ea*ch*) fresh mozzarella cheese pearls, drained
⅓	cup minced fresh basil
1	tablespoon minced fresh parsley
2	teaspoons minced fresh mint
¼	cup lemon juice
¼	cup olive oil
¾	teaspoon salt
¼	teaspoon pepper
2	medium ripe avocados, peeled and chopped

1. In a large bowl, combine the tomatoes, cheese, basil, parsley and mint; set aside.
2. In a small bowl, whisk the lemon juice, oil, salt and pepper. Pour over tomato mixture; toss to coat. Cover and refrigerate for at least 1 hour before serving.
3. Just before serving, stir in avocados. Serve with a slotted spoon.

YIELD: 8 servings.

slow-cooked pork & beans

SUE LIVERMORE ⌖ DETROIT LAKES, MINNESOTA

Bacon adds subtle smokiness to this hearty side dish that's loaded with flavor. Brown sugar, vinegar and a hint of molasses make the sauce irresistible!

1	package (1 pound) sliced bacon, chopped
1	cup chopped onion
2	cans (15 ounces ea*ch*) pork and beans, undrained
1	can (16 ounces) kidney beans, rinsed and drained
1	can (16 ounces) butter beans, rinsed and drained
1	can (15¼ ounces) lima beans, rinsed and drained
1	can (15 ounces) black beans, rinsed and drained
1	cup packed brown sugar
½	cup cider vinegar
1	tablespoon molasses
2	teaspoons garlic powder
½	teaspoon ground mustard

1. In a large skillet, cook bacon and onion over medium heat until bacon is crisp. Remove to paper towels to drain.
2. In a 4-qt. slow cooker, combine the remaining ingredients; stir in bacon mixture. Cover and cook on low for 6-8 hours or until heated through.

YIELD: 12 servings.

antipasto picnic salad

MICHELE LARSON 🏴 BADEN, PENNSYLVANIA

1 package (16 ounces) medium pasta shells

2 jars (16 ounces *each*) giardiniera

1 pound fresh broccoli florets

½ pound cubed part-skim mozzarella cheese

½ pound hard salami, cubed

½ pound deli ham, cubed

2 packages (3½ ounces *each*) sliced pepperoni, halved

1 large green pepper, cut into chunks

1 can (6 ounces) pitted ripe olives, drained

DRESSING:

½ cup olive oil

¼ cup red wine vinegar

2 tablespoons lemon juice

1 teaspoon Italian seasoning

1 teaspoon coarsely ground pepper

½ teaspoon salt

1. Cook pasta according to package directions. Meanwhile, drain giardiniera, reserving ¾ cup liquid. In a large bowl, combine the giardiniera, broccoli, mozzarella, salami, ham, pepperoni, green pepper and olives. Drain pasta and rinse in cold water; stir into meat mixture.

2. For dressing, in a small bowl, whisk the oil, vinegar, lemon juice, Italian seasoning, pepper, salt and reserved giardiniera liquid. Pour over salad and toss to coat. Refrigerate until serving.

YIELD: 25 servings (1 cup each).

EDITOR'S NOTE: Giardiniera, a pickled vegetable mixture, is available in mild and hot varieties and can be found in the Italian or pickle section of your grocery store.

picnic potato salad

SHERI NEISWANGER ↣ RAVENNA, OHIO

10 medium red potatoes, cubed
⅔ cup canola oil
2 tablespoons cider vinegar
4 teaspoons honey
1 teaspoon dried basil
1 teaspoon ground mustard
½ teaspoon salt
½ teaspoon dried thyme
¼ teaspoon dried marjoram
¼ teaspoon dried mint
Dash cayenne pepper

1. Place potatoes in a large saucepan and cover with water. Cover and bring water to a boil over medium-high heat; cook for 15-20 minutes or until tender. Drain and place in a large bowl.
2. Combine the remaining ingredients; pour over potatoes and toss to coat. Cool to room temperature. Cover and refrigerate until serving.

YIELD: 12 servings.

crunchy coleslaw

JULIE VAVROCH ⚑ MONTEZUMA, IOWA

*This cabbage salad is so easy to put together that we often have it for
spur-of-the-moment picnics or when unexpected company stops by. We love its nutty flavor.*

⅓ cup canola oil
1 package (3 ounces) beef ramen noodles
½ teaspoon garlic salt
1 package (16 ounces) shredded coleslaw mix
1 package (5 ounces) sliced almonds

1. In a small saucepan, heat oil. Stir in contents of noodle seasoning packet and garlic salt; cook for 3-4 minutes or until blended.

2. Meanwhile, crush the noodles and place in a bowl. Add coleslaw mix and almonds. Drizzle with oil mixture and toss to coat. Serve immediately.

YIELD: 6-8 servings.

apple mallow salad

PAULA MARCHESI ⚑ ROCKY POINT, NEW YORK

*I enjoy picking fresh apples at local orchards, and using both red and green apples
makes this a festive-looking dish to serve at parties and family gatherings.*

1 can (20 ounces) crushed pineapple
½ cup sugar
1 tablespoon all-purpose flour
1 to 2 tablespoons white vinegar
1 egg, beaten
1 carton (12 ounces) frozen whipped topping, thawed
2 medium red apples, diced
2 medium green apples, diced
4 cups miniature marshmallows
1 cup honey-roasted peanuts

1. Drain pineapple, reserving juice; set pineapple aside. In a saucepan, combine sugar, flour, vinegar and reserved juice until smooth. Bring to a boil; cook and stir for 2 minutes or until thickened. Remove from the heat. Stir a small amount of hot mixture into egg; return all to the pan, stirring constantly. Bring to a gentle boil; cook and stir for 2 minutes. Remove from the heat; cool.

2. Fold in whipped topping. Fold in the apples, marshmallows and reserved pineapple. Cover and refrigerate for 1 hour. Just before serving, fold in the peanuts.

YIELD: 16-20 servings.

After sampling a similar pasta dish at a market in Florida, I came home to develop my own version.

confetti tortellini salad

SUZANNE ZICK ⮞ LINCOLNTON, NORTH CAROLINA

1½ cups refrigerated *or* frozen cheese tortellini
1 cup *each* cauliflowerets and broccoli florets
2 medium carrots, cut into ¼-inch slices
2 tablespoons thinly sliced green onions
1 garlic clove, minced
¼ cup grated Parmesan cheese
½ cup Italian salad dressing
¼ teaspoon hot pepper sauce

1. In a large saucepan, cook tortellini according to the package directions; drain. In a bowl, combine the tortellini, vegetables and garlic. Sprinkle with Parmesan cheese. Combine the salad dressing and the hot pepper sauce; pour over salad and toss gently. Cover and refrigerate until serving.

YIELD: 6 servings.

KEEPING HANDS CLEAN
Even in outdoor settings, hand washing is important. Be sure to bring along a water jug, soap and paper towels, or use packaged towelettes or hand sanitizer to keep hands clean while preparing food.

COOKIES, BROWNIES & BARS

My family just loves these chewy chocolate and peanutty bars. They're perfect for dessert and snacks. I make them whenever I get a craving for something sweet.

triple-layer cookie bars

DIANE BRADLEY ☞ SPARTA, MICHIGAN

CRUST:

- 1¼ cups all-purpose flour
- ⅔ cup sugar
- ⅓ cup baking cocoa
- ¼ cup packed brown sugar
- 1 teaspoon baking powder
- ¼ teaspoon salt
- ½ cup butter
- 2 eggs, lightly beaten

TOPPING:

- 1 package (7 ounces) flaked coconut
- 1 can (14 ounces) sweetened condensed milk
- 2 cups (12 ounces) semisweet chocolate chips
- ½ cup creamy peanut butter

1. In a mixing bowl, combine the first six ingredients. Cut in butter until crumbly. Add eggs; mix well. Spread in a greased 13-in. x 9-in. x 2-in. baking pan. Bake at 350° for 8 minutes.

2. Sprinkle coconut on top. Drizzle sweetened condensed milk evenly over coconut. Return to the oven for 20-25 minutes or until lightly browned. In a saucepan over low heat, melt the chocolate chips and the peanut butter, stirring until smooth. Spread over the bars. Cool.

YIELD: 2-3 dozen.

chocolate macadamia nut cookies

ARLIENE HILLINGER ➢ RANCHO PALOS VERDES, CALIFORNIA

I've been hosting an annual Christmas cookie exchange for over 35 years now.
Each guest brings six dozen cookies to share. This is always a favorite.

10 tablespoons butter, softened
¾ cup packed brown sugar
1 teaspoon vanilla extract
1 egg, lightly beaten
1 cup all-purpose flour
¾ teaspoon baking powder
⅛ teaspoon baking soda
⅛ teaspoon salt
1½ cups semisweet chocolate chips
¾ cup coarsely chopped macadamia nuts
¾ cup coarsely chopped pecans

CARAMEL GLAZE:
12 caramels
2 tablespoons heavy whipping cream

1. In a mixing bowl, cream butter, sugar and vanilla. Add egg. Combine flour, baking powder, baking soda and salt; add to creamed mixture and mix well. Fold in chocolate chips and nuts.
2. Drop by teaspoonfuls 2 in. apart onto greased baking sheets. Bake at 350° for 10-12 minutes or until golden. Cool on a wire rack.
3. For glaze, melt the caramels and cream in a saucepan over low heat, stirring until smooth. Drizzle over cooled cookies.

YIELD: 2 dozen.

BRING BARS AND BROWNIES
Bars and brownies are perfect desserts to take along to tailgate parties because they are so easy to transport. If it's a hot day, stay away from frosted bars or cookies with lots of chips, as the frosting or chips can melt.

soft sugar cookies

MABEL SHIRK ➢ FAIR PLAY, SOUTH CAROLINA

I was born in Africa and grew up enjoying cardamom. Through the years, I've experimented with this
spice in a variety of recipes, including these old-fashioned delights that are ideal for parties.

1 cup butter, softened
2¼ cups sugar, *divided*
2 eggs
5 cups all-purpose flour
1 teaspoon baking soda
½ teaspoon baking powder
1½ teaspoons ground cardamom, *divided*
½ cup milk

1. In a large mixing bowl, cream the butter and 2 cups of the sugar. Add eggs, one at a time, beating well after each addition. Combine the flour, baking soda, baking powder and 1 teaspoon of the cardamom; add to creamed mixture alternately with milk.
2. In a small bowl, combine the remaining sugar and cardamom; dip rounded teaspoonfuls of dough into sugar mixture. Place on greased baking sheets. Bake at 375° for 10-12 minutes or until lightly browned. Cool on wire racks.

YIELD: about 6 dozen.

These chewy delights are big on taste but need only a little effort. They are handy to make when the weather is hot, since the oven never has to be turned on.

no-bake bars

SUSIE WINGERT ⚑ PANAMA, IOWA

4 cups Cheerios
2 cups crisp rice cereal
2 cups dry roasted peanuts
2 cups M&M's
1 cup light corn syrup
1 cup sugar
1½ cups creamy peanut butter
1 teaspoon vanilla extract

1. In a large bowl, combine the first four ingredients; set aside. In a large saucepan, bring corn syrup and sugar to a boil. Cook and stir just until sugar is dissolved.
2. Remove from the heat; stir in peanut butter and vanilla. Pour over cereal mixture and toss to coat evenly. Spread into a greased 15-in. x 10-in. x 1-in. baking pan. Cool. Cut into square bars.

YIELD: 15 bars.

watermelon cookies

RUTH WITMER ⚑ STEVENS, PENNSYLVANIA

¾ cup butter, softened
¾ cup sugar
1 egg
½ teaspoon almond extract
2¼ cups all-purpose flour
¼ teaspoon *each* salt and baking powder
Red and green food coloring
Dried currants
Sesame seeds

1. In a mixing bowl, cream butter, sugar, egg and extract until light and fluffy. Combine flour, salt and baking powder; stir into creamed mixture and mix well. Remove 1 cup of dough; set aside. At low speed, beat in enough red food coloring to tint dough deep red. Roll into a 3½-in.-long tube; wrap in plastic wrap and refrigerate until firm, about 2 hours.

2. Divide 1 cup of reserved dough into two pieces. To one piece, add enough green food coloring to tint dough deep green. Do not tint remaining piece of dough. Wrap each piece separately in plastic wrap; chill until firm, about 1 hour.

3. On a floured sheet of waxed paper, roll untinted dough into an 8½-in. x 3½-in. rectangle. Place red dough along short end of rectangle. Roll up and encircle red dough with the untinted dough; set aside.

4. On floured waxed paper, roll the green dough into a 10-in. x 3½-in. rectangle. Place tube of red/untinted dough along the short end of green dough. Roll up and encircle tube with green dough. Cover tightly with plastic wrap; refrigerate at least 8 hours.

5. Unwrap dough and cut into ⅛-in. slices. Place 1 in. apart on ungreased baking sheets. Lightly press dried currants and sesame seeds into each slice to resemble watermelon seeds. Bake at 375° for 6-8 minutes or until cookies are firm but not brown. While still warm, cut each cookie in half or into pie-shaped wedges. Remove to a wire rack to cool.

YIELD: 3 dozen.

Who wouldn't enjoy these cute delights? Kids and adults alike just love them. Dried currants and sesame seeds make the edible seeds for these treats that are perfect for a party.

apple-chip cookies

MRS. DEAN ZAHS ⚑ AINSWORTH, IOWA

These scrumptious apple cookies never last for long in our cookie jar. They're perfect for fall.

¼ cup butter, softened
1 cup packed brown sugar
½ cup heavy whipping cream
1 egg
2 cups all-purpose flour
½ teaspoon baking soda
½ teaspoon salt
¼ teaspoon ground nutmeg
1 cup chopped peeled apple
½ cup chocolate *or* butterscotch chips
1 cup chopped nuts

GLAZE:
3 tablespoons butter, melted
1 teaspoon ground cinnamon
2 tablespoons heavy whipping cream
2 cups confectioners' sugar

1. In a mixing bowl, cream butter and sugar. Beat in cream and egg. Combine the dry ingredients; add to creamed mixture. Fold in apples, chips and nuts. Drop by teaspoonfuls onto greased baking sheets.
2. Bake at 350° for 12-15 minutes. Do not overbake. For glaze, combine all ingredients; spread over cooled cookies.

YIELD: about 3 dozen.

chewy oatmeal cookies

RUTH O'DONNELL ⚑ ROMEO, MICHIGAN

When our family gathered at my aunt's summer home on Mackinac Island a few years back, she pulled out her tried-and-true recipe and made these wholesome cookies. I think of her and that memorable vacation every time I make these for my own family.

1 cup butter, softened
1 cup sugar
1 cup packed brown sugar
2 eggs
1 teaspoon vanilla extract
1½ cups all-purpose flour
1 teaspoon baking soda
1 teaspoon baking powder
1 teaspoon salt
2 cups quick-cooking oats
2 cups cornflakes
1 cup flaked coconut
1 cup salted peanuts

1. In a mixing bowl, cream butter and sugars. Add the eggs, one at a time, beating well after each addition. Beat in vanilla. Combine flour, baking soda, baking powder and salt; gradually add to the creamed mixture.
2. Stir in remaining ingredients. Drop by level tablespoonfuls 2 in. apart onto ungreased baking sheets. Bake at 350° for 10-12 minutes or until lightly browned. Remove to wire racks to cool.

YIELD: about 6½ dozen.

STORING COOKIES
Flavors will blend during storage, so don't store strong-flavored cookies with delicate-flavored ones. Arrange cookies in a container with waxed paper between each layer.

Homemade chocolate frosting adds a special touch to these moist brownies prepared from a mix.

football brownies

TASTE OF HOME TEST KITCHEN

1 package fudge brownie mix
  (13-inch x 9-inch x 2-inch pan size)

6 tablespoons butter, softened

2¾ cups confectioners' sugar

½ cup baking cocoa

⅓ cup milk

1 teaspoon vanilla extract

¼ cup vanilla *or* white chips

1. Prepare the brownie batter according to package directions. Spread into a greased 15-in. x 10-in. x 1-in. baking pan. Bake at 350° for 13-15 minutes or until a toothpick comes out clean. Cool on a wire rack.

2. In a mixing bowl, cream butter, sugar, cocoa, milk and vanilla. Spread over cooled brownies. Loosely cover and chill for 1 hour or until frosting is set. With a sharp knife, make lengthwise 1½-in. parallel cuts from a short side to a long side to form diamonds.

3. In a microwave, melt vanilla chips at 50% power; stir until smooth. Place in a small heavy-duty resealable plastic bag; cut a small hole in a corner of bag. Pipe laces on brownies.

YIELD: about 3 dozen.

butter pecan cookies

MARTHA THENFIELD ▷ CEDARTOWN, GEORGIA

1¾ cups chopped pecans
1 tablespoon plus 1 cup butter, softened, *divided*
1 cup packed brown sugar
1 egg, *separated*
1 teaspoon vanilla extract
2 cups self-rising flour
1 cup pecan halves

1. Place chopped pecans and 1 tablespoon butter in a baking pan. Bake at 325° for 5-7 minutes or until toasted and browned, stirring frequently. Set aside to cool.

2. In a mixing bowl, cream brown sugar and remaining butter. Beat in egg yolk and vanilla. Gradually add flour. Cover and refrigerate for 1 hour or until easy to handle. Roll into 1-in. balls, then roll in toasted pecans, pressing nuts into dough. Place 2 in. apart on ungreased baking sheets.

3. Beat egg white until foamy. Dip pecan halves in egg white, then gently press one into each ball. Bake at 375° for 10-12 minutes or until golden brown. Cool for 2 minutes before removing to wire racks.

YIELD: about 4 dozen.

EDITOR'S NOTE: As a substitute for each cup of self-rising flour, place 1½ teaspoons baking powder and ½ teaspoon salt in a measuring cup. Add all-purpose flour to measure 1 cup.

blonde brownies

ANNE WEILER ⚑ PHILADELPHIA, PENNSYLVANIA

My family has enjoyed these bars at potlucks, in brown bags and as an anytime snack throughout the years. Butterscotch or peanut butter chips can be used in place of the chocolate chips.

¼ cup butter-flavored shortening
1½ cups packed brown sugar
2 eggs
½ teaspoon vanilla extract
1 cup all-purpose flour
1½ teaspoons baking powder
½ teaspoon salt
1 cup chopped walnuts
½ cup semisweet chocolate chips

1. In a mixing bowl, cream shortening and brown sugar. Add eggs, one at a time, beating well after each addition. Beat in vanilla. Combine flour, baking powder and salt; gradually add to the creamed mixture. Stir in nuts and chips.
2. Spread into a greased 11-in. x 7-in. x 2-in. baking pan. Bake at 350° for 25-30 minutes or until a toothpick inserted near the center comes out clean. Cool on wire rack. Cut into bars.

YIELD: 2 dozen.

ginger nut crisps

DELLENE LOVE ⚑ HOOD RIVER, OREGON

The only problem with these is that it's hard to eat just one! I came up with this recipe when my mother shared a large supply of ginger. We love these spice cookies.

1 cup butter, softened
1 cup sugar
¾ cup honey
3 cups all-purpose flour
1 cup whole wheat flour
1 tablespoon ground cinnamon
1 tablespoon ground cloves
2 to 3 teaspoons ground ginger
1½ teaspoons baking soda
1 teaspoon salt
1½ cups finely chopped pecans *or* almonds

1. In a mixing bowl, cream butter and sugar. Beat in honey. Combine the flours, cinnamon, cloves, ginger, baking soda and salt; gradually add to the creamed mixture. Stir in nuts. Shape into two 11-in. rolls; wrap each in plastic wrap. Refrigerate for 3 hours or until firm.
2. Unwrap and cut into ¼-in. slices. Place 2 in. apart on ungreased baking sheets. Bake at 375° for 8-11 minutes or until firm. Remove to wire racks to cool.

YIELD: 6 dozen.

toffee chip cookies

KAY FRANCES RONNENKAMP ✍ ALBION, NEBRASKA

These cookies combine several mouth-watering flavors. The generous size of the batch gives me plenty of scrumptious cookies to have on hand and extras to send to our sons at college.

1 cup butter, softened
½ cup canola oil
1 cup sugar
1 cup packed brown sugar
1 teaspoon vanilla extract
2 eggs
3½ cups all-purpose flour
1 teaspoon cream of tartar
1 teaspoon baking soda
1 teaspoon salt
3 cups crisp rice cereal
1 cup quick-cooking oats
1 cup flaked coconut
1 cup chopped pecans
1 cup English toffee bits *or* almond brickle chips

1. In a large mixing bowl, cream butter, oil, sugars and vanilla. Add eggs, one at a time, beating well after each addition. Combine the flour, cream of tartar, baking soda and salt; add to creamed mixture. Stir in remaining ingredients.
2. Drop by tablespoonfuls 2 in. apart onto ungreased baking sheets. Bake at 350° for 10-12 minutes or until lightly browned. Remove to wire racks to cool.

YIELD: 12 dozen.

spiced apple bars

EVELYN WINCHESTER ✍ FORT MYERS, FLORIDA

I bake chopped walnuts and hearty oats into these moist apple and cinnamon squares.

½ cup butter, softened
1 cup sugar
2 eggs
1 cup all-purpose flour
1 cup quick-cooking oats
1 tablespoon baking cocoa
1 teaspoon baking powder
1 teaspoon ground cinnamon
½ teaspoon baking soda
½ teaspoon salt
½ teaspoon ground nutmeg
¼ teaspoon ground cloves
1½ cups diced peeled tart apples
½ cup chopped walnuts
Confectioners' sugar

1. In a mixing bowl, cream butter and sugar. Add the eggs, one at a time, beating well after each. Combine dry ingredients; add to creamed mixture and mix well. Stir in apple and nuts.
2. Spread into a greased 13-in. x 9-in. x 2-in. baking pan. Bake at 375° for 20-25 minutes or until a toothpick comes out clean. Cool. Dust with confectioners' sugar. Cut into bars.

YIELD: about 2½ dozen.

> *People love these very rich brownies so much that I never take them anywhere without bringing along several copies of the recipe to hand out. These treats are wonderful to take on a picnic because you don't have to worry about frosting melting.*

chocolate chip brownies

BRENDA KELLY ⚑ ASHBURN, VIRGINIA

1 cup butter
3 cups sugar
6 eggs
1 tablespoon vanilla extract
2¼ cups all-purpose flour
½ cup baking cocoa
1 teaspoon baking powder
½ teaspoon salt
1 cup (6 ounces) semisweet chocolate chips
1 cup (about 6 ounces) vanilla *or* white chips
1 cup chopped walnuts

1. In a mixing bowl, cream butter and sugar. Add eggs and vanilla; mix well. Combine flour, cocoa, baking powder and salt; stir into creamed mixture just until blended (do not overmix).

2. Pour into two greased 9-in. square baking pans. Sprinkle with chips and nuts. Bake at 350° for 35-40 minutes or until toothpick inserted near the center comes out clean.

YIELD: 3-4 dozen.

fudgy nut brownies

RUTH STERN SHADOW HILLS, CALIFORNIA

2½ cups semisweet chocolate chips
1 cup butter
1 cup sugar
¼ teaspoon salt
4 eggs, lightly beaten
2 teaspoons vanilla extract
¾ cup all-purpose flour
1 cup coarsely chopped hazelnuts *or* almonds, toasted

TOPPING:

12 squares (1 ounce *each*) semisweet chocolate
1 tablespoon shortening
3 squares (1 ounce *each*) white baking chocolate

1. In a saucepan over low heat, melt chocolate chips and butter; remove from heat. Add sugar and salt; stir until dissolved. Cool for 10 minutes. Stir in eggs, vanilla, flour and nuts.

2. Spread into a greased 15-in. x 10-in. x 1-in. baking pan. Bake at 350° for 25-30 minutes or until a toothpick inserted near the center comes out with moist crumbs (do not overbake). Cool completely on a wire rack.

3. For topping, in a heavy saucepan or microwave, heat semisweet chocolate and shortening just until melted. Spread over brownies. Melt white chocolate. Pour into a small heavy-duty resealable plastic bag; cut a small hole in corner of bag.

4. Pipe thin lines 1 in. apart widthwise. Beginning about 1 in. from a wide side, gently pull a toothpick through the lines to the opposite side. Wipe toothpick clean. Then pull toothpick through lines in opposite directions. Repeat over entire top at 1-in. intervals. Cut into bars.

YIELD: about 2½ dozen.

cashew blondies

KATHEY SKARIE ⚑ VERGAS, MINNESOTA

These easy-to-make white chocolate brownies are a hit at potlucks and other gatherings—I always come home with an empty plate and lots of compliments.

2 eggs
⅔ cup sugar
1 teaspoon vanilla extract
8 squares (1 ounce *each*) white baking chocolate, melted and cooled
⅓ cup butter, melted
1½ cups all-purpose flour
1½ teaspoons baking powder
¼ teaspoon salt
½ to 1 cup chopped salted cashews *or* pecans

1. In a mixing bowl, beat eggs, sugar and vanilla on medium speed for 1 minute. Beat in chocolate and butter. Combine the flour, baking powder and salt; gradually add to chocolate mixture. Stir in cashews.
2. Spread into a greased 9-in. square baking pan. Bake at 350° for 25-30 minutes or until a toothpick inserted near the center comes out clean. Cool on a wire rack. Cut into bars.

YIELD: 2 dozen.

almond sugar cookies

LINDA HOLT ⚑ WICHITA FALLS, TEXAS

We made these crisp cookies often when I worked in the lunchroom at our daughters' grade school. Students just gobbled them up! The almond flavor makes them more unique than plain sugar cookies.

2 cups butter-flavored shortening
1 cup sugar
1 cup packed brown sugar
2 eggs
1 teaspoon vanilla extract
1 teaspoon almond extract
4 cups all-purpose flour
2 teaspoons baking soda
2 teaspoons cream of tartar
Additional sugar *or* colored sugar

1. In a large mixing bowl, cream the shortening and sugars. Add eggs, one at a time, beating well after each addition. Beat in extracts. Combine the flour, baking soda and cream of tartar; gradually add to creamed mixture.
2. Drop by tablespoonfuls 2 in. apart onto ungreased baking sheets. Flatten with a glass dipped in sugar. Bake at 350° for 10-12 minutes or until lightly browned. Remove to wire racks to cool.

YIELD: 5 dozen.

FREEZING BARS
You can freeze a pan of uncut bars in an airtight container or resealable plastic bag. Or, wrap individual bars in plastic wrap and stack in an airtight container.

strawberry jam bars

KAREN MEAD PITTSBURGH, PENNSYLVANIA

½ cup butter, softened
½ cup packed brown sugar
 1 egg
 1 package (18¼ ounces) white cake mix
 1 cup finely crushed cornflakes
 1 cup strawberry jam *or* preserves

1. In a mixing bowl, cream butter and brown sugar until smooth. Add egg; mix well. Gradually add dry cake mix and cornflakes. Set aside 1½ cups for topping. Press remaining dough into a greased 13-in. x 9-in. x 2-in. baking pan.
2. Carefully spread jam over crust. Sprinkle with reserved dough; gently press down. Bake at 350° for 30 minutes or until golden brown. Cool completely on a wire rack. Cut into bars.

YIELD: 2 dozen.

cranberry oat cookies

MARJORIE GOERTZEN ⚑ CHASE, KANSAS

These cookies that I adapted from another recipe call to mind ones my mother used to bake.
Instead of stirring in raisins like she did, though, I add bright red cranberries for festive flair.

⅔ cup butter, softened
⅔ cup brown sugar
2 eggs
1½ cups all-purpose flour
1½ cups old-fashioned oats
1 teaspoon baking soda
1 teaspoon ground cinnamon
½ teaspoon salt
1¼ cups dried cranberries
1 cup chopped pecans, toasted
⅔ cup vanilla *or* white chips

1. In a mixing bowl, cream butter and brown sugar. Add eggs; mix well. Combine the dry ingredients; gradually add to the creamed mixture. Stir in the remaining ingredients.
2. Drop by tablespoonfuls 3 in. apart onto ungreased baking sheets. Bake at 375° for 10-12 minutes or until golden brown. Remove to wire racks to cool.

YIELD: about 4 dozen.

classic lemon bars

MELISSA MOSNESS ⚑ LOVELAND, COLORADO

My from-scratch dessert comes together in a snap, but can be made
with a prepared graham cracker crust when time is tight.

½ cup butter, softened
¼ cup sugar
1 cup all-purpose flour
FILLING:
2 eggs
¾ cup sugar
3 tablespoons lemon juice
2 tablespoons all-purpose flour
¼ teaspoon baking powder
Confectioners' sugar

1. In a small mixing bowl, cream the butter and sugar; gradually add the flour. Press into an ungreased 8-in. square baking dish. Bake at 375° for 12 minutes. Cool slightly.
2. Meanwhile, in another mixing bowl, beat the eggs, sugar, lemon juice, flour and baking powder until frothy. Pour over warm crust. Bake for 15-20 minutes or until lightly browned. Cool on a wire rack. Dust with confectioners' sugar. Cut into bars.

YIELD: 9 servings.

fruit 'n' nut bars

JOHN NAGEL ➢ DEERBROOK, WISCONSIN

*Children are sure to enjoy this healthy treat. For convenient snacking,
wrap bars individually in plastic wrap so they can snack on the go!*

1¼ cups chopped almonds
 1 jar (2 ounces) sesame seeds
 4 cups quick-cooking oats
 1 cup dark seedless raisins
 1 cup light corn syrup
⅔ cup canola oil
½ cup hulled sunflower kernels
½ cup toasted wheat germ
½ cup nonfat dry milk powder
 2 teaspoons ground cinnamon
 1 teaspoon vanilla extract
½ teaspoon salt

1. In a large bowl, combine all ingredients; mix well. Press mixture firmly and evenly into a greased 15-in. x 10-in. x 1-in. baking pan. Bake at 350° for 25 minutes or until golden brown. Cool in pan on wire rack at least 2 hours. Store in refrigerator.
YIELD: 18 bars.

USE GREASE FOR EASE
When a recipe calls for greased baking sheets or pans, grease them with shortening or nonstick cooking spray. For even easier removal, line the bottom of the pan with parchment paper instead.

five-chip cookies

SHARON HEDSTROM ➢ MINNETONKA, MINNESOTA

With peanut butter, oats and five kinds of chips, these make a hearty snack that appeals to kids of all ages. I sometimes double the recipe to share with friends and neighbors.

1 cup butter, softened
1 cup peanut butter
1 cup sugar
⅔ cup packed brown sugar
2 eggs
1 teaspoon vanilla extract

2 cups all-purpose flour
1 cup old-fashioned oats
2 teaspoons baking soda
½ teaspoon salt
⅔ cup *each* milk chocolate chips, semisweet chocolate chips, peanut butter chips, vanilla chips and butterscotch chips

1. In a large mixing bowl, cream butter, peanut butter and sugars. Add eggs, one at a time, beating well after each addition. Beat in vanilla. Combine flour, oats, baking soda and salt; gradually add to creamed mixture. Stir in chips.
2. Drop by rounded tablespoonfuls 2 in. apart onto ungreased baking sheets. Bake at 350° for 10-12 minutes or until lightly browned. Cool for 1 minute before removing to wire racks.
YIELD: 4½ dozen.

My family can't possibly eat all of the sweets I whip up, so my co-workers are more than happy to sample them—particularly these rich, chewy brownies that are full of gooey caramel, chocolate chips and crunchy walnuts.

caramel brownies

CLARA BAKKE COON RAPIDS, MINNESOTA

 2 cups sugar
¾ cup baking cocoa
 1 cup canola oil
 4 eggs
¼ cup milk
1½ cups all-purpose flour
 1 teaspoon salt
 1 teaspoon baking powder
 1 cup (6 ounces) semisweet chocolate chips
 1 cup chopped walnuts, *divided*
 1 package (14 ounces) caramels
 1 can (14 ounces) sweetened condensed milk

1. In a mixing bowl, combine the sugar, cocoa, oil, eggs and milk. Combine the flour, salt and baking powder; add to egg mixture and mix until combined. Fold in chocolate chips and ½ cup walnuts. Spoon two-thirds of the batter into a greased 13-in. x 9-in. x 2-in. baking pan. Bake at 350° for 12 minutes.

2. Meanwhile, in a saucepan, heat the caramels and condensed milk over low heat until caramels are melted. Pour over baked brownie layer. Sprinkle with remaining walnuts. Drop remaining batter by teaspoonfuls over caramel layer; carefully swirl brownie batter with a knife.

3. Bake 35-40 minutes longer or until a toothpick inserted near the center comes out with moist crumbs. Cool brownies on a wire rack.

YIELD: 2 dozen.

This is a good brownie to take to gatherings because it won't crumble in your hand. It's easy to achieve the attractive marbled effect.

chocolate cream cheese brownies

LISA GODFREY 🏴 TEMPLE, GEORGIA

1 package (4 ounces) German sweet chocolate
3 tablespoons butter
2 eggs
¾ cup sugar
½ cup all-purpose flour
½ teaspoon baking powder
¼ teaspoon salt
1 teaspoon vanilla extract
¼ teaspoon almond extract
½ cup chopped nuts

FILLING:
1 package (3 ounces) cream cheese, softened
2 tablespoons butter, softened
¼ cup sugar
1 egg
1 tablespoon all-purpose flour
½ teaspoon vanilla extract

1. In a microwave, melt chocolate and butter; stir until smooth. Cool. In a small mixing bowl, beat eggs. Gradually add sugar, beating until thick and pale yellow. Combine the flour, baking powder and salt; add to egg mixture. Stir in melted chocolate, extracts and nuts. Pour half of the batter into a greased 8-in. square baking dish; set aside.

2. For filling, in a small mixing bowl, beat cream cheese and butter until light and fluffy. Gradually add the sugar until light and fluffy. Beat in the egg, flour and vanilla; mix well. Pour over batter in pan. Spoon remaining batter over filling. Cut through batter with a knife to swirl the chocolate.

3. Bake at 325° for 35-40 minutes or until a toothpick inserted near the center comes out clean. Cool on a wire rack. Cut into bars. Store in the refrigerator.

YIELD: about 2 dozen.

apple crumb bars

BARBARA PICKARD ⚑ UNION LAKE, MICHIGAN

This has been a favorite recipe of mine for many years. Whether I make the apple bars for parties or family, they're always a hit.

1½ cups packed brown sugar

1½ cups rolled oats

  3 cups all-purpose flour

  ¾ teaspoon baking soda

1¼ cups butter, *divided*

  5 to 6 cups thinly sliced peeled apples

  1 cup sugar

  3 tablespoons cornstarch

  1 cup boiling water

  1 teaspoon vanilla extract

1. In a bowl, combine the brown sugar, oats, flour, baking soda and 1 cup plus 2 tablespoons butter. Reserve 2 cups for topping; lightly pat remaining crumbs into a greased 13-in. x 9-in. x 2-in. baking pan. Arrange apples over the top; set aside.

2. In a saucepan, combine the sugar, cornstarch, water, vanilla and remaining butter. Bring to a boil and cook until thick; spread on the apples. Sprinkle reserved crumbs on top. Bake at 350° for 35-45 minutes or until top lightly browned.

YIELD: 3-4 dozen.

make-ahead glazed brownies

BARBARA ROBBINS ⚑ DELRAY BEACH, FLORIDA

I often rely on these moist brownies for last-minute treats. It's a sweet snack I've been making for years.

½ cup butter, softened

1 cup sugar

1 egg

¼ cup sour cream

1 cup all-purpose flour

½ cup baking cocoa

½ teaspoon baking powder

¼ teaspoon salt

½ cup milk

GLAZE:

¼ cup butter, softened

½ cup confectioners' sugar

2 tablespoons baking cocoa

3 tablespoons milk

½ cup chopped pecans

½ teaspoon vanilla extract

1. In a large mixing bowl, cream butter and sugar. Beat in egg and sour cream. Combine the flour, cocoa, baking powder and salt; add to creamed mixture alternately with milk. Spread into a greased 13-in. x 9-in. x 2-in. baking pan. Bake at 350° for 20-25 minutes or until a toothpick inserted near the center comes out clean.

2. Meanwhile, in a small mixing bowl, cream butter. Gradually beat in confectioners' sugar, cocoa and milk. Stir in pecans and vanilla. Spread over warm brownies. Cool on a wire rack. Cover and freeze for up to 1 month. Thaw and cut into bars.

YIELD: 2 dozen.

lemon star cookies

TASTE OF HOME TEST KITCHEN

Family and friends will cheer when they see these patriotic cookies. Make them throughout the year by using different cookie cutters and food coloring.

1 cup butter, softened
2 cups confectioners' sugar
2 eggs
2 tablespoons lemon juice
4 teaspoons half-and-half cream
2 teaspoons grated lemon peel
3¼ cups all-purpose flour
½ cup ground almonds
½ teaspoon baking soda
⅛ teaspoon salt
GLAZE:
2 cups confectioners' sugar
¼ cup light corn syrup
2 tablespoons lemon juice
Red and blue food coloring

1. In a large bowl, cream butter and confectioners' sugar until light and fluffy. Add eggs, one at a time, beating well after each addition. Beat in the lemon juice, cream and lemon peel.
2. Combine flour, almonds, baking soda and salt; gradually add to creamed mixture. Cover and refrigerate for 2 hours or until easy to handle.
3. On a lightly floured surface, roll out dough to ⅛-in. thickness. Cut with a floured star-shaped cookie cutter. Place 1 in. apart on ungreased baking sheets. Bake at 350° for 8-10 minutes or until lightly browned. Remove to wire racks to cool.
4. For glaze, in a small bowl, combine the confectioners' sugar, corn syrup and lemon juice until smooth. Divide into three bowls. Tint one portion red and one portion blue; leave the third portion white. Spread over cookies; let stand overnight for glaze to harden.

YIELD: about 5½ dozen.

peanut butter crunch bars

CHRISTIE PORTER ⚑ SHIPSHEWANA, INDIANA

Kids will love these colorful, crunchy bars. They're a fun twist on the traditional marshmallow crispy treats. And because they're so easy, older kids could whip up a batch on their own!

30 large marshmallows
3 tablespoons butter
1 tablespoon peanut butter
6 cups Peanut Butter Cap'n Crunch
1½ cups milk chocolate M&M's

1. In a large saucepan, combine the marshmallows, butter and peanut butter. Cook and stir over medium-low heat until melted. Remove from the heat. Stir in the cereal and M&M's.
2. Pat into a 13-in. x 9-in. pan coated with cooking spray. Cool. Cut into bars.

YIELD: 2 dozen.

deluxe chocolate marshmallow bars

ESTHER SHANK HARRISONBURG, VIRGINIA

¾ cup butter, softened
1½ cups sugar
3 eggs
1 teaspoon vanilla extract
1⅓ cups all-purpose flour
3 tablespoons baking cocoa
½ teaspoon baking powder
½ teaspoon salt
½ cup chopped nuts, optional
4 cups miniature marshmallows

TOPPING:
1⅓ cups semisweet chocolate chips
1 cup peanut butter
3 tablespoons butter
2 cups crisp rice cereal

1. In a small bowl, cream butter and sugar until light and fluffy. Add eggs, one at a time, beating well after each addition. Beat in vanilla.
2. Combine the flour, cocoa, baking powder and salt; gradually add to creamed mixture. Stir in nuts if desired. Spread into a greased 15-in. x 10-in. x 1-in. baking pan.
3. Bake at 350° for 15-18 minutes or until set. Sprinkle marshmallows over the top; bake 2-3 minutes longer or until melted. Place pan on a wire rack. Using a knife dipped in water, gently spread marshmallows evenly over the top. Cool the bars completely.
4. For topping, combine the chocolate chips, peanut butter and butter in a small saucepan. Cook and stir over low heat until blended. Remove from the heat; stir in cereal. Spread over bars immediately. Chill.

YIELD: about 3 dozen.

I like to serve these spiced treats with a dollop of lemon sherbet. They're great to cool off with on hot summer days.

ginger thins

ELEANOR SENSKE ☞ ROCK ISLAND, ILLINOIS

  6 tablespoons butter, softened
  ½ cup plus 2 tablespoons sugar, *divided*
  2 tablespoons molasses
  1 tablespoon cold strong brewed coffee
1¼ cups all-purpose flour
  ¾ teaspoon ground ginger
  ½ teaspoon baking soda
  ½ teaspoon ground cinnamon
  ¼ teaspoon ground cloves
  ⅛ teaspoon salt

1. In a mixing bowl, cream butter and ½ cup sugar; set remaining sugar aside. Add molasses and coffee to creamed mixture; mix well. Combine the remaining ingredients; add to creamed mixture. Mix well (dough will be soft).
2. Cover and freeze for 15 minutes. Shape dough into a 7-in. roll; flatten to 1-in. thickness. Wrap in plastic wrap. Freeze for 8 hours or overnight.
3. Unwrap dough and cut into ⅛-in. slices; place 2 in. apart on parchment paper-lined baking sheets. Sprinkle with reserved sugar. Bake at 350° for 8-10 minutes or until firm. Remove to wire racks to cool.

YIELD: 3½ dozen.

white chocolate cereal bars

ANNE POWERS ⚑ MUNFORD, ALABAMA

*A friend gave me this recipe. The white candy coating provides
a delicious twist on the traditional crisp rice treats.*

- 4 cups miniature marshmallows
- 8 ounces white candy coating, broken into pieces
- ¼ cup butter, cubed
- 6 cups crisp rice cereal

1. In a microwave-safe bowl, combine the marshmallows, candy coating and butter. Microwave, uncovered, on high for 2 minutes or until melted, stirring every minute. Add cereal; stir to coat.

2. Transfer to a greased 13-in. x 9-in. x 2-in. pan and gently press mixture evenly into pan. Cut into squares.

YIELD: about 3 dozen.

EDITOR'S NOTE: This recipe was tested in a 1,100-watt microwave.

cookie brittle

BETTY BYRNES CONSBRUCK ⚑ GAINESVILLE, FLORIDA

*This recipe originally called for chocolate chips, but my family likes it
better when I use peanut butter chips. And so do I!*

- 1 cup butter, softened
- 1 cup sugar
- 2 cups all-purpose flour
- 1¼ cups peanut butter chips
- ½ cup coarsely chopped pecans

1. In a mixing bowl, cream butter and sugar. Gradually add flour; mix well. Stir in peanut butter chips. Line a 15-in. x 10-in. x 1-in. baking pan with foil; coat with nonstick cooking spray. Gently press dough into the pan; sprinkle with pecans and press into dough.

2. Bake at 350° for 20-25 minutes or until golden brown. Cool in pan on a wire rack. Invert pan and remove foil. Break brittle into pieces; store in an airtight container.

YIELD: about 4 dozen.

Glowing campfire coals are not needed to enjoy the traditional taste of s'mores with this recipe. The tasty take-along treat makes a sweet snack any time of the day.

s'mores bars

KRISTINE BROWN ⚑ RIO RANCHO, NEW MEXICO

8 to 10 whole graham crackers (about 5 inches x 2½ inches)

1 package fudge brownie mix (13-inch x 9-inch x 2-inch pan size)

2 cups miniature marshmallows

1 cup (6 ounces) semisweet chocolate chips

⅔ cup chopped peanuts

1. Arrange graham crackers in a single layer in a greased 13-in. x 9-in. x 2-in. baking pan. Prepare brownie batter according to package directions. Spread over crackers.

2. Bake at 350° for 25-30 minutes or until a toothpick inserted near the center comes out clean. Sprinkle with the marshmallows, chocolate chips and peanuts. Bake 5 minutes longer or until the marshmallows are slightly puffed and golden brown. Cool on a wire rack before cutting.

YIELD: 2 dozen.

These individual brownie-like cupcakes studded with pecan pieces are simply delicious. The crinkly tops of the chewy treats are so pretty that they don't even need frosting.

brownie cups

MERRILL POWERS 🏁 SPEARVILLE, KANSAS

1 cup butter
1 cup (6 ounces) semisweet chocolate chips
1 cup chopped pecans
4 eggs
1½ cups sugar
1 cup all-purpose flour
1 teaspoon vanilla extract

1. In a saucepan over low heat, melt the butter and chocolate chips, stirring until smooth. Cool. Add pecans; stir until well-coated.

2. In a large bowl, combine the eggs, sugar, flour and vanilla. Fold in chocolate mixture. Fill paper-lined muffin cups two-thirds full. Bake at 325° for 35-38 minutes or until a toothpick inserted near the center comes out clean.

YIELD: about 1½ dozen.

frosted cinnamon zucchini bars

BONITA HOLZBACHER ⚑ BATESVILLE, INDIANA

*I figure you can never have enough recipes calling for zucchini! These cake-like
bars with a cinnamon-flavored frosting are unbelievably good.*

¾ cup butter, softened
½ cup sugar
½ cup packed brown sugar
2 eggs
1 teaspoon vanilla extract
1¾ cups all-purpose flour
1½ teaspoons baking powder
2 cups shredded zucchini
1 cup flaked coconut
¾ cup chopped walnuts
FROSTING:
2 cups confectioners' sugar
1 teaspoon ground cinnamon
2 tablespoons butter, melted
1 teaspoon vanilla extract
2 to 3 tablespoons milk

1. In a mixing bowl, cream butter and sugars. Add
the eggs, one at a time, beating well after each
addition. Beat in vanilla. Combine flour and
baking powder; gradually add to the creamed
mixture. Stir in zucchini, coconut and nuts.
2. Spread into a greased 15-in. x 10-in. x 1-in.
baking pan. Bake at 350° for 25-30 minutes or
until a toothpick inserted near the center comes
out clean. Cool on a wire rack.
3. In a bowl, combine sugar and cinnamon. Stir
in butter, vanilla and enough milk until frosting
reaches spreading consistency. Frost cooled
bars; cut.
YIELD: about 5 dozen.

peanut butter cookie cups

KRISTI TACKETT ⚑ BANNER, KENTUCKY

*I'm a busy schoolteacher and pastor's wife who always looks for shortcuts.
I wouldn't dare show my face at a church dinner or bake sale without these tempting
peanut butter treats. They're quick and easy to make and always a hit.*

1 package (17½ ounces) peanut butter
cookie mix
36 miniature peanut butter cups, unwrapped

1. Prepare cookie mix according to package
directions. Roll the dough into 1-in. balls. Place
in greased miniature muffin cups. Press dough
evenly onto bottom and up sides of each cup.
2. Bake at 350° for 11-13 minutes or until set.
Immediately place a peanut butter cup in each
cup; press down gently. Cool for 10 minutes;
carefully remove from pans.
YIELD: 3 dozen.

EDITOR'S NOTE: 2¼ cups peanut butter cookie dough of
your choice can be substituted for the mix.

These colossal cookies taste best when they're golden around the edges and moist and chewy in the center. My grandchildren can polish them off in no time.

giant cherry oatmeal cookies

IRENE MCDADE ⚑ CUMBERLAND, RHODE ISLAND

½ cup shortening
½ cup butter, softened
¾ cup packed brown sugar
½ cup sugar
2 eggs
1 teaspoon vanilla extract
2½ cups old-fashioned oats
1⅓ cups all-purpose flour
2 teaspoons apple pie spice
½ teaspoon baking powder
¼ teaspoon baking soda
¼ teaspoon salt
1½ cups dried cherries, chopped
½ to 1 teaspoon grated orange peel

1. In a large mixing bowl, cream shortening, butter and sugars. Beat in the eggs and vanilla. Combine the oats, flour, apple pie spice, baking powder, baking soda and salt; gradually add to the creamed mixture. Stir in cherries and orange peel.

2. Drop by ⅓ cupfuls onto an ungreased baking sheet. Press to form a 4-in. circle. Bake at 375° for 9-12 minutes or until golden brown. Let stand for 1 minute before removing to wire racks to cool.

YIELD: 1 dozen.

A sweet raspberry filling is sandwiched between a crispy crust and a crunchy brown sugar topping in these satisfying snack bars.

raspberry walnut shortbread

PAT HABIGER SPEARVILLE, KANSAS

1¼ cups plus 2 tablespoons all-purpose flour, *divided*
½ cup sugar
½ cup cold butter
½ cup raspberry jam
2 eggs
½ cup packed brown sugar
1 teaspoon vanilla extract
⅛ teaspoon baking soda
1 cup finely chopped walnuts

1. In a bowl, combine 1¼ cups flour and sugar; cut in butter until crumbly. Press into a greased 9-in. square baking pan. Bake at 350° for 20-25 minutes or until edges are lightly browned. Place on a wire rack. Spread jam over hot crust.
2. In a mixing bowl, beat eggs, brown sugar and vanilla. Combine baking soda and remaining flour; stir into the egg mixture just until combined. Fold in walnuts. Spoon over jam; spread evenly. Bake for 17-20 minutes or until golden brown and set. Cool completely on a wire rack before cutting.

YIELD: 16 servings.

really rocky road brownies

BRENDA WOOD ⚑ EGBERT, ONTARIO

This rich, fudgy dessert recipe came from a family reunion cookbook that I compiled. My niece Olivia Fallon contributed the recipe.

8 squares (1 ounce *each*) unsweetened chocolate
1½ cups butter
6 eggs
3 cups sugar
1 tablespoon vanilla extract
1½ cups all-purpose flour
1 cup chopped walnuts, optional

TOPPING:
2 cups miniature marshmallows
1 square (1 ounce) unsweetened chocolate, melted

1. In a heavy saucepan over medium heat, cook and stir chocolate and butter until melted; cool slightly. In a mixing bowl, beat eggs for 2 minutes. Gradually add sugar; beat until thick, about 3 minutes. Stir in chocolate mixture and vanilla. Fold in flour and nuts if desired.

2. Pour into two greased and floured 9-in. square baking pans. Bake at 350° for 25-30 minutes or until a toothpick inserted in the center comes out with moist crumbs (do not overbake). Sprinkle each pan with 1 cup of marshmallows. Broil until marshmallows are golden brown, about 30-60 seconds. Drizzle with melted chocolate.

YIELD: 4 dozen.

EDITOR'S NOTE: For easier cutting, refrigerate brownies for several hours.

crispy peanut butter treats

LISA HORNISH ⚑ GRAND FORKS AIR FORCE BASE, NORTH DAKOTA

I don't make these crispy bars very often because it's hard to stop eating them! The peanut butter ribbon in the middle makes them eye-catching at any party.

2 cups (12 ounces) semisweet chocolate chips
¾ cup peanut butter
7 cups crisp rice cereal
1 package (10 ounces) peanut butter chips
¼ cup butter
2 tablespoons water
½ teaspoon vanilla extract
1 cup confectioners' sugar

1. In a large microwave-safe bowl, heat chocolate chips and peanut butter, uncovered, on high for 45 seconds; stir. Microwave 15-30 seconds longer until chips are melted; stir until smooth. Stir in cereal until evenly coated. Pat half into a greased 13-in. x 9-in. x 2-in. dish.

2. In a microwave, heat peanut butter chips and butter on high for 45 seconds; stir. Microwave 10-15 seconds longer or until chips are melted; stir until smooth. Stir in water, vanilla and confectioners' sugar until smooth. Carefully spread over the cereal layer. Gently press remaining cereal mixture over peanut butter layer. Chill for at least 1 hour. Cut into squares.

YIELD: 3 dozen.

EDITOR'S NOTE: This recipe was tested in a 1,100-watt microwave.

raspberry patch crumb bars

LEANNA THORNE ⚑ LAKEWOOD, COLORADO

To give these fresh, fruity bars even more crunch, add a sprinkling of nuts to the yummy crumb topping. Everyone will want to indulge.

3 cups all-purpose flour
1½ cups sugar, *divided*
1 teaspoon baking powder
¼ teaspoon salt
¼ teaspoon ground cinnamon
1 cup shortening
2 eggs, lightly beaten
1 teaspoon almond extract
1 tablespoon cornstarch
4 cups fresh *or* frozen raspberries

1. In a large bowl, combine flour, 1 cup sugar, baking powder, salt and cinnamon. Cut in shortening until mixture resembles coarse crumbs. Stir in eggs and extract. Press two-thirds of the mixture into a greased 13-in. x 9-in. baking dish.
2. In a large bowl, combine the cornstarch and remaining sugar; add berries and gently toss. Spoon over the crust. Sprinkle with remaining crumb mixture.
3. Bake at 375° for 35-45 minutes or until bubbly and golden brown. Cool on a wire rack. Cut into bars. Store in the refrigerator.

YIELD: 3 dozen.

EDITOR'S NOTE: If using frozen raspberries, do not thaw before tossing with cornstarch mixture.

caramel butter-pecan bars

MARY JEAN HLAVAC ⚑ MCFARLAND, WISCONSIN

These melt-in-your-mouth bars are simply to die for. They go together in minutes, and even though the chocolate layer takes time to harden, these treats are definitely worth the wait.

2 cups all-purpose flour
1 cup packed brown sugar
¾ cup cold butter
1½ cups chopped pecans
1 jar (12 ounces) caramel ice cream topping, warmed
1 package (11½ ounces) milk chocolate chips

1. In a large bowl, combine the flour and brown sugar; cut in butter until crumbly. Press into an ungreased 13-in. x 9-in. baking dish. Top with pecans. Drizzle the caramel topping evenly over pecans.
2. Bake at 350° for 15-20 minutes or until caramel is bubbly. Place on a wire rack. Sprinkle with chocolate chips. Let stand for 5 minutes. Carefully spread chips over caramel layer. Cool at room temperature for at least 6 hours or until chocolate is set. Cut into bars.

YIELD: 4 dozen.

salty peanut squares

WANDA BORGEN ⚑ MINOT, NORTH DAKOTA

1 package (10 ounces) corn chips, lightly crushed, *divided*

1 cup unsalted peanuts, *divided*

1 cup light corn syrup

1 cup sugar

1 cup peanut butter

½ cup milk chocolate chips, melted

1. Place half of the corn chips and peanuts in a greased 13-in. x 9-in. pan; set aside. In a large saucepan, bring the corn syrup and sugar to a boil. Stir in peanut butter until blended. Drizzle half over corn chip mixture in pan.

2. Add remaining corn chips and peanuts to remaining syrup; stir until combined. Spoon over mixture in pan; press down lightly. Drizzle with melted chocolate. Cool before cutting.

YIELD: 2 dozen.

Kids and adults will gobble up these yummy granola bars. Take a batch of them to your next tailgate party and see for yourself.

chewy granola bars

DEENA MCCARTER ⌐ CORONACH, SASKATCHEWAN

6 cups quick-cooking oats
1½ cups dried fruit bits
1 cup packed brown sugar
1 cup butter, melted
1 cup corn syrup
½ cup miniature chocolate chips
½ cup flaked coconut
Vanilla frosting and yellow food coloring, optional

1. In a large bowl, combine first seven ingredients; mix well. Spread into a greased 15-in. x 10-in. x 1-in. baking pan. Bake at 350° for 20-25 minutes or until the edges are golden brown. Cool on a wire rack.
2. Use a knife to cut into squares or cookie cutters to cut into shapes. If desired, tint frosting and frost bars. Store in a covered container or wrap individually.
YIELD: about 3 dozen.

butterscotch popcorn bars

CAROL STONE ⚑ WAVERLY, TENNESSEE

Dotted with peanuts and raisins, these chewy squares are easy to whip together on the stovetop.

2 quarts unsalted popped popcorn
1 cup salted peanuts
1 cup raisins
½ cup butter
1 package (10½ ounces) miniature marshmallows
1 cup butterscotch chips

1. In a large bowl, combine the popcorn, peanuts and raisins. In a large saucepan over low heat, melt butter. Stir in the marshmallows and chips until melted and smooth.
2. Pour over popcorn mixture and stir until evenly coated. Immediately pour into a greased 13-in. x 9-in. x 2-in. pan and press down evenly. Cool before cutting.

YIELD: 3 dozen.

baby ruth cookies

ELINOR NIELD ⚑ SOQUEL, CALIFORNIA

Pack a few of these chewy delights the next time you're headed to a party. They taste just like the candy bar.

½ cup butter, softened
¾ cup sugar
1 egg
½ teaspoon vanilla extract
1⅓ cups all-purpose flour
½ teaspoon baking soda
½ teaspoon salt
2 Baby Ruth candy bars (2.1 ounces *each*), chopped

1. In a mixing bowl, cream butter and sugar. Add egg and vanilla; mix well. Combine flour, baking soda and salt; add to the creamed mixture. Stir in candy bars.
2. Drop by rounded teaspoonfuls 2 in. apart onto greased baking sheets. Bake at 350° for 10 minutes or until the edges are lightly browned. Immediately remove cookies to wire racks to cool.

YIELD: 4 dozen.

MAKE THEM THE SAME
For even baking, it's important that you make cookies the same size. Use a teaspoon or tablespoon from your flatware set or a small ice cream scoop.

These are so tasty, we bake them a few times a month. For a change of pace, use butterscotch chips or mix different ones together.

peanut butter chip cookies

ANNE WEGENER ⚑ SPRINGVILLE, INDIANA

½ cup butter, softened
½ cup peanut butter
¾ cup packed brown sugar
¼ cup sugar
1 egg
2 tablespoons milk
1 teaspoon vanilla extract
1¾ cups all-purpose flour
1 teaspoon baking soda
½ teaspoon salt
¾ cup semisweet chocolate chips
Additional sugar

1. In a mixing bowl, cream butter, peanut butter and sugar. Beat in egg, milk and vanilla. Combine the flour, baking soda and salt; add to creamed mixture and mix well. Stir in chocolate chips.
2. Roll into 1-in. balls; roll in additional sugar. Place 2 in. apart on ungreased baking sheets. Flatten if desired. Bake at 375° for 7-9 minutes or until golden brown. Remove to wire racks to cool.

YIELD: 4 dozen.

SWEET
TREATS

Everyone gets fired up when they see my Racetrack Cake. For the track and pit stop area, I use gray icing outlined with yellow frosting. Green glitter designates the grass areas, and miniature racecars look so cute speeding around the track.

racetrack cake

AMBER KIMMICH ⚐ POWHATAN, VIRGINIA

 1 package (18-1/4 ounces) white cake mix
 1 package (18-1/4 ounces) chocolate cake mix
 10 cups buttercream frosting
 Black, yellow and red food coloring
 Green edible glitter
 4 miniature cars
 2 miniature checkered flags

1. Prepare and bake each cake according to package directions, using greased 13-in. x 9-in. baking pans. Cool for 10 minutes before inverting onto wire racks to cool completely.

2. Transfer cakes to a covered board and position side by side. Frost tops of cakes with 5-1/3 cups of frosting. Tint 1-1/2 cups frosting black. Cut a small hole in the corner of a pastry or plastic bag; fill with black frosting. Outline edge of cake. Using a #17 star tip, pipe a checkered pattern on sides of cake with 1 cup white frosting and remaining black frosting.

3. Tint 2/3 cup frosting gray; create an oval racetrack in middle of cake. Tint 3/4 cup frosting yellow; pipe lines around track and infield. For grass, sprinkle green glitter on infield.

4. Tint 1/2 cup frosting red; pipe lettering on corners of cake. Position the cars and checkered flags as desired.

YIELD: 24-30 servings.

EDITOR'S NOTE: Edible glitter is available from Wilton Industries. Call 800-794-5866 or visit wilton.com.

old-fashioned apple cake

IOLA EGLE ⚑ MCCOOK, NEBRASKA

Everyone enjoys biting into this moist, dark cake—they're greeted with an abundance of apples, nuts and chocolate!

1 cup butter, softened
2 cups sugar
3 eggs
½ cup water
1 tablespoon vanilla extract
¼ teaspoon almond extract
2½ cups all-purpose flour
2 tablespoons baking cocoa
1 teaspoon baking powder
¾ teaspoon ground cardamom
¾ teaspoon ground cinnamon
½ teaspoon ground allspice
½ teaspoon baking soda
½ teaspoon salt
2 medium tart apples, peeled and shredded
1 cup chopped walnuts
½ cup semisweet chocolate chips

CARDAMOM SUGAR:
½ cup sugar
¼ teaspoon ground cardamom

1. In a mixing bowl, cream butter and sugar until fluffy. Add eggs, one at a time, beating well after each addition. Beat in water and extracts. Combine dry ingredients; add to creamed mixture. Stir in apples, nuts and chips. Pour into a greased and floured 10-in. fluted tube pan.
2. Bake at 325° for 60-70 minutes or until a toothpick inserted near the center comes out clean. Cool in pan for 10 minutes; remove to a wire rack. Combine sugar and cardamom in a blender; process for 1 minute. Sprinkle 3-5 tablespoons over cooled cake. Store remaining sugar in an airtight container for another use.

YIELD: 12-15 servings.

chocolate snack cake

DEBI PESCHKA ⚑ BROKEN ARROW, OKLAHOMA

This is a moist, delicious snack cake, so good that icing is not necessary. It never fails to satisfy my sweet tooth.

1 cup boiling water
¼ cup butter
1 egg
1 teaspoon vanilla extract
1 cup all-purpose flour
1 cup sugar
3 tablespoons baking cocoa
1 teaspoon baking powder
½ teaspoon baking soda
¼ teaspoon salt
Confectioners' sugar

1. In a mixing bowl, beat water and butter until butter is melted. Beat in egg and vanilla. Combine flour, sugar, cocoa, baking powder, baking soda and salt; add to the egg mixture. Beat for 2 minutes.
2. Pour into a greased 8-in. square baking pan. Bake at 350° for 25-30 minutes or until a toothpick inserted near the center comes out clean. Cool on a wire rack. Dust with confectioners' sugar.

YIELD: 9 servings.

picnic cupcakes

FLORENCE LEINWEBER ⚐ ENDICOTT, WASHINGTON

These tender cupcakes don't need frosting, so they're perfect for a picnic or traveling.

1 package (18½ ounces) chocolate *or* yellow cake mix

FILLING:

1 package (8 ounces) cream cheese, softened

1 egg

⅓ cup sugar

1 cup (6 ounces) semisweet chocolate chips

1. Mix cake according to package directions. Spoon batter into 24 greased or paper-lined muffin cups, filling two-thirds full.
2. In a mixing bowl, beat cream cheese, egg and sugar until smooth. Fold in the chips. Drop by tablespoonfuls into batter. Bake at 350° for 20 minutes or until a toothpick inserted near the center of cupcakes comes out clean.

YIELD: 2 dozen.

coconut cupcakes

JUDY WILSON ⚐ SUN CITY WEST, ARIZONA

I took these yummy treats to a picnic for our computer club one year, and they went like hotcakes! I should have made a double batch. With their creamy topping and sprinkling of coconut, they appeal to kids and adults.

1½ cups butter, softened

2 cups sugar

5 eggs

1 to 1½ teaspoons vanilla extract

1 to 1½ teaspoons almond extract

3 cups all-purpose flour

1 teaspoon baking powder

½ teaspoon baking soda

½ teaspoon salt

1 cup buttermilk

1¼ cups flaked coconut

CREAM CHEESE FROSTING:

1 package (8 ounces) cream cheese, softened

¾ cup butter, softened

½ teaspoon vanilla extract

½ teaspoon almond extract

2¾ cups confectioners' sugar

Additional flaked coconut, toasted

1. In a large mixing bowl, cream butter and sugar until light and fluffy. Add eggs, one at a time, beating well after each addition. Beat in extracts. Combine the flour, baking powder, baking soda and salt; add to creamed mixture alternately with buttermilk. Fold in coconut.
2. Fill paper-lined muffin cups two-thirds full. Bake at 350° for 18-20 minutes or until a toothpick comes out clean. Cool for 10 minutes before removing from pans to wire racks to cool completely.
3. For frosting, in a mixing bowl, beat the cream cheese, butter and extracts until smooth. Gradually beat in the confectioners' sugar. Frost the cupcakes; sprinkle with toasted coconut.

YIELD: 2½ dozen.

I received this recipe from my sister more than 25 years ago, and it's still popular in our family.

blushing apple cream pie

MARNY EULBERG WHEAT RIDGE, COLORADO

¾ cup heavy whipping cream
2 tablespoons red-hot candies
½ teaspoon ground cinnamon
1 cup sugar
¼ cup all-purpose flour
2 tablespoons white vinegar
4½ cups thinly sliced peeled tart apples
Pastry for double-crust pie (9 inches)

1. In a mixing bowl, combine first six ingredients; mix well. Add apples and stir gently to mix. Pour into a pastry-lined pie plate. Roll out remaining pastry to fit top of pie.
2. Cut slits in top crust; place over apples. Seal and flute edges. Bake at 400° for 50 minutes or until pastry is golden and apples are tender.

YIELD: 8 servings.

buttermilk pound cake

GRACIE HANCHEY ⚐ DE RIDDER, LOUISIANA

1 cup butter, softened
3 cups sugar
4 eggs
3 cups all-purpose flour
¼ teaspoon baking soda
1 cup buttermilk
1 teaspoon vanilla extract
Confectioners' sugar, optional

1. In a mixing bowl, cream butter and sugar. Add the eggs, one at a time, beating well after each addition. Combine flour and baking soda; add alternately with the buttermilk and beat well. Stir in vanilla.

2. Pour into a greased and floured 10-in. fluted tube pan. Bake at 325° for 1 hour and 10 minutes or until a toothpick inserted near the center comes out clean. Cool in pan for 15 minutes before removing to a wire rack to cool completely. If desired, dust with confectioners' sugar.

YIELD: 16-20 servings.

magic wands

RENEE SCHWEBACH ⚑ DUMONT, MINNESOTA

These fun and colorful magic wands don't take a magician to make. You can change the colors for any theme party, too!

1½ cups vanilla *or* white chips
1 package (10 ounces) pretzel rods
Colored candy stars *or* sprinkles
Colored sugar *or* edible glitter

1. In a microwave, melt chips; stir until smooth. Dip each pretzel rod halfway into melted chips; shake off the excess. Sprinkle with candy stars and colored sugar. Place on a wire rack for 15 minutes or until set. Store in an airtight container.
YIELD: 2 dozen.

peanut butter sheet cake

BRENDA JACKSON ⚑ GARDEN CITY, KANSAS

I received this recipe from a minister's wife, and my family loves it.

2 cups all-purpose flour
2 cups sugar
1 teaspoon baking soda
½ teaspoon salt
1 cup water
¾ cup butter
½ cup chunky peanut butter
¼ cup canola oil
2 eggs
½ cup buttermilk
1 teaspoon vanilla extract
GLAZE:
⅔ cup sugar
⅓ cup evaporated milk
1 tablespoon butter
⅓ cup chunky peanut butter
⅓ cup miniature marshmallows
½ teaspoon vanilla extract

1. In a large mixing bowl, combine flour, sugar, baking soda and salt; set aside. In a saucepan, bring water and butter to a boil; stir in peanut butter and oil until blended. Add to dry ingredients; mix well. Combine eggs, buttermilk and vanilla; add to peanut butter mixture. Mix well.
2. Pour into a greased 15-in. x 10-in. x 1-in. baking pan. Bake at 350° for 16-20 minutes or until a toothpick inserted near the center comes out clean.
3. Meanwhile, combine sugar, milk and butter in a saucepan. Bring to a boil, stirring constantly; cook and stir for 2 minutes. Remove from the heat; stir in the peanut butter, marshmallows and vanilla until marshmallows are melted. Spoon over warm cake and carefully spread over the top. Cool completely.
YIELD: 20-24 servings.

EDITOR'S NOTE: Reduced-fat or generic brands of peanut butter are not recommended for this recipe.

These moist, old-fashioned molasses cupcakes were my grandmother's specialty. To keep them from disappearing too quickly, she used to store them out of sight. Somehow, we always figured out her hiding places!

shoofly cupcakes

BETH ADAMS ⚐ JACKSONVILLE, FLORIDA

4   cups all-purpose flour
2   cups packed brown sugar
¼   teaspoon salt
1   cup cold butter, cubed
2   teaspoons baking soda
2   cups boiling water
1   cup molasses

1. In a large bowl, combine the flour, brown sugar and salt. Cut in butter until crumbly. Set aside 1 cup for topping. Add baking soda to remaining crumb mixture. Stir in water and molasses.
2. Fill paper-lined muffin cups two-thirds full. Sprinkle with reserved crumb mixture. Bake at 350° for 20-25 minutes or until a toothpick comes out clean. Cool for 10 minutes before removing from pans to wire racks to cool.

YIELD: 2 dozen.

EDITOR'S NOTE: This recipe does not use eggs.

mom's peach pie

SALLY HOLBROOK ⚑ PASADENA, CALIFORNIA

1 egg white
1 unbaked pastry shell (9 inches)
¾ cup all-purpose flour
½ cup packed brown sugar
⅓ cup sugar
¼ cup cold butter, cut into 6 pieces
6 cups sliced peeled fresh peaches

1. Beat egg white until foamy; brush over bottom and sides of the pastry. In a small bowl, combine the flour and sugars; cut in butter until mixture resembles fine crumbs.

2. Sprinkle two-thirds into the bottom of pastry; top with peaches. Sprinkle with remaining crumb mixture. Bake at 375° for 40-45 minutes or until filling is bubbly and peaches are tender.

YIELD: 6-8 servings.

A delightful summertime pie, this dessert is ripe with fresh peach flavor. Each sweet slice is packed with old-fashioned appeal. The streusel topping makes this pie a little different than the ordinary and adds homemade flair.

football cake

RUTH ANDREWSON ⚑ LEAVENWORTH, WASHINGTON

This delicious chocolate cake will be a hit at a Super Bowl gathering, taken along for tailgating with the gang, or even as the star at a football fan's birthday party!

½ cup boiling water
1 bar (4 ounces) German sweet chocolate, chopped
1 cup butter, softened
2 cups sugar
4 eggs, *separated*
1 teaspoon vanilla extract
2½ cups cake flour
1 teaspoon baking soda
½ teaspoon salt
1 cup buttermilk

FROSTING/FILLING:
1 cup sugar
1 tablespoon cornstarch
1 cup evaporated milk
3 egg yolks, beaten
½ cup butter, melted
1 teaspoon vanilla extract
2½ cups flaked coconut

Green food coloring
1 can (16 ounces) vanilla frosting
2 tablespoons baking cocoa
6 white pipe cleaners

1. In a small bowl, pour water over chocolate; set aside. In a large bowl, cream butter and sugar until light and fluffy. Add egg yolks, one at a time, beating well after each. Add cooled chocolate and vanilla. Combine flour, baking soda and salt; add to creamed mixture alternately with buttermilk.

2. In another bowl, beat egg whites until soft peaks form. Fold into batter. Grease and flour one 8-in. round baking pan and one 13-in. x 9-in. baking pan. If desired, line bottoms with waxed paper; grease and flour paper.

3. Pour 2½ cups batter into round baking pan. Pour the remaining batter into the rectangular pan. Bake at 350° for 25-30 minutes (round) and 35-40 minutes (rectangular) or until a toothpick comes out clean. Cool in pans for 10 minutes before removing to wire racks. Remove waxed paper and cool completely.

4. For frosting, combine sugar and cornstarch in a saucepan. Stir in milk and egg yolks until smooth. Add butter; bring to a boil over medium heat until thickened and bubbly, stirring constantly. Boil for 2 minutes. Remove from the heat; stir in vanilla and coconut.

5. Cool completely; set aside ¾ cup. Tint remaining frosting green. Place rectangular cake on serving platter; frost top and sides with green frosting. Place ½ cup vanilla frosting in a decorator tube; pipe yard lines across cake.

6. For football, slice a 2-in.-wide strip from the center of round cake (save for another use). Spread reserved coconut frosting between layers of cake, forming the football. Place cut side down on a flat surface.

7. Combine remaining vanilla frosting with cocoa; frost top and sides of football. Use decorator tube to pipe laces on football. With a large spatula, carefully lift football and place on the green cake. Use three pipe cleaners at each end of cake to form goalposts.

YIELD: 20-24 servings.

dirt dessert

KRISTI LINTON ⚑ BAY CITY, MICHIGAN

1 package (8 ounces) cream cheese, softened

¼ cup butter, softened

1 cup confectioners' sugar

3½ cups cold 2% milk

2 packages (3.4 ounces *each*) instant vanilla pudding mix

1 carton (12 ounces) frozen whipped topping, thawed

1 package (16.6 ounces) cream-filled chocolate sandwich cookies

Shaved white chocolate, optional

1. In a large bowl, beat cream cheese, butter and confectioners' sugar until smooth. In a large bowl, whisk milk and pudding mixes for 2 minutes; let stand for 2 minutes or until soft-set. Gradually stir into the cream cheese mixture. Fold in whipped topping.

2. Spread 1⅓ cups of crushed cookies into an ungreased 13-in. x 9-in. dish. Layer with half of the pudding mixture and half of the remaining cookies. Repeat layers. Refrigerate for at least 1 hour before serving. Serve with shaved white chocolate if desired.

YIELD: 20 servings.

Folks who enjoy homemade chocolate cupcakes are even more impressed when they bite into these treats and find a fluffy cream filling. These are great in a lunch box.

cream-filled cupcakes

EDIE DESPAIN LOGAN, UTAH

3 cups all-purpose flour
2 cups sugar
⅓ cup baking cocoa
2 teaspoons baking soda
1 teaspoon salt
2 eggs
1 cup milk
1 cup canola oil
1 cup water
1 teaspoon vanilla extract
FILLING:
¼ cup butter, softened
¼ cup shortening
2 cups confectioners' sugar
3 tablespoons milk
1 teaspoon vanilla extract
Pinch salt
Chocolate frosting

1. In a mixing bowl, combine the first five ingredients. Add eggs, milk, oil, water and vanilla. Beat until smooth, about 2 minutes. Fill paper-lined muffin cups half full.
2. Bake at 375° for 15-20 minutes or until a toothpick inserted near the center comes out clean. Remove from pans to wire racks to cool completely.
3. In a mixing bowl, combine butter, shortening, confectioners' sugar, milk, vanilla and salt; beat until fluffy, about 5 minutes.
4. Insert a very small tip into a pastry or plastic bag; fill with cream filling. Push the tip through the bottom of paper liner to fill each cupcake. Frost tops with chocolate frosting.
YIELD: 3 dozen.

cherry crumb pie

ANDREA CHAPMAN 🏴 HELENA, OKLAHOMA

I keep a file of simple recipes and a variety of ingredients on hand so my grandkids can choose what they want when they stop by. This is a most-requested treat!

1 tablespoon cornstarch
1 tablespoon cold water
1 can (21 ounces) cherry pie filling
1 graham cracker crust (9 inches)
TOPPING:
⅓ cup all-purpose flour
⅓ cup quick-cooking oats
2 tablespoons sugar
2 tablespoons brown sugar
3 tablespoons cold butter

1. In a bowl, combine cornstarch and water until smooth. Stir in pie filling. Pour into crust. For topping, combine flour, oats and sugars in a small bowl; cut in the butter until crumbly. Sprinkle over filling.
2. Bake at 375° for 35-40 minutes or until crust is golden brown and filling is bubbly. Cool on a wire rack; refrigerate until chilled.

YIELD: 6-8 servings.

luscious lemon cake roll

DARLENE BRENDEN 🏴 SALEM, OREGON

A co-worker shared the recipe for this elegant cake roll. It's perfect for rounding out a special meal. Plus, it travels well for take-and-go gatherings.

4 eggs, *separated*
¾ cup sugar, *divided*
1 tablespoon canola oil
1 teaspoon lemon extract
⅔ cup cake flour
1 teaspoon baking powder
¼ teaspoon salt
Confectioners' sugar
CREAMY LEMON FILLING:
1 can (14 ounces) sweetened condensed milk
⅓ cup lemon juice
2 teaspoons grated lemon peel
7 drops yellow liquid food coloring, *divided*
1½ cups whipped topping
½ teaspoon water
½ cup flaked coconut

1. Line a greased 15-in. x 10-in. x 1-in. baking pan with waxed paper and grease the paper; set aside. In a large mixing bowl, beat egg yolks until lemon-colored. Gradually beat in ¼ cup sugar. Stir in oil and lemon extract; set aside.
2. In another large mixing bowl, beat egg whites on medium speed until soft peaks form. Gradually add the remaining sugar, 2 tablespoons at a time, beating until stiff glossy peaks form and sugar is dissolved. Fold into egg yolk mixture. Combine the flour, baking powder and salt; fold into egg mixture.
3. Transfer to prepared pan. Bake at 375° for 10-12 minutes or until cake springs back when lightly touched. Cool for 5 minutes. Turn cake onto a kitchen towel dusted with confectioners' sugar. Gently peel off waxed paper. Roll up cake in towel, starting with a short side. Cool completely on a wire rack.
4. For filling, in a small bowl, combine the milk, lemon juice, lemon peel and 5 drops of food coloring. Fold in whipped topping. Unroll cake; spread half of the filling over cake to within 1 in. of edges. Roll up again. Place seam side down on a platter. Spread remaining filling over cake.
5. In a large resealable plastic bag, combine water and remaining food coloring; add coconut. Seal bag and shake to tint. Sprinkle the coconut over cake. Refrigerate for at least 2 hours before serving. Refrigerate leftovers.

YIELD: 10 servings.

favorite chocolate sheet cake

MARY LEWIS ⚑ ESCONDIDO, CALIFORNIA

My mother adapted this family pleaser from a recipe for vanilla cake that was in a church cookbook.
The cake is so flavorful, it wouldn't need frosting—but I always feel you can never have enough chocolate!

1	cup butter, softened
2	cups sugar
4	eggs
2	teaspoons vanilla extract
2¼	cups cake flour
1	teaspoon baking soda
1	teaspoon salt
1	cup buttermilk
3	squares (1 ounce each) bittersweet chocolate, melted

FROSTING:

¼	cup baking cocoa
⅓	cup milk
½	cup butter
1	teaspoon vanilla extract
3½	cups confectioners' sugar

1. In a mixing bowl, cream butter and sugar. Add eggs, one at a time, beating well after each addition. Beat in vanilla. Combine the flour, baking soda and salt; add to creamed mixture alternately with buttermilk. Beat in chocolate until combined. Pour into a greased 15-in. x 10-in. x 1-in. baking pan. Bake at 350° for 23-27 minutes or until a toothpick inserted near the center comes out clean. Cool on a wire rack.

2. For frosting, in a saucepan, bring cocoa and milk to a boil over medium heat, stirring constantly. Remove from the heat; stir in butter and vanilla until butter is melted. Whisk in confectioners' sugar until smooth. Drizzle over cake and spread quickly. Let stand until set.

YIELD: 24 servings.

macaroon apple cobbler

PHYLLIS HINCK ⚑ LAKE CITY, MINNESOTA

Especially when I'm just serving a dessert, I like to prepare this. It's great as a treat for get-togethers.

4	cups thinly sliced peeled tart apples
⅓	cup sugar
½	teaspoon ground cinnamon
½	cup flaked coconut
¼	cup chopped pecans

TOPPING:

½	cup butter, softened
½	cup sugar
1	egg
½	teaspoon vanilla extract
¾	cup all-purpose flour
¼	teaspoon baking powder

1. Place the apples in an ungreased 9-in. pie plate. Combine sugar and cinnamon; sprinkle over apples. Top with coconut and pecans; set aside.

2. In a mixing bowl, cream butter and sugar. Add egg and vanilla; mix well. Combine the flour and baking powder; add to the creamed mixture until blended. Carefully spread over apples. Bake at 350° for 25-30 minutes or until top is golden brown and fruit is tender. Serve warm.

YIELD: 6-8 servings.

A crust of vanilla wafer crumbs and crushed peanuts provides this cool and creamy dessert with an extra tasty base. It's almost guaranteed that I'll bring home an empty pan when I take it to a potluck.

chocolate peanut torte

ARDYCE PIEHL ⚑ WISCONSIN DELLS, WISCONSIN

2 cups crushed vanilla wafers

⅓ cup butter, melted

1 cup salted peanuts, finely chopped, *divided*

1 package (8 ounces) cream cheese, softened

1 cup confectioners' sugar

½ cup peanut butter

4 cups whipped topping, *divided*

3 cups cold milk

2 packages (3.9 ounces *each*) instant chocolate pudding mix

1 milk chocolate candy bar (1.55 ounces), grated

1. In a large bowl, combine the wafer crumbs, butter and ⅔ cup peanuts. Press into an ungreased 13-in. x 9-in. x 2-in. baking dish. Bake at 350° for 8-10 minutes or until lightly browned. Cool.

2. In a large mixing bowl, beat the cream cheese, sugar and peanut butter until smooth. Fold in 2 cups of whipped topping. Spread over crust.

3. In another large mixing bowl, beat milk and pudding mixes on low for 2 minutes. Carefully spread over the cream cheese layer. Cover and refrigerate for 4-6 hours.

4. Just before serving, carefully spread remaining topping over the pudding layer. Sprinkle with grated chocolate and the remaining peanuts.

YIELD: 16-20 servings.

If you like chocolate-covered pretzels, you'll love these simple snacks. They're fun to make any time of year because you can color-coordinate the M&M's to each holiday or to your favorite team's colors!

chocolate pretzel rings

KIM SCURIO ⚑ CAROL STREAM, ILLINOIS

48 to 50 pretzel rings *or* mini twists
1 package (8 ounces) milk chocolate kisses
¼ cup M&M's

1. Place the pretzels on greased baking sheets; place a chocolate kiss in the center of each ring. Bake at 275° for 2-3 minutes or until chocolate is softened. Remove from the oven.
2. Place an M&M on each, pressing down slightly so chocolate fills the ring. Refrigerate for 5-10 minutes or until chocolate is firm. Store in an airtight container at room temperature.
YIELD: about 4 dozen.

chocolate caramel apples

LINDA SMITH FREDERICK, MARYLAND

1 package (14 ounces) caramels
2 tablespoons water
4 wooden sticks
4 large tart apples
2 cups chopped pecans *or* peanuts
1 cup (6 ounces) semisweet chocolate chips
1 teaspoon shortening
1 cup English toffee bits *or* almond brickle chips

1. In a microwave-safe bowl, combine the caramels and water. Microwave, uncovered, on high for 45 seconds; stir. Microwave 20-40 seconds longer or until the caramels are melted. Insert wooden sticks into apples; dip apples into the caramel mixture, turning to coat. Coat with nuts; set on waxed paper to cool.

2. Melt chocolate chips and shortening; drizzle over apples. Sprinkle with toffee bits. Set on waxed paper to cool. Cut into wedges to serve.

YIELD: 8 servings.

EDITOR'S NOTE: This recipe was tested in an 1,100-watt microwave.

Caramel apples get dressed up with chocolate, nuts and toffee bits. Cut into wedges, these scrumptious apples are easy to share.

cherry berry pie

WANDA VAN VOORHIS ⚑ PLAIN CITY, OHIO

*I'm always looking for new treats to serve my family, but this dessert is
one I turn to again and again, especially in summer.*

1½ cups sugar
¼ cup plus 2 teaspoons quick-cooking tapioca
⅛ teaspoon salt
2½ cups fresh *or* frozen pitted tart cherries, thawed
1½ cups fresh *or* frozen unsweetened raspberries, thawed
1 teaspoon lemon juice
Pastry for double-crust pie (9 inches)
1 tablespoon butter

1. In a large bowl, combine the sugar, tapioca and salt. Add the cherries, raspberries and lemon juice; gently toss to coat. Let stand for 15 minutes.
2. Line a 9-in. pie plate with bottom pastry. Trim to 1 in. beyond edge of pie plate. Pour filling into crust; dot with butter. Roll out remaining pastry; make a lattice crust. Trim, seal and flute edges.
3. Cover edges loosely with foil. Bake at 400° for 30 minutes. Remove foil; bake 5-10 minutes longer or until crust is golden brown and filling is bubbly. Cool on a wire rack.

YIELD: 6-8 servings.

chocolate peanut butter cake

BRENDA MELANCON ⚑ GONZALES, LOUISIANA

*The two great flavors of chocolate and peanut butter come together in this
oh-so-easy and delicious cake. Kids of every age will be all over this one!*

2 cups miniature marshmallows
1 package (18¼ ounces) chocolate cake mix
1¼ cups water
¾ cup peanut butter
⅓ cup canola oil
3 eggs
1 cup (6 ounces) semisweet chocolate chips

1. Sprinkle marshmallows into a greased 13-in. x 9-in. baking pan. In a large bowl, combine the cake mix, water, peanut butter, oil and eggs; beat on low speed for 30 seconds. Beat on medium for 2 minutes or until smooth. Pour over marshmallows; sprinkle with chocolate chips.
2. Bake at 350° for 30-35 minutes or until a toothpick inserted near the center comes out clean. Cool on a wire rack.

YIELD: 12-15 servings.

Highlight the natural sweetness of peak summertime fruit with brown sugar, butter and a squeeze of lemon juice. Foil packets make this a go-anywhere dessert.

grilled peaches 'n' berries

SHARON BICKETT ⚑ CHESTER, SOUTH CAROLINA

2 medium ripe peaches, halved and pitted
½ cup fresh blueberries
1 tablespoon brown sugar
2 teaspoons lemon juice
4 teaspoons butter

1. Place two peach halves, cut side up, on each of two double thicknesses of heavy-duty foil (12 in. square). Sprinkle each with blueberries, brown sugar and lemon juice; dot with butter. Fold foil around peaches and seal tightly.

2. Grill, covered, over medium-low heat for 18-20 minutes or until tender. Open foil carefully to allow steam to escape.

YIELD: 2 servings.

Folks love these rich, yummy cupcakes at parties. They're so easy to make because the mini peanut butter cups eliminate the need to frost them.

peanut butter cup cupcakes

HEIDI HARRINGTON ✐ STEUBEN, MAINE

⅓ cup shortening
⅓ cup peanut butter
1¼ cups packed brown sugar
2 eggs
1 teaspoon vanilla extract
1¾ cups all-purpose flour
1¾ teaspoons baking powder
1 teaspoon salt
1 cup milk
16 miniature peanut butter cups

1. In a large mixing bowl, cream the shortening, peanut butter and brown sugar until light and fluffy. Add eggs, one at a time, beating well after each addition. Add vanilla. Combine the flour, baking powder and salt; add to creamed mixture alternately with milk.

2. Fill paper-lined muffin cups with ¼ cup of batter. Press a peanut butter cup into the center of each until top edge is even with batter. Bake at 350° for 22-24 minutes or until a toothpick inserted on an angle toward the center of the cupcakes comes out clean. Cool for 10 minutes before removing from pans to wire racks to cool completely.

YIELD: 16 cupcakes.

ginger pear pie

DELILAH STAUFFER ⚐ MT. PLEASANT MILLS, PENNSYLVANIA

My mother, who collected many recipes over the years, made this delicious pie often.

3 tablespoons cornstarch
¼ teaspoon ground ginger
½ cup water
½ cup dark corn syrup
1 teaspoon lemon juice
⅛ teaspoon grated lemon peel
4 large pears, peeled and thinly sliced
1 tablespoon butter
1 unbaked pastry shell (9 inches)

TOPPING:
½ cup all-purpose flour
¼ cup packed brown sugar
⅛ teaspoon ground ginger
¼ cup cold butter
¼ cup chopped pecans

1. In a saucepan, combine the first six ingredients until blended. Gently stir in pears. Bring to a boil over medium heat, stirring occasionally; boil for 1 minute. Add butter. Pour into pastry shell.

2. For topping, combine flour, brown sugar and ginger in bowl. Cut in butter until mixture resembles coarse crumbs. Stir in pecans. Sprinkle over pears. Bake at 425° for 20-25 minutes or until topping is golden brown.

YIELD: 6 servings.

chocolate chip caramel cake

MICHELE VANDEWERKER ⚐ ROSEBOOM, NEW YORK

When I want to serve a treat that's pretty and delicious, I make this scrumptious cake. Dotted with chocolate chips and topped with caramel icing, pecans and a chocolate drizzle, it's absolutely irresistible!

1 package (18¼ ounces) white cake mix
1½ cups vanilla yogurt
4 egg whites
1 teaspoon baking soda
½ teaspoon baking powder
1 cup (6 ounces) miniature semisweet chocolate chips

CARAMEL TOPPING:
¼ cup butter, cubed
1 cup confectioners' sugar
⅓ cup packed brown sugar
2 to 3 tablespoons evaporated milk
½ teaspoon vanilla extract
¼ cup chopped pecans

CHOCOLATE GLAZE:
¼ cup semisweet chocolate chips
½ teaspoon shortening

1. In a large mixing bowl, beat the first five ingredients on medium speed for 2 minutes. Stir in chocolate chips. Spread into a well-greased and floured 10-in. fluted tube pan.

2. Bake at 350° for 50-55 minutes or until a toothpick inserted near the center comes out clean. Cool for 10 minutes before removing from pan to a wire rack to cool completely.

3. For topping, in a small heavy saucepan, cook butter over medium heat for 5-7 minutes or until golden brown. Pour into a small mixing bowl and beat in the confectioners' sugar, brown sugar, milk and vanilla. Drizzle over cake. Sprinkle with nuts.

4. In a microwave, melt chips and shortening; stir until smooth. Drizzle over top.

YIELD: 12-16 servings.

play ball cake

SUE GRONHOLZ ⟶ BEAVER DAM, WISCONSIN

You won't need fancy pans to make this sporting dessert. Our kids and their cousins all wanted pieces that had the red licorice lacing! Fresh, pliable licorice works the best for forming the laces on the curved ball cake.

1/2 cup shortening
1-1/2 cups sugar
2 eggs
1 teaspoon vanilla extract
2-1/2 cups cake flour
2 teaspoons baking powder
1/2 teaspoon salt
1 cup milk

FROSTING:
1/2 cup shortening
1/2 cup butter, softened
3 cups confectioners' sugar
4 tablespoons milk, *divided*
1/2 teaspoon vanilla extract
1/4 teaspoon almond extract
Dash salt
1/4 cup baking cocoa
Shoestring red licorice

1. In a large bowl, cream shortening and sugar until light and fluffy. Add eggs, one at a time, beating well after each. Beat in vanilla. Combine the flour, baking powder and salt; add alternately with milk to the creamed mixture, beating well after each addition. Pour 1-1/2 cups batter into a greased and floured 3-cup ovenproof bowl.

2. Pour remaining batter into a greased and floured 9-in. round baking pan. Bake both cakes at 325° for 40-45 minutes or until a toothpick inserted near the center comes out clean. Cool for 10 minutes before removing to wire racks to cool completely.

3. For frosting, in a large bowl, beat the shortening, butter and confectioners' sugar until smooth. Beat in 3 tablespoons milk, extracts and salt until smooth. Set aside 1 cup.

4. To remaining frosting, beat in cocoa and remaining milk. Cut a 3-in. x 1-in. oval for the thumb opening from an edge of the 9-in. cake. Place cake on an 11-in. covered board. Frost with chocolate frosting.

5. With four pieces of licorice, form two crosses over thumb opening for laces in mitt. Frost the rounded cake with white frosting. Use licorice pieces to form laces of ball. Place on mitt cake opposite the thumb opening.

YIELD: 8-10 servings.

MIXING CAKE BATTER
Adding dry and wet ingredients alternately to cake batter helps to limit beating. Overbeating can cause the cake's texture to become tough. In general, plan to alternate wet and dry ingredients about three times.

hot quick banana boats

SHEILA PARKER ⚑ RENO, NEVADA

These delicious warm bananas are great on campouts or in the backyard. You can eat them right out of the foil bowl, which makes cleanup easy.

4 large unpeeled bananas
8 teaspoons semisweet chocolate chips
8 teaspoons trail mix
¼ cup miniature marshmallows

1. Place each banana on a 12-in. square of foil; crimp and shape foil around the bananas so they sit flat.
2. Cut each banana lengthwise about ½ in. deep, leaving ½ in. uncut at both ends. Gently pull each banana peel open, forming a pocket. Fill pockets with chocolate chips, trail mix and marshmallows.
3. Grill bananas, covered, over medium heat for 4-5 minutes or until marshmallows are melted and golden brown.

YIELD: 4 servings.

cocoa cola cake

ANNA BAKER ☞ BLAINE, WASHINGTON

2 cups all-purpose flour
2 cups sugar
1 teaspoon baking soda
1 cup butter
3 tablespoons baking cocoa
1 cup cola
½ cup buttermilk
2 eggs, beaten
1 teaspoon vanilla extract
1 cup miniature marshmallows
ICING:
½ cup butter
2 to 3 tablespoons baking cocoa
6 tablespoons cola
3¼ cups confectioners' sugar
1 cup coarsely chopped nuts

1. In a mixing bowl, combine the flour, sugar and baking soda; set aside. In a saucepan, bring butter, cocoa and cola to a boil; stir into dry ingredients. Stir in buttermilk, eggs, vanilla and marshmallows; mix well. Pour into a greased 13-in. x 9-in. x 2-in. baking pan.
2. Bake at 350° for 35 minutes or until a toothpick inserted near the center comes out clean. For icing, combine butter, cocoa and cola in a saucepan; bring to a boil. Remove from heat; stir in confectioners' sugar and mix well. Spread over hot cake. Sprinkle with nuts. Cool before cutting.
YIELD: 8-10 servings.

buttermilk chocolate cupcakes

ELLEN MOORE 🏁 SPRINGFIELD, NEW HAMPSHIRE

½ cup butter, softened

1½ cups sugar

2 eggs

1 teaspoon vanilla extract

1½ cups all-purpose flour

½ cup baking cocoa

1 teaspoon baking soda

¼ teaspoon salt

½ cup buttermilk

½ cup water

FROSTING:

½ cup butter, softened

3¾ cups confectioners' sugar

2 squares (1 ounce *each*) unsweetened chocolate, melted

2 tablespoons evaporated milk

1 teaspoon vanilla extract

¼ teaspoon salt

Chocolate sprinkles

1. In a large mixing bowl, cream butter and sugar until light and fluffy. Add eggs, one at a time, beating well after each addition. Beat in vanilla. Combine the flour, cocoa, baking soda and salt. Add dry ingredients to creamed mixture alternately with buttermilk and water.

2. Fill paper-lined muffin cups two-thirds full. Bake at 375° for 15-20 minutes or until a toothpick comes out clean. Cool for 10 minutes before removing from pans to wire racks to cool completely.

3. For frosting, in a small mixing bowl, beat butter and confectioners' sugar until smooth. Beat in the melted chocolate, milk, vanilla and salt. Frost cupcakes and garnish with chocolate sprinkles.

YIELD: 2 dozen.

Good any time of the year, cupcakes make a great get-up-and-go treat for summer baseball games or fall football parties.

carrot sheet cake

DOTTIE COSGROVE ⚐ SOUTH EL MONTE, CALIFORNIA

We sold pieces of this cake at an art show, and before long, sold out of the 10 cakes we had made!

4 eggs
1 cup canola oil
2 cups sugar
2 cups all-purpose flour
2 teaspoons baking soda
¼ teaspoon baking powder
2 teaspoons ground cinnamon
½ teaspoon salt
3 cups shredded carrots
⅔ cup chopped walnuts

FROSTING:

1 package (8 ounces) cream cheese, softened
½ cup butter, softened
1 teaspoon vanilla extract
4 cups confectioners' sugar
⅔ cup chopped walnuts

1. In a mixing bowl, beat eggs, oil and sugar until smooth. Combine flour, baking soda, baking powder, cinnamon and salt; add to egg mixture and beat well. Stir in carrots and walnuts.
2. Pour into a greased 15-in. x 10-in. x 1-in. baking pan. Bake at 350° for 35 minutes or until a toothpick inserted near the center comes out clean. Cool on a wire rack.
3. For frosting, beat cream cheese, butter and vanilla in a mixing bowl until smooth; beat in sugar. Spread over cake. Sprinkle with nuts.

YIELD: 24-30 servings.

dipped fruit on a stick

PAULA MARCHESE ⚐ ROCKY POINT, NEW YORK

Our five grown sons loved these when they were tots. Nowadays, it's our grandchildren who request the flavorful snacks.

2 cups (12 ounces) semisweet chocolate chips
2 tablespoons shortening
3 medium firm ripe bananas
3 medium tart apples, cored
10 wooden *or* craft sticks
1 cup finely chopped walnuts
1 cup flaked coconut

1. In a saucepan over low heat, melt chocolate and shortening until smooth. Cut bananas in half crosswise. Cut apples in half, starting at stem end. Insert sticks into fruit; dip into chocolate, coating fruit completely. Roll in nuts or coconut.
2. Place on a waxed paper-lined baking sheet. Freeze for at least 20 minutes. Remove from freezer 10 minutes before serving.

YIELD: 12 servings.

A dusting of cocoa powder deliciously tops off these pretty cupcakes. They're so scrumptious, no one ever guesses they're lighter.

cappuccino cupcakes

CAROL FORCUM ⚑ MARION, ILLINOIS

2 cups all-purpose flour
1½ cups sugar
½ cup baking cocoa
1 teaspoon baking soda
½ teaspoon salt
¼ cup instant coffee granules
½ cup hot water
2 eggs
½ cup prune baby food
¼ cup canola oil
2 teaspoons vanilla extract
1½ cups reduced-fat whipped topping
Additional baking cocoa

1. In a large bowl, combine the flour, sugar, cocoa, baking soda and salt. Dissolve coffee granules in hot water. In another bowl, whisk the eggs, baby food, oil, vanilla and coffee mixture. Stir into dry ingredients just until moistened.

2. Fill paper-lined muffin cups two-thirds full. Bake at 350° for 18-20 minutes or until a toothpick comes out clean. Cool for 10 minutes before removing from pans to wire racks to cool completely.

3. Just before serving, frost cupcakes with whipped topping and sprinkle with cocoa.

YIELD: 17 cupcakes.

granola banana sticks

DIANE TOOMEY ⚑ ALLENTOWN, PENNSYLVANIA

¼ cup peanut butter

2 tablespoons plus 1½ teaspoons honey

4½ teaspoons brown sugar

2 teaspoons milk

3 medium firm bananas

6 Popsicle sticks

2 crunchy oat and honey granola bars, crushed

1. In a small saucepan, combine the peanut butter, honey, brown sugar and milk; cook until heated through, stirring occasionally.

2. Peel bananas and cut in half widthwise; insert a Popsicle stick into one end of each banana half. Spoon peanut butter mixture over bananas to coat completely. Sprinkle with granola. Serve immediately or place on a waxed paper-lined baking sheet and freeze.

YIELD: 6 servings.

glazed apple pan pie

BARBARA KEITH ⚑ FAUCETT, MISSOURI

*Potluck gatherings keep us busy throughout the year, so I appreciate foods that can
feed a crowd. With a sweet filling and delicious crust, this pan pie is always a hit.*

5 cups all-purpose flour
4 teaspoons sugar
½ teaspoon salt
½ teaspoon baking powder
1½ cups shortening
2 egg yolks
⅔ cup ice water

FILLING:

14 cups thinly sliced peeled tart apples
4 teaspoons lemon juice
1 teaspoon vanilla extract
¾ cup sugar
¾ cup packed brown sugar
2 teaspoons ground cinnamon
¼ teaspoon salt
3 tablespoons butter
2 tablespoons milk

GLAZE:

½ cup confectioners' sugar
1 tablespoon water
⅛ teaspoon vanilla extract

1. Combine first four ingredients; cut in shortening until crumbly. Beat egg yolks and water; add to flour mixture, tossing with a fork until dough forms a ball. Divide in half.

2. Roll out one half to fit the bottom and sides of an ungreased 15-in. x 10-in. x 1-in. baking pan. Toss apples with lemon juice and vanilla; set aside. Combine sugars, cinnamon and salt. Place half of apples in crust; sprinkle with half of the sugar mixture. Repeat; dot with butter.

3. Roll out remaining dough to fit top of pie; place over filling. Seal and flute edges. Brush with milk. Bake at 375° for 50-55 minutes or until golden brown. Cool 10 minutes. Combine glaze ingredients; drizzle over pie.

YIELD: 24 servings.

rocky road pizza

TASTE OF HOME TEST KITCHEN

*Looking for an interesting new dessert to offer your bunch? Chocolate lovers will relish this palate-pleasing pizza
that cleverly captures the flavor of rocky road ice cream. Folks will have a hard time eating just one slice!*

Pastry for single-crust pie (9 inches)
¾ cup semisweet chocolate chips
½ cup miniature marshmallows
¼ cup salted peanuts

1. On a lightly floured surface, roll pastry into a 9-in. circle; place on a lightly greased baking sheet. Prick with a fork. Bake at 450° for 8-10 minutes or until lightly browned. Sprinkle with chocolate chips. Bake for 1-2 minutes longer or until chocolate is softened.

2. Spread chocolate over crust to within ½ in. of edges. Sprinkle with marshmallows. Bake for 1-2 minutes or until marshmallows puff slightly and are golden brown. Sprinkle with peanuts. Remove to wire rack to cool.

YIELD: 6-8 servings.

ALPHABETICAL INDEX

BEVERAGES (continued)
Mulled Dr Pepper, 63
Peachy Spiced Cider, 65
Spiced Coffee, 65

BROCCOLI
Bacon-Broccoli Cheese Ball, 29
Beef Stir-Fry on a Stick, 115
Cheesy Floret Soup, 210

BURGERS
All-American Hamburgers, 122
Bacon-Stuffed Burgers, 136
Basil Burgers, 93
BBQ Bacon Burgers, 130
Chili Burgers, 128
Chipotle Cheeseburgers, 119
Firecracker Burgers, 104
Giant Mushroom Burger, 116
Grilled Italian Meatball Burgers, 98
Healthy Turkey Burgers, 85
Horseradish Burgers, 113
Portobello Burgers, 134
Smoked Linkburgers, 132
Stuffed Bacon Burgers, 106
Tender Turkey Burgers, 89

CABBAGE & SAUERKRAUT
Brats with Sauerkraut, 120
Corned Beef & Cabbage
 Sandwiches, 148
Creamy Coleslaw, 293
Crunchy Coleslaw, 243
Fruit Slaw in a Cabbage Bowl, 231
Tangy Coleslaw, 220

CAKES & CUPCAKES
Buttermilk Chocolate
 Cupcakes, 303
Buttermilk Pound Cake, 284
Cappuccino Cupcakes, 305
Carrot Sheet Cake, 304
Chocolate Chip Caramel Cake, 299
Chocolate Peanut Butter Cake, 296
Chocolate Snack Cake, 281
Cocoa Cola Cake, 302
Coconut Cupcakes, 282
Cream-Filled Cupcakes, 290
Favorite Chocolate Sheet Cake, 292

Football Cake, 288
Luscious Lemon Cake Roll, 291
Old-Fashioned Apple Cake, 281
Peanut Butter Cup Cupcakes, 298
Peanut Butter Sheet Cake, 285
Picnic Cupcakes, 282
Play Ball Cake, 300
Racetrack Cake, 280
Shoofly Cupcakes, 286

CHEESE
Bacon-Broccoli Cheese Ball, 29
Beef 'n' Cheese Wraps, 165
Cheesy Beef Taco Dip, 34
Cheesy Floret Soup, 210
Cheesy Pecan Roll, 23
Chili Cheese Popcorn, 30
Chipotle Cheeseburgers, 119
Chocolate Cream Cheese
 Brownies, 262
Crab and Cream Cheese Dip, 14
Creamy Taco Dip, 19
Eggplant-Portobello Sandwich
 Loaf, 124
Fancy Ham 'n' Cheese, 160
Fresh Mozzarella & Tomato
 Salad, 240
Fruit 'n' Cheese Kabobs, 21
Garlic-Onion Cheese Spread, 53
Grilled Cheese Loaf, 95
Grilled Greek Crostini Topping, 24
Grilled Parmesan Potatoes, 89
Grilled Steak Appetizers with
 Stilton Sauce, 47
Ham & Cheese Sandwich Loaf, 96
Ham Cheddar Chowder, 208
Horseradish Cheese Spread, 31
Individual Grilled Pizzas, 127
Marinated Mozzarella Cubes, 22
Salmon Cheese Spread, 18

CHERRIES
Cherry Barbecue Sauce, 180
Cherry Berry Pie, 296
Cherry Crumb Pie, 291
Cherry Punch, 58
Giant Cherry Oatmeal Cookies, 271

CHICKEN
Baja Chicken & Slaw Sliders, 25
Barbecue Chicken Wings, 32

Barbecued Chicken, 117
BBQ Chicken Sandwiches, 139
Beer-Can Chicken, 85
Brunswick Stew, 203
California Clubs, 147
Caribbean Jerk Chicken, 125
Cheesy Pecan Roll, 23
Chicken Fajitas, 129
15-Minute Marinated Chicken, 120
Fruity Tortellini Salad, 238
Grilled Glazed Drummies, 42
Grilled Jerk Chicken Wings, 110
Grilled Orange Chicken Strips, 107
Grilled Tarragon Chicken, 107
Guacamole Chicken Roll-Ups, 161
Honey-Citrus Chicken
 Sandwiches, 94
Honey-Glazed Chicken Kabobs, 91
Honey-Mustard Chicken
 Kabobs, 105
Mexican Chicken Wings, 13
Picnic Chicken Pitas, 142
Pita Pocket Chicken Salad, 159
Santa Fe Chicken Chili, 213
Sweet and Spicy Grilled
 Chicken, 115
White Chili, 199

CHILI
Barbecued Beef Chili, 205
Bold Bean and Pork Chili, 201
Chili Verde, 195
Garden Harvest Chili, 206
Heartwarming Chili, 204
Santa Fe Chicken Chili, 213
Sausage Onion Chili, 192
Super-Duper Chili, 192
Turkey Chili, 196
White Chili, 199
Wild West Chili, 198

CHOCOLATE
Brownie Cups, 269
Buttermilk Chocolate
 Cupcakes, 303
Cappuccino Cupcakes, 305
Caramel Brownies, 261
Caramel Butter-Pecan Bars, 274
Chocolate Caramel Apples, 295
Chocolate Chip Brownies, 255
Chocolate Chip Caramel Cake, 299